Narrative, Race, and Ethnicity in the United States

EDITED BY

James J. Donahue

Jennifer Ann Ho

Shaun Morgan

THE OHIO STATE UNIVERSITY PRESS | COLUMBUS

Library of Congress Cataloging-in-Publication Data
Names: Donahue, James J., editor. | Ho, Jennifer Ann, 1970– editor. | Morgan, Shaun, 1977– editor.
Title: Narrative, race, and ethnicity in the United States / James J. Donahue, Jennifer Ann Ho, Shaun Morgan, editors.
Other titles: Theory and interpretation of narrative series.
Description: Columbus : The Ohio State University Press, [2017] | Series: Theory and interpretation of narrative | Includes bibliographical references and index.
Identifiers: LCCN 2017023517 | ISBN 9780814213544 (cloth ; alk. paper) | ISBN 0814213545 (cloth ; alk. paper)
Subjects: LCSH: Race in literature. | Ethnicity in literature. | Narration (Rhetoric) | American literature—History and criticism—Theory, etc.
Classification: LCC PS374.R32 N37 2017 | DDC 810.9/3552—dc23
LC record available at https://lccn.loc.gov/2017023517

Cover design by Susan Zucker
Cover image by Melissa Hlavac
Text design by Juliet Williams
Type set in Adobe Minion Pro

9 8 7 6 5 4 3 2 1

CONTENTS

ACKNOWLEDGMENTS

NO VOLUME such as this would be possible without the hard work, commitment, and enthusiasm of a host of people, as well as the support of various institutions. First and foremost, the editors would like to extend their thanks to everyone who participated in the 2011 Project Narrative Summer Institute, where, unbeknownst to us at the time, this project was originally conceived. The various participants—Emily Anderson, Leah Anderst, Todd Cesaratto, Bruce Fudge, Lasse Gammelgaard, Summer Allison, Urania Milevski, Jeanne-Marie Musto, Jannike Hegdal Nilssen, Elizabeth Stone, Jo-Ann Triner, Janine Utell, Laura Wagner, Kathleen Wells, and Neal Wyatt—were open to our questions of the place of race and ethnicity in the study of narrative and helped us to ask the various questions that, in many ways, are tackled in this volume. In particular, we would like to thank Leah Anderst, Janine Utell, and the seminar leaders Jim Phelan and Frederick Aldama, who have over the years helped to shape this volume in ways too many to note.

We would also like to thank the dedicated and professional staff at The Ohio State University Press. At every stage, from initial submission through the various readers' reports, everyone who has worked on this book has helped to produce a volume we are proud to have included in the Theory and Interpretation of Narrative series and for its audience of students, scholars, and interested readers of narrative. We would like to extend a special thanks to Lindsay Martin, whose expertise was matched only by her excitement for the project. Her sure hands and steady guidance helped to turn a series of questions and ideas into a coherent volume.

James J. Donahue would first like to thank his coeditors, Jennifer and Shaun, for sharing their thoughts, their questions, and most of all their time spent on this project. Further, he needs to thank his colleagues at SUNY Potsdam for their support, guidance, and help unwinding when it was time to step away from the desk. In this regard, he notes the mentorship of Derek Maus, who helped him cut his teeth on the work of editing a scholarly collection, and whose house in Montreal was always a comfortable destination when it was time to recharge. He would also like to thank his friends, who are far too many to name. But a special word of thanks goes to Jo Luloff and Laurel Ralston, who spent more time than anyone can expect listening to him ramble on about this project and work out various ideas.

Jennifer Ann Ho would like to thank her coeditors, Jim and Shaun, first and foremost. What began as a throwaway thought on Facebook, that she wished there was a volume that married her interests in narrative and critical race theory, turned into a passion project with two brilliant and generous friends. Though her colleagues and friends are too numerous to mention, a special nod goes to Sue Kim, who introduced her to PNSI and assured her that there was a place for people interested in race and narratology. Finally, Jennifer thanks her husband, Matthew Grady, for his unconditional love and support.

Shaun Morgan would like to thank his coeditors, Jennifer and Jim, for being wonderful colleagues, mentors, and friends. He thanks his many friends and colleagues who have listened to him drone on about narrative theory, race, and the work of editing manuscripts. He would especially like to thank Allen Dunn, who introduced him to narrative theory and who impressed upon him the joys and the significance of attending to words and ideas. Lastly, Shaun thanks his wife, Erin, for her love and for her support of his academic habit these many years.

Finally, and most importantly, we would like to thank all of the contributors to this volume. Without their hard work, their various insights and expertise, and their commitment to the project, all of the pages between these covers would be blank.

Narrative, Race, and Ethnicity in the United States

JAMES J. DONAHUE

IN HER LANDMARK study of race and American literature *Playing in the Dark* (1992), Toni Morrison argued that literary history has taken for granted a certain set of assumptions, including the understanding that "American literature is free of, uninformed, and unshaped by the four-hundred-year-old presence of, first, Africans and then African Americans in the United States" and that "this presence . . . had no significant place or consequence in the origin and development of that culture's literature" (4–5). Morrison's work provides a thoughtful and insightful study of race in American fiction and has inspired a generation of scholars to study the complexities of race and ethnicity in American literature. However, much (though certainly not all) of this work focuses its attention on the study of literary texts as cultural artifacts, as representations of moments of cultural diversity in the United States. In one respect, the academy has answered Morrison's charge with a robust and thought-provoking (if at times contentious[1]) discussion of the role played by African Americans—as well as Asian Americans, Native Americans, Latino/as, and other ethnic populations—in the development of the rich tapestry that we call the American literary canon. However, the editors of this volume would like to suggest that the academy has only recently begun addressing the full implica-

---

1. For example, one need only remember the conflicted reception of Kenneth W. Warren's *What Was African American Literature?* (2011). For an introduction to the debate that followed in the wake of this book, the reader is directed to Marlon B. Ross's review in *Callaloo* 35.3 (2012): 604–12, as well as the "theories and methodologies" section of *PMLA* 128.2 (March 2013): 386–409.

tions of Morrison's charge. Just prior to the above passage, Morrison writes, "For some time now I have been thinking about the validity or vulnerability of a certain set of assumptions conventionally accepted among literary historians and critics and circulated as 'knowledge'" (4). While there has been much ink spilled by a variety of literary critical schools of thought, there is one major literary critical tradition that, as yet, has not fully[2] explored issues of race and ethnicity, either as a subject in its own right or as a means by which to challenge the methodological assumptions of that school: narrative theory.

This is an exciting time to be working with narrative theories. I use the plural "theories" because there are currently a number of theoretical approaches to the study of narrative. And narrative theorists, in the best tradition of the history of literary theory, have been eagerly employing the work of scholars in other disciplines—from such disparate fields as critical legal studies and cognitive neuroscience, to name but two—to gain new insights into the nature and operations of narrative. This diversity—as well as the current limitations in the field—may best be represented by the relatively recent publication of *Narrative Theory: Core Concepts & Critical Debates* (2012), an introduction to the study of narrative whose purpose is to introduce readers to four major schools under the umbrella of "narrative theory": rhetorical, feminist, mind-oriented, and antimimetic (now generally called "unnatural") approaches to narrative. Organized around a variety of topics, this primer does an excellent job of introducing the reader to the ways that these four critical schools address their major concerns. More importantly, the strength of this work exists in the contributors' responses to each others' sections, allowing the reader to witness part of a developing conversation on the uses (and limitations) of various approaches to the study of narrative. However, as a narrative theorist who is primarily interested in the study of ethnic American literature—and as such invested in explorations of race and ethnicity in the construction and interpretation of fictional narratives—I quickly noticed that neither race nor ethnicity were foundational categories for any of the four represented schools of thought. In her introduction to the feminist approach to narrative, Robyn Warhol notes that "class, race, nation, gender, sexuality, ethnicity, dis/ability: feminist narrative theory tries to keep as many of those balls in the air as possible" (12). An admirable enterprise, certainly. That said, her own contributions to the volume do not explicitly address race; instead, her analysis of Jane Austen's *Persuasion* is focused on "ways in which Austen's novel deconstructs binary oppositions underlying mainstream assumptions about gender, sexuality, and class" (11). Jim Phelan and Peter J. Rabinowitz,

---

2. Some notable work in this area is currently being done, and will be noted throughout.

in their introduction to the rhetorical approach to narrative, discuss race as an aspect of Mark Twain's *The Adventures of Huckleberry Finn*; however, these discussions are in passing, as parts (albeit important parts) to a different set of concerns. Upon finishing this book, one might be tempted to ask: are race and ethnicity not core concepts in the study of narrative?

Of course they are, and the contributors to that volume certainly recognize that fact. The above-mentioned authors—as well as numerous other narrative theorists—have increasingly studied works produced by writers from a variety of racial and ethnic groups, and have remarked on the importance of narrative in expressing social, cultural, and political concerns of those different groups. While there are numerous examples of narrative theorists who turn their attention to nonwhite authors,[3] only recently has there been an attempt at studying race and ethnicity that provides, in Sue J. Kim's words, "theoretically and methodologically sustained engagement in the manner of Robyn Warhol and Susan Lanser on the relationship between feminist theory and narratology" (233). In other words, only recently have there been attempts not merely to discuss issues of race and ethnicity *in* narratives (print, film, and television), but to explore how race and ethnicity might force us to reconsider what we know about the *nature of* narrative (what Morrison would call "knowledge" regarding narrative form). More importantly, it is only recently that narrative theorists have asked the question: how do texts from "ethnic" literary traditions force us to rethink the tools of narrative theory?[4]

In one respect, the editors of and contributors to this volume take their lead from feminist narratologists, whose work has forced narrative theorists to reconsider some of the foundational principles of narrative, as well as exposed much of the underlying gender-based assumptions of scholars and readers alike. The scholars involved in this collection all, in diverse ways, explore how race and ethnicity operate as foundational components of narrative, as well as develop methodological tools that can assist other scholars in continuing this project. That said, we wish to note that this does not mean merely applying the existing tools in the narrative toolbox to the study of race. In short, a critical race narratology must be more than the application of existing tools

---

3. Of course, James Phelan immediately comes to mind. Whether it is his exploration of character narration in John Edgar Wideman's "Doc's Story" (*Living*) or his discussion of the controversy surrounding voice and voicelessness in Zora Neale Hurston's *Their Eyes Were Watching God* ("Voice"), Phelan has spent much time turning his critical attention to narratives produced by African Americans.

4. In his contribution to *Teaching Narrative Theory* (2010), Frederick Luis Aldama outlines a three-pronged approach to "integrate effectively the teaching of narrative theory with the teaching of so-called ethnic literature" that may serve as a useful starting point, especially for classroom use ("Ethnicity" 252).

to the study of race and ethnicity.[5] Although there has been no single work that launched the study of race and ethnicity in narrative in the way that one might argue that Susan Lanser's article "Toward a Feminist Narratology" (1986) inaugurated feminist narratology, there have been a number of works whose chief concern has been outlining the possible parameters of such critical investigations. For example, Frederick Luis Aldama's collection *Analyzing World Fiction: New Horizons in Narrative Theory* (2011) collects essays that were birthed during a Project Narrative symposium on "Multicultural Narratives and Narrative Theory." Covering literature, film, and television programs from multiple cultural traditions and national canons, this collection works to understand narrative in a global as well as multicultural context.[6] Similarly, Sue J. Kim edited a special issue of *JNT: Journal of Narrative Theory* (42.3 [Fall 2012]) on "Decolonizing Narrative Theory," featuring essays that offer a "reconsideration of narratology in relation to ethnic and postcolonial studies" (234).

As Dan Shen has noted, "contextualist narratologies and formal narrative poetics have nourished each other over the past twenty years or so," and there exists a "mutually-benefitting relationship between classical narrative poetics and contextualized narrative criticism," with "the former providing technical tools for the latter, which in turn helps the former to gain current relevance" (142–43). The inclusion of feminist narratology in such a collection as *Narrative Theory: Core Concepts & Critical Debates* demonstrates just such a beneficial relationship and points to the ways that formal approaches to narrative may be employed by a wider range of feminist scholars in interdisciplinary approaches to the study of sex and gender in a variety of narrative instances. However, for the purposes of this present collection, feminist narratology also stands as a model for other contextualist approaches. In fact, at its inception, feminist narratology alluded to the other possible contextualist approaches that could—and soon would—become important in the development of narrative theory. In establishing the ground upon which she built her methodology, Lanser presciently wrote, "There are compelling reasons why feminism (*or any explicitly political criticism*) and narratology (*or any largely*

---

5. That is to say, just as the social, cultural, and political concerns faced by a variety of minority groups may be similar, nobody would suggest that (for example) women and African Americans face the same pressures in the same ways. Similarly, these various tensions do not manifest in the same ways in narrative texts. The study of race and ethnicity is similar to, but not coterminous with, the study of gender, sexuality, class, and so on.

6. In many ways, *Analyzing World Fiction* can be read as a follow-up project to Aldama's *Postethnic Narrative Criticism: Magicorealism in Oscar "Zeta" Acosta, Ana Castillo, Julie Dash, Hanif Kureshi, and Salman Rushdie* (2003), which is as much a primer for the study of multicultural narrative production as it is a bold statement in genre criticism.

formal poetics) might seem incompatible" ("Toward" 343; emphasis added). Although she notes why these two approaches may appear to be incompatible, the remainder of her landmark essay goes on to demonstrate how these two approaches are better understood as complementary.[7] And just as, for Lanser, the "most obvious question feminism would ask of narratology is simply this: upon what body of texts, upon what understandings of the narrative and referential universe, have the insights of narratology been based?" ("Toward" 343), so too does the present collection ask, "upon what body of texts have the insights of narratology been based?" Robyn Warhol has similarly noted that "narratology, in its original forms, seems to be gender-blind" (*Gendered Interventions* 3). No longer "gender-blind" as a result of the work done by feminist narratologists, in many ways narrative theory still appears to be "race/ethnicity-blind."

Although there is a growing trend toward analyzing works by authors from a variety of racial and ethnic backgrounds, much of the current narratological framework has been built upon insights gained while reading a limited array of texts. From Gérard Genette's *Narrative Discourse: An Essay in Method* to Alber and Fludernik's *Postclassical Narratology: Approaches and Analyses,* narrative theory is founded, as Susan Lanser has noted, upon the study of literature that is "heavily European, white, canonical, and restricted primarily to the nineteenth and early twentieth centuries" ("Susan S. Lanser" 101). Certainly, I do not mean to suggest that such work is inherently problematic. Neither does the present volume fully address this deficiency. Our goal is not to erase what has come before, but to productively add to it in some small but significant way, in the spirit of collaboration that characterizes feminist narratology, as well as such volumes as *Narrative Theory: Core Concepts & Critical Debates.* Lanser later noted that "sex is a common if not constant element of narrative *so long as we include its absence as a narratological variable*" ("Sexing" 87; emphasis original), and (quoting Gerald Prince) that "whether absent or present, and sometimes more interestingly when absent, sex is a 'technical feature' of narrative that, like other narratologically significant elements, 'can lead to the construction of meaning'" ("Sexing" 90). Similarly, this present volume explores the variety of ways that race and ethnicity function as technical features of narrative, or otherwise provide new insights into the operations of narrative and help to construct new tools (or sharpen old tools) in the postclassical narratological toolbox. In short, what new questions can be asked, and how can new—and perhaps more nuanced—answers be given to existing questions?

---

7. Of course, this mode of thinking—approaching diversity by engaging with complementary methodologies—has long been the foundation of feminist literary and critical practice.

Although race and ethnicity are not explicitly mentioned in Jan Alber and Monika Fludernik's *Postclassical Narratology: Approaches and Analyses* (2010),[8] these concepts—as the present volume demonstrates—help narrative theorists to "expose the limits but also [exploit] the possibilities of the older, structuralist models" (qtd. in Alber and Fludernik 1) of narratology, as David Herman defines postclassical narratology. As some contributors to this volume demonstrate, by pointing the narratological lens at texts by nonwhite authors—authors working within literary and cultural traditions that may be informed by non-European traditions of storytelling and aesthetics—the study of race and ethnicity as component parts of the narrative construct will force, in the words of Alber and Fludernik, a "reconceptualization of the theoretical models and even the discipline of narratology" (Introduction 3). Similarly, just as it is now more apt to speak of feminist narrato*logies* in the plural, given the variety of approaches to the study of sex and gender in narrative forms (including social, political, and aesthetic as well as purely formal and structural concerns), so too should we speak of race- and ethnicity-based theo*ries* of narrative currently being developed.[9] The aforementioned texts all contribute to this new development in the study of narrative by bringing to bear a multiplicity of concerns, methodologies, and even activist purposes to the study of narrative texts in literature, film, and television.

In that spirit, the present volume enters this conversation by offering an exclusive focus on texts produced in the United States by writers who were born in or who produced their work while living in the United States, and working with the historical developments of the study of race and ethnicity that have characterized American society broadly as well as American literature specifically. This is due to the fact that the United States (like many nations and geopolitical regions) has a specific development of the concept of race as a social construct, and the recognition that the literature produced by authors from particular regions will to some degree be a product of those specific cultural tensions. To date, much of the work done exploring race, ethnicity, and narrative has focused on, in Aldama's words, "first understanding narrative fiction within its worldwide dimension and then analyzing its myriad expressions as particularities in each time and place" ("How To" viii). Aldama's work—in both *Postethnic Narrative Criticism* and *Analyzing*

[handwritten margin notes: insights from scholarship; sampling; study of race/ethnic outside/inside literature; race as particular social construct]

---

8. Neither term merits a mention in the index.

9. For a fascinating exploration of how the study of race and ethnicity can productively work alongside feminist narratology, see Brandon Manning's essay "'I Felt Like I Was Part of the Troop': Satire, Feminist Narratology, and Community," where he establishes the parameters of a "black feminist narratology" (126) by providing a thoughtful analysis of ZZ Packer's short story "Brownies." Similarly, I have elsewhere argued for an expansion of the operations of focalization to include considerations of cultural background; see my article "Focalization."

World Fiction—is consciously engaged with what are often termed "world literatures," as is *JNT*'s special issue on "Decolonizing Narrative Theory." While such work provides much-needed insights into the operations of narrative—asking, as Brian Richardson does, "two related questions: how can narrative theory help us better understand U.S. ethnic and postcolonial fiction, and what are the larger implications of these narrative practices for narrative theory as a whole?" ("U.S. Ethnic" 3)—the editors of the present volume believe that there is merit in a more localized study of the impact of race and ethnicity in American narrative expression. The essays that follow examine the intersections of race, ethnicity, and narrative in texts produced by authors with ties to the United States, a region that has seen the widespread sale of African slaves as well as the inheritance of a legacy of slavery on the descendants of those slaves, the decimation of indigenous peoples in the wake of European colonialism and the enforced paternalism of tribal populations in the following years, the hybridization and ostracizing of settler-colonials with roots in Spain, and the systematic mistreatment of Asian immigrants, as well as a cultural history that has needed to be ever-mindful of that heritage. It is the belief of the editors that, for all the racial and ethnic diversity represented by the various authors and works under study, these writers and their works participate in a larger cultural history, particularly with respect to issues of racial and ethnic identity, and that narratives produced by artists in the United States reflect that shared history. As Sue J. Kim has noted, "there can be no wholly decontextualized narrative because humans and the knowledge that we produce always emerges from *somewhere*" (241; emphasis original); the present volume acknowledges this by providing an explicit focus on a particular "*somewhere*."

In a similar vein, the present volume also hopes to contribute to the growing discussion surrounding the idea of the "postracial" in American society and cultural production.[10] Since the election of Barack Obama to the office of president of the United States, there has been a growing sentiment that America is in a "postracial" phase of cultural development, or even that America has moved past racism. However, as Ramón Saldívar (among others) has argued in "The Second Elevation of the Novel," this couldn't be further from the truth. Instead, Saldívar wishes to "use the term 'postrace' as Colson Whitehead and other writers have suggested that we do: under erasure and with full ironic force" (2). In his compelling article—in which he develops a case for demarcating a new phase of literary history after postmodernism out of reading the novels of Colson Whitehead, not dissimilar to Genette's development of clas-

---

10. The editors recommend the following texts for an introduction to this discussion: Ali, *Mixed-Race*; Bonilla-Silva, *Racism*; Markus and Moya, *Doing Race*; Touré, *Who's Afraid?*

sical narratology from a reading of Proust's *À la recherche du temps perdu*—Saldívar argues that "twenty-first century US ethnic writers have initiated a new stage in the history of the novel" (3). He details the "four features of the postrace aesthetic" (4): that this aesthetic is in dialog with postmodernism, that it consists of a mixture of generic forms, that it is particularly invested in speculative realism, and that it focuses on race as a theme in twenty-first-century fiction. The editors of the current volume believe that just as there is much productive work to be done in narrative theory with respect to race and ethnicity, there is much potential in following Saldívar's lead in bringing "postracial" considerations to a variety of diverse narrative texts, in film and television as well as in print.

To give but one of a number of examples that could be drawn from current literary criticism, Mark McGurl, in his award-winning study *The Program Era: Postwar Fiction and the Rise of Creative Writing* (2009), argues that "put baldly, what Roth knows about the Jewish experience, and Morrison knows about the African American experience, writers like Powers, DeLillo, and Pynchon know about the second law of thermodynamics, cybernetic causality, communications and media theory, and the like" (62). While I would not argue against Powers and others being fully conversant in those areas, their knowledge is *not* in fact akin to the kind of knowledge (and identity construction) that comes with identifying as part of an ethnic group and working within specific racial categories; in other words, "technicity" is not "ethnicity" (63), and any claims to elide the two work to eliminate whiteness as a racial category worthy of study. Later in his study, McGurl equates "writers of color" with writers who are "ethnically-marked" (236), as if white writers are somehow not marked ethnically. This, of course, is common in much literary criticism today, evidenced by casual remarks such as noting that Sandra Cisneros's *House on Mango Street* is "a classic text of ethnic American literature" (339). Why is it not a classic text of "American literature"? Why is Thomas Wolfe's *Look Homeward, Angel* a "major American novel" (79) rather than a "major white American novel"?

The following essays all work at the intersection of narrative theory and race/ethnicity studies. It is the editors' hope that these essays open up some of the many avenues for discussion that exist at this exciting intersection. As such, this volume is intended not as the final word, but as an opening salvo; we hope we have demonstrated not the limitations of the potential threads that can be teased out of the larger fabric, but rather the variety of possibilities that exist. Similarly, readers will inevitably note gaps and identify further avenues for study. We hope for this volume to serve as invitation for those readers to develop the necessary tools and approaches to fill such gaps. The essays that

[margin annotations: "category of people"; "lit crit as observing, objective, as writers/whiteness"; "key"]

follow all, at times explicitly, address one another directly; the reader is eagerly invited to this conversation as well.

The first essays all work to combine theoretical practices from the fields of narrative theory and what we might broadly term "cultural studies." Opening this collection, in "What Asian American Studies and Narrative Theory Can Do for Each Other," Sue J. Kim demonstrates how we can sharpen and redeploy some of the tools in the "narrative toolbox" by highlighting the common ground shared by the seemingly disparate fields of narrative theory and Asian American literary criticism. By identifying paradigmatic texts from both traditions and reading them alongside one another, Kim opens up space for a more nuanced study of contextualist narratologies. Working in a similar manner, Christopher González uses his chapter "Reading Latina/o Fiction: Narrative Form, Ideal Readerships, and Oscar 'Zeta' Acosta's *The Autobiography of a Brown Buffalo*" to use the tools of narrative theory—in particular, David Herman's notion of "storyworlds" as paired with a grounding in reception theory—to highlight issues of audience reception and audience expectation of Latina/o narratives. For González, Acosta's *Autobiography* serves as a paradigmatic case study for teasing apart the tensions between an actual audience and an ideal audience, and how that tension informs the reception of—and expectations for—Latino/a literature. González's essay can also serve as a model for the reworking of existing narrative theoretical concepts that can be productively employed alongside other areas of aesthetic criticism.

In "Narrative Disidentification: Beginnings in Toni Morrison's *Song of Solomon*," Catherine Romagnolo weaves together feminist narratology and postcolonial theory, using the work of Toni Morrison to demonstrate how narrative can be used to disrupt hierarchical constructions based on race and gender. Romagnolo explores the relationship between form, content, and ideology to explore the means by which Morrison (as a paradigmatic example of "minoritized writers") constructs a disidentificatory black subject that highlights for the reader how power and agency operate in narrative fiction. Stephen Spencer follows suit in "Text and Context in Leslie Marmon Silko's *Ceremony*" by providing another way to usefully combine narrative and postcolonial theories, focusing on the means by which Leslie Marmon Silko's work demonstrates a resistance to colonial constructions of identity. For Spencer, Silko's classic novel dissolves narrative boundaries in ways parallel to how it dissolves cultural boundaries, operations that are brought into full relief by the simultaneous use of Bakhtin's understanding of double-voiced discourse and Lanser's feminist narratology, which have in their own ways engaged similar narratological concerns. Blake Wilder then places critical race theory and narrative theory into conversation in his essay "Black World / White World:

Narrative Worldmaking in Jim Crow America" to explore the social and political importance of narrative worldmaking in James Baldwin's fiction. Wilder identifies how separate racial worlds in both our material existence and our narrative constructs inform (and create) one another.

The next essays all, in some capacity, study race and identity through the various lenses of narrative theory. In "Postblack Unnatural Narrative—Or, Is the Implied Author of Percival Everett's *I Am Not Sidney Poitier* Black?," Christian Schmidt reads the work of Percival Everett through the lens of the developing field of unnatural narrative poetics, with implications for the racial construction of the implied author in works produced by "ethnic" American writers. In doing so, he unpacks the racialized complications of Everett's implied author and suggests a means by which we might understand the previously unacknowledged racialized assumptions that have unwittingly accompanied our existing narratological abstractions. Stephanie Li, in "The Presumptions of Whiteness in Ann Petry's *Country Place*," follows suit by exploring the operations of racialization in narrative, emphasizing the distinction between the narrator and the implied author to show how Ann Petry critiques the false entitlements of whiteness. Li highlights the means by which the subjective nature of storytelling reveals a racialized desire to possess the stories of others. Along similar lines, Patrick E. Horn explores Monique Truong's use of paralepsis in his essay "'One Silence Had Led to Another': Strategic Paralepsis and a Non-Normative Narrator in *Bitter in the Mouth*" to reevaluate the importance of imposed identity categories over self-generated representations, and how narrative devices can be used to mask cultural information. Just as importantly, his essay serves as a reminder that silence can be just as powerful a tool—narratively as well as socially—as the text that is written down.

Exploring identity in narrative in a different vein, in "Rhetorical Narrative Theory and Native American Literature: The Antimimetic in Thomas King's *Green Grass, Running Water*," Joseph L. Coulombe demonstrates how King's novel operates as an example of the means by which contemporary Native American/First Nations written narratives employ narrative flexibility in order to disrupt and reject static notions of cultural identity. King's use of both Native American/First Nations and Euro-American myths and stories also serves as a useful model by which scholars can engage multiple theoretical traditions in the study of narrative. And Sterling Lecater Bland Jr. weaves together multiple threads from postclassical narrative theory in his essay "Narration on the Lower Frequencies in Ralph Ellison's *Invisible Man*" to outline the means by which *Invisible Man*'s unnamed narrator constructs his racial identity through the act of narration. The unnamed—but, as Bland notes, not unraced—narrator operates as a microcosm of the nation itself, as it too is racially marked, albeit in ways often unnamed and unremarked upon.

The final essays all point outward, by both explicitly attacking stereotypes as well as providing points of departure for the interested reader and suggesting new possibilities for the study of race and ethnicity in narrative. In his essay "Race as Interpretive Lens: Focalization and Critique of Globalization in Jhumpa Lahiri's 'Sexy,'" Shaun Morgan unpacks the means by which Lahiri uses two levels of focalization to critique the racial ideology of globalization. In her story, internal focalization is employed to highlight racial anxieties considered taboo and kept from public expression and scrutiny, while external focalization is employed to demonstrate the falsity of racial harmony that is often presented to paper over the material disparities that exist between different racial communities. Similarly addressing race in a global context, Claudia Breger uses her essay "Race, Cosmopolitanism, and the Complexities of Belonging in the *Open City*: Teju Cole's Transcontinental Aesthetics" to extend Susan Lanser's work in feminist narratology to transcontinental literatures to explore how narrative theory can productively work with African diaspora aesthetics. The transcontinental, cosmopolitan aesthetics engaged by Cole's work are emphasized by their narrative complexity, gesturing toward the connections between globalization and narrative worldmaking. Looking toward the Caribbean, Deborah Noel in "Caribbean Book Nerds: Narrative Moves and Possible Worlds in Judith Cofer and Junot Díaz" intertwines different theories of narrative worldmaking to demonstrate how the narrators of *The Latin Deli* and *The Brief Wondrous Life of Oscar Wao* move beyond the ideological orientations of their parents and peers to create unique identities by means of their own reading of speculative narrative fiction. These possible worlds exist as sites of resistance to the ideological pressures of cultural identity. Similarly, in "Homo-narrative Capture and the Queer Latino Child," Roy Pérez reads both textual and televisual narratives to explore the practice he designates "homo-narrative capture," or how the use of racially marked children is embraced by a neoliberal gay identity politics. This exploration considers the role of the racialized and sexualized corporeal body in the various operations of narrative media.

·

On a final note, I'd like to point out that the present volume was—unbeknownst to us at the time—born in 2011, at the Project Narrative Summer Institute hosted by The Ohio State University. Jennifer, Shaun, and I immediately bonded over our discussions—both on and off campus—related to issues of race and ethnicity in narrative. When we brought these conversations to the attention of the rest of the group, we were met with enthusiastic support and thoughtful suggestions. Additionally, the institute's directors—James Phelan and Frederick Luis Aldama—provided us with much-needed encouragement as well as the benefit of many years' combined study in narrative theories, adding to our growing reading list and pointing us in the most useful directions. We three continued our discussions long after "narrative summer camp" was dismissed, and the volume you hold in your hands represents only the first in what we hope will be many productive conversations (in person, in print, and online) regarding the intersections of narrative theories and the theories and methodologies of race and ethnicity studies.

CHAPTER 1

What Asian American Studies and Narrative Theory Can Do for Each Other

SUE J. KIM

ARE NARRATOLOGY and Asian American literary studies fundamentally incompatible? That is, are the intellectual and political aims, methods, and praxes of these two intellectual formations irreconcilable? Such a question, of course, has no simple answer. Both fields are heterogeneous, with arguments about the nature and scope of the fields marking their earliest days, and both fields have changed and grown a great deal over the decades. But the relationship between narratology and Asian American literary studies—or ethnic studies of any sort—has often been fitful, even contentious, and calls for further thought of the kind included in this volume. So I start by posing this deliberately provocative question to face head-on some of the challenges posed in doing narrative theory and studying ethnicity, in this case Asian American literary studies.[1]

Narratology, despite the emergence of contextualist narrative theories as well as the actual heterogeneity of its pioneers, has historically been seen as a structuralist enterprise seeking to map out the elements of narratives across historical contexts; narratology seeks a poetics or grammar of narrative functions. In contrast, Asian American literary studies has always maintained that race, history, and politics are inextricable from literature. While classical nar-

---

1. The author would like to thank the editors of this volume (Jennifer Ann Ho, Jim Donahue, and Shaun Morgan) as well as the series editors (James Phelan and Robyn Warhol) for their invaluable feedback on this essay.

ratology has been charged with universalizing insights derived from narratives by a handful of canonical, mostly European and/or American, writers (Austen, Proust, Fielding, James), Asian Americanist literary criticism emphasizes the specificity and historicity of every subject, community, and narrative, focusing particularly on texts by Asian American writers. These fields have distinct genealogies and institutional formations, and narrative theory and Asian Americanist criticism have significant differences epistemologically, politically, and even ontologically. Where, then, are the possible points of convergence?

In recent decades, both narrative theory and Asian American studies have embraced poststructuralism, in the sense of *after*-structuralist narratology as well as in the sense of privileging heterogeneity, deconstruction, performativity, and so on. Thus, although contemporary work in each field still tends to take place in different arenas, resonances are perhaps more evident than in previous eras. In this essay, however, I suggest that revisiting early, foundational texts in each field reveals not only productive differences but also surprising resonances between early Asian Americanist and narratological texts. Moreover, in bringing together these intellectual formations, I seek to reframe how these fields are usually discussed. The usual genealogy of narratology describes the addition of contextualist concerns as relative newcomers, but part of my argument here is that historical contexts are embedded into the apparently ahistorical concepts and that formal concerns and even structuralist approaches are present in even the most politically committed Asian American literary criticism.

In this essay, I focus on texts by American structuralist narratologists—Gerald Prince's *A Grammar of Stories: An Introduction* (1973), Seymour Chatman's *Story and Discourse* (1978), and Dorrit Cohn's *Transparent Minds* (1978)—as well as Wayne Booth's *The Rhetoric of Fiction* (1961).[2] In Asian American literary studies, the texts include selections from the feminist anthology *Asian Women* (1971); the well-known *Aiiieeeee!: An Anthology*

---

2. Although Booth's *Rhetoric* was published before he knew anything about structuralism and even before the coining of the term "narratologie," I include it in this group of early texts because it has been so foundational in the field of narrative theory. Furthermore, his attempts to identify fundamental elements of narrative beyond individual texts is arguably more in line with the structuralist narratologists than with the later contextualist and poststructuralist generations. Also, because I focus on the U.S. context, I have not included key early narrative theorists such as Gérard Genette, Franz Stanzel, and Mieke Bal. I realize this distinction is tenuous given that narrative theory has, then as now, been transatlantic, but it would be too complex here to go into the different ethnic and racial histories of France, Austria, and the Netherlands. Furthermore, the U.S. narrative theorists would at least have had some opportunity, however minimal, of coming into contact with the Asian Americanist criticism.

of Asian-American Writers, edited by Frank Chin, Jeffrey Paul Chan, Lawson Inada, and Shawn Wong (1974); the lesser-known literary anthology, *Asian-American Heritage* (1974), edited by David Hsin-Fu Wand; *Counterpoint: Perspectives on Asian America,* edited by Emma Gee et al. (1976); and Elaine Kim's *Asian American Literature* (1982).[3] Writing by and about Asian Americans existed before the 1970s (e.g., Sui Sin Far, Carlos Bulosan, etc.), as did theories about narrative form (Victor Shklovsky, Mikhail Bakhtin), but the articulation of these specific fields of study in the United States really developed between roughly 1960 and 1980.

I do not, of course, maintain that the shapes of these emerging fields are identical or, perhaps, even similar, but I do argue we can identify more common ground than generally supposed. The concerns of these two fields have often been opposed, implicitly and explicitly. Asian American literary criticism is interpretative, contextualist, extrinsic, and praxis-oriented; narrative theory is concerned with articulating a formal poetics and is formalist, intrinsic, and abstract. Dan Shen, for instance, defines narratology relatively narrowly: "In the early 1960s through 1970s, the term 'narratology' had a clear reference: the systematic description of the structures . . . of (verbal, fictional) narrative, aimed at establishing a universal grammar and a poetics of fiction" (143). While arguing that formalist narratology needs contextualist approaches to stay relevant, Shen nevertheless seeks to retain a formal poetics distinct from contextualist concerns.[4] By almost any measure, Asian Americanist literary criticism, particularly in its early years, falls firmly into the contextualist camp.

In this essay, however, I explore a number of points of consonance, if not equivalence. First, both fields arise in response to a perceived need for a more refined and complete understanding of the elements and operations of literature as they exist in history. As Patrick Horn, drawing on Susan Lanser's work, points out in this volume, the history or context in question may be an

---

3. The anthologies *Asian Women* and *Counterpoint* include many kinds of essays, including history, social commentary, political tracts, and other genres, but for reasons of focus and space, in this essay I focus on the literary criticism. In Asian American literary criticism, however, such inter- and cross-disciplinary concerns are integral to literary studies, which goes to the point of this essay.

4. For instance, Shen argues that the feminist and cognitivist approaches of, respectively, Robyn Warhol and David Herman actually draw on and utilize "decontextualized" narratological concepts in their discussions of narrative qua narrative: "Once an attempt is made to theorize those non-structural elements [such as gender, sex, race, class, etc.] as 'narratological' categories, it also becomes necessary to lift the texts out of their contexts and to distill from them the distinguishing properties concerned. Such non-structural elements, that is to say, cannot enter into the realm of narratological *theory* unless they *are transformed into decontextualized formal distinctions*" (153, emphasis original).

unmarked dominant norm, whether one speaks of characters, implied readers, narrators, or causality, but that context nevertheless exists. But if narrative
theory cannot avoid being situated in history, the Asian Americanist criticism,
despite its political and social emphasis, does not avoid formal literary concerns. Second, both critical discourses see literature as making arguments in
social discourse. Third, the two fields share an engagement with the dynamics
of representing minds in literature. Lest the emphasis on social structures risk
obliterating agency, there is a sense of the mind—depicted in and interacting
with narratives—that the emphasis on power and discourse in late twentieth-
century poststructuralist theory overshadowed to some degree, and which has
become the focus of the recent cognitive turn. While conceptions of mind and
agency are not identical, I would argue that we can identify a shared interest
in understanding the ways in which fictional narratives operate within larger
social structures as well as an investment in the scrutiny of how minds and
subjectivity work in and through narratives.

CONTEXT AND FORM

Both fields arise as an intervention in literary studies, responding to a perceived need for a more refined and complete understanding of the elements
and operations of literature as they exist in history. That is, rather than starting with abstractions, both endeavors started with lived material. Structuralist
narratology does not make its claims out of whole cloth; it starts with existing
narratives. In doing so, these critical fields help to articulate and refine two of
the most important arenas of understanding literature: social-historical context—including and especially race—and literary form. While the New Critics
eschewed the former and had a relatively narrow conception of the latter (e.g.,
resolution of tensions), Asian Americanist criticism insisted on the centrality of Asian American history to understand the literature, and narratology
sought a wide-reaching theory of narrative that would account for how all
fictional narratives work. But while the common understanding is that Asian
Americanist critics do context and narratologists do formal poetics, the actual
history is more complicated.

Certainly, Asian Americanist literary criticism stresses the importance of
Asian American history to understand the literature; every early text includes
an account of Asian American histor(ies), including Asian American literary
history. The bulk of both *Asian Women* and *Counterpoint* are essays on Asian
American history (or "herstory," in *Asian Women*), with a few sections of literature. The editors of *Aiiieeeee!* root the literature in that history: "the vitality

of literature stems from its ability to codify and legitimize common experience . . . and to celebrate life as it is lived" (Chin et al. xxxvi). "Fifty Years of Our Whole Voice," the introductory essay of *Aiiieeeee!*, provides a history of Chinese, Japanese, and Filipino American literature, while Wand includes an account of Polynesian (i.e., Pacific Islander) oral literature (Chin et al. 3–58; Wand 9–13). Elaine Kim's *Asian American Literature,* the first critical monograph solely focused on Asian American literature published in the United States, seeks to illuminate the "topography and texture" of Asian American literature from the nineteenth century to 1982. While she acknowledges that "literary" concerns are important, she makes a conscious decision "to emphasize how the literature elucidates the social history of Asians in the United States," because that social context is key to comprehending the literature (Kim xv). For instance, she notes, if Louis Chu's *Eat A Bowl of Tea* is not understood in the context of immigration laws that barred women and the "Chinatown ghetto of aging bachelors," the novel may seem "simply soft-core pornography" rather than "a novel of manners" (xviii). Stressing "the importance of social context" leads to a number of common critical concerns among early critics, including the literature's "reaction to racism" (Ling 89–90). In *Counterpoint,* Bruce Iwasaki argues that Asian American literature is "the above surface manifestation of the churning psycho-cultural frictions and social-political conflicts which Asian communities take part in. . . . The experience of struggle in the broadest sense is the basis; literature is part of the expression of that" (452).

Narratology would seem to be at the opposite end of the form-context spectrum of concerns, but narratologists do not—and do not claim to—create narratological concepts out of a vacuum. Structuralist and neo-Aristotelian enterprises of formulating narrative poetics are based on examination of existing narratives. If the formal elements are themselves products of history, the historical (or contextual) factors constituting them can arguably be understood as fundamental aspects of the narratives themselves.[5] Dan Shen has notably argued that "formal narrative poetics (in the shape of newly-established decontextualized structural models), in effect, has appeared continuously in contextual narratologies, which have also drawn quite extensively on classical narrative poetics in contextual criticism" (142). I agree with Shen that contextualist narratology has employed formal narrative poetics (164), but

---

5. Take, for instance, Sue Lanser's arguments in *Fictions of Authority* about female authors' use of communal voice or Robyn Warhol in *Gendered Interventions* on the prevalence of engaging narrators in Victorian women's novels. Dan Shen argues that the concepts of gender and sex are not integral to Lanser's and Warhol's readings, but I would argue that gender is integral to producing these formal variations.

rather than separating narratology proper from contextual concerns, I would contend that context—or history—informs even the most abstract attempt at structuralist narratology. Structuralist narratology cannot but refer to context continually, and history haunts even early narratology in at least two ways: in the history of existing literature that constitutes its body of evidence, and in the cultural contexts of those narratives.

It is true that many early narrative theorists seek ahistorical abstraction. In his 1961 study of fiction as rhetoric, Wayne Booth writes, "I am aware . . . I have arbitrarily isolated technique from all of the social and psychological forces that affect authors and readers. For the most part I have had to rule out different demands made by different audiences in different times" (*Rhetoric* xiii–xiv). Likewise, Seymour Chatman claims, "Narrative theory has no critical axe to grind. Its objective is a grid of possibilities, through the establishment of the minimal narrative constitute features" (18–19). Narrative poetics is a "rationalist discipline" that asks, "What are the necessary components—and only those—of a narrative?" (Chatman 19). Gerald Prince seeks to identify "a finite number of explicit rules [that] could account for the structure of all . . . stories," a grammar of narrative regardless of culture and historical era (5, 9).

Despite these aims, early narratologists cannot avoid acknowledging, however reluctantly, the importance of context. Wayne Booth's rhetorical and ethical approach leads him in later decades to embrace more explicitly the importance of social context.[6] Chatman is likewise forced to admit that narrative form cannot actually be isolated from its content, context (or "substance"), and medium (22, 25). In his discussion of macro typologies of plot, Chatman points out "the relativism inherent in comprehending narratives"; for instance, "Aristotle's moral presuppositions" are inadequate to assess "modern characters and situation" (89). Thus, he writes, "the characterization of plot into macrostructures and typologies depends upon an understanding of cultural codes and their interplay with literary and artistic codes and codes of ordinary life" (95).

Even Prince, who wants to extract content as well as context—"a grammar of stories does not have to be concerned with the study of subjects and themes"—cannot limit himself strictly to form (13). For Prince, the basic unit of narrative is content-based: "the basic units constituting any story are units of content" (17). He defines a "minimal story" as "the smallest series of events conjoined by the minimum number of conjunctive features and constituting a story" (19). Chronology and causality are integral, Prince argues:

---

6. See also Booth's admission in the second edition's afterword that his 1961 book "is more time- and culture-bound than my younger self suspected," and that while contextual concerns are integral to narrative theory, he is not sure yet how this integration can be done (414).

A minimal story consists of three conjoined events. The first and third events are stative, the second is active. Furthermore, the third event is the inverse of the first. Finally the three events are conjoined by three conjunctive features in such a way that (a) the first event precedes the second in time and the second precedes the third, and (b) the second event causes the third. (31)

In other words, in order for a series of events to constitute a narrative, the first and third events should express states or conditions (e.g., "John was rich"), and the second statement should describe an action that produces the change in conditions (e.g., "John was unhappy, then he met a woman, then, as a result, he was happy").

Prince's overall argument is more complex and involved, seeking a scientific grammar for all possible stories of varying complexities, but let us examine his basic formulation of a minimal story. If we bring Prince's formulation into conversation with early Asian Americanist literary critics, two principal complications arise: (1) the blurry line between a state and an action, as evidenced by the project of articulating "Asian America" and Asian American literature, and (2) the necessity of context to determine causality. First, in terms of stative and active statements, we might ask, into which category does a statement such as "Maxine is Asian American" belong? Today, particularly in studies of race and ethnicity, we take the interconnection between stative and active statements as a given; the work of Judith Butler, Yen Le Espiritu, Michael Omi and Howard Winant, Kandice Chuh, and others have helped us understand that racial and ethnic identities are constituted through actions, or what we call "performativity." Indeed, it is in part the actions of these early critics defining "Asian American" that constitute that state. Each of these early Asian Americanist critical texts include a statement of the diversity within the category and the tension of accepting—however resistantly—a homogenizing category imposed by the power structure as a grouping. Moreover, these critical texts note the ways in which these tensions are embedded within the literary texts.[7]

Furthermore, the concept of causality is nonsensical without cultural and historical context. Take, for example, the following statement: "Ichiro is unhappy, then his mother dies, then, as a result, Ichiro is relieved." As Elaine Kim notes, without knowledge of the Japanese internment and questions 27 and 28 of the loyalty questionnaire, John Okada's *No-No Boy* might be read as a typical narrative of postwar American angst or a typical story of tension between generations; she argues, "Ichiro's anguish cannot be fully understood

---

7. See Wand 2–5, 9–13; Kim xii; and Chin et al. vii.

apart from the context of the internment of Japanese American during World War II" (xviii). But I would add that *even if* this specific history is not known to the reader, postwar American youth angst or a "typical" story of tension between generations stems from some particular historical-cultural context; that is, the dominant cultural context is unmarked and naturalized. Bruce Iwasaki puts it more bluntly:

> White critics . . . should not be deprived of the warm and reassuring knowledge that whites, as a race, have a particularized value laden sensibility. Not universal essence of humankind. They could then share something. For Third World people, oppression is among other things, never taking leave of the sense of being racial or ethnic minorities. For a long time the effect was us believing that People were whites, that we were variations. Supplements. (455)

Other examples of context-specific causality arise from the early Asian American literature and criticism. Take, for example, the following: "Frank is Asian American, then John loves Frank, then, as a result, Frank is angry." This could be a story of homophobia or "racist love," or "white racist supremacy passed off as love and acceptance"; as King-Kok Cheung has noted, the articulation of racist love is one of the contributions of *Aiiieeeee!* A blunter example might be "John was happy, then John looked at Mary, then, as a result, John died"; in the unmarked "normal" context in which both John and Mary are white and heterosexual, this minimal narrative might be a metaphor for transcendent love or sexual pleasure. In the context of racial violence and the policing of white femininity, this narrative might be very literal. In other words, in what actual narrative is causality separable from cultural context?

But if history haunts narratology, formalism haunts early Asian American literary studies. For instance, in *Counterpoints,* E. San Juan Jr., one of the most enduring Marxist critics of Asian American and postcolonial literatures, anchors his analysis of the politics of Carlos Bulosan's *America Is in the Heart* in its formal features:

> Bulosan acquired a passionate and searching comprehension of actually existing tendencies in society by consistently identifying himself with the victims, outcasts, the insulted and injured. In doing so he transformed the exploited class from its condition of being simply a static category into a dynamic agency for its liberation, from a class-in-itself to a class-for-itself. One can observe the growth of this consciousness in the transaction of "I" and "We," the private and collective, in this meditative sequence. (190)

San Juan goes on to discuss the narrator's use of "I" versus "we"/"us" in *America Is in the Heart*, contrasting the narrator's development from "I was very young when I landed [in the United States]" to "The McDuffie-Tydings Law has affected us so much. It has thrown us into dungeons; it violated our rights and civil liberties" (190). Thus, although San Juan does not use the terms, he is essentially discussing concepts such as communal voice or distancing/engaging narrator. Such narratological tools, developed in feminist narrative theory, may be useful here, and those tools can be further refined by widening the field of literary texts and criticism with which narratology engages.

Although the focus of early Asian American literary criticism is on history and politics—partly to intervene in the dominant literary canon and partly to question the very standards by which literature is evaluated—aesthetics cannot be ignored. For instance, although his focus is on the literature as an expression of "the Asian experience in America," Iwasaki admits, "one can overdo this rather sociological view. Because the second fact which strikes you about Asian American literature is its range—its variety of form, voice, subject, consciousness, theme. Lots of stuff happening" (452). The highly politicized Iwasaki—who, as Chris Lee points out, "ultimately grants no role for literature unless it can be subsumed under the demands of identity politics" (55)—admits that questions central to the study of Asian American literature also include "issues of audience, language, [and] style" (Iwasaki 453). For instance, Iwasaki spends some time examining Hisaye Yamamoto's use of the "child focused-character" (457). In other words, in conversations about literature, the formal concerns of the narrative theorists can no more be ignored than the contextual considerations of the Asian Americanists.

SOCIAL MINDS

Both critical discourses also see literature as making arguments in social discourse. That is, rather than conceiving of literature as an autonomous aesthetic object, a simple reflection of dominant political forces, or part of an institution of art disconnected from daily life, both the Asian Americanists and the narratologists see literature as making various arguments on both macro and micro levels, in a social-political arena of contestation. Asian Americanist literary criticism, of course, is manifestly seeking to change academic, literary, and popular discourses; this intellectual, aesthetic, and political fight is, to some extent, its reason for coming into being. Early Asian Americanist criticism reads the literature as depicting and critiquing aspects of racism (including racist love) and issues of gender. Asian American literature is in part "a critique of America from people who are uniquely prepared to provide one, discouraged from doing so, and able to illuminate how these two conditions are related" (Iwasaki 452). Indeed, even the articulation of "Asian American" as an identity group and "Asian American literature" as a field constitutes significant intervention in academic, literary, and popular spheres.

Of the early narrative theorists, Wayne Booth is most obviously interested in the kinds of arguments that narratives make through their style. Famously, he reads Jane Austen's *Emma* as an exercise in rhetorical persuasion. As opposed to characterizations of Austen as an "unconscious [of her craft] spinster with her knitting needles," Booth reads *Emma* as produced by Austen's masterful manipulation of narrative techniques (*Rhetoric* 244). Indeed, he makes his case for the concept of the implied author based on the ethical effects invited (although not guaranteed) by the formal elements of such a narrative, seeking to retain the notion of an author (an active agent) who seeks to communicate something to a reader: "The 'author herself'—not necessarily the real Jane Austen but an implied author, represented in this book by a reliable narrator—heightens the effects by directing our intellectual, moral, and emotional progress" (*Rhetoric* 256). Booth outlines how the narrator enables judgment of Emma's foolish, selfish, or unkind actions through the oscillation of distance between the narrator's and Emma's points of view. This process makes this novel's marriage plot substantively different from more conventional ones: "the critical difference lies in the precise quality of the values appealed to and the precise quality of the characters who violate or realize them" (*Rhetoric* 260). Thus, for Booth, an implied author like Jane Austen, a "friend and guide" in *Emma*, "is thus fully as important as any other element in the story" (*Rhetoric* 264, 266).[8]

> Her "omniscience" is thus a much more remarkable thing than is ordinarily implied by the term. All good novelists know all about their characters—all that they need to know. And the question of how their narrators are to find out all that *they* need to know, the question of "authority," is a relatively simple one. The real choice is much more profound than this would imply. It is a choice of the moral, not merely the technical, angle of vision from which the story is to be told. (*Rhetoric* 265, emphasis original)

Of course, the question of authority is *not* a simple one, even within the bounds of a fictional world, but the emphasis on the perspectives from which stories are told and the moral implications of those angles is important.[9]

8. In light of feminist criticism, Booth goes on to reassess Austen's complicity with patriarchy in *The Company We Keep* (1989).

9. This emphasis on perspective and moral implications stems from Booth's treatment of narrative as rhetoric, which is quite different from a more purely structuralist taxonomy of narrative.

Although in the first edition of *The Rhetoric of Fiction,* Booth does not explicitly draw politics and power into his discussions, by the second edition (published in 1983) he has begun to extend his earlier sentiments, noting, "I am even more interested today in pursuing questions about the artist's ethical and political obligations and about how we can talk about the 'morality of technique' without making fools of ourselves" (*Rhetoric* 419). First clarifying that he does *not* equate morality and religion, he goes on to admit that "moral questions" are not irrelevant to technique. He writes, "The 'well-made phrase' in fiction must be much more than 'beautiful': it must serve larger ends, and the artist has a moral obligation, contained as an essential part of his aesthetic obligation to 'write well,' to do all that is possible in any given instance to realize his world as he intends it" (*Rhetoric* 388). Booth disparages the idea of writing some "science of fiction":

> Once I had chosen to look at fiction in a rhetorical perspective, once I had chosen to study the technique of fiction, "viewed as the art of communicating with readers," the art of "imposing fictional world" on readers, I was of course obliged to take seriously everything that those "worlds" entailed; I could hardly dodge the way in which all narratives both depend on and impose what I called "beliefs" and "norms," what modern jargon calls "values," and what Bakhtin and other continental critics call "ideology." All stories, even the most seemingly neutral, depend, both in what they say and in their silences, on appeals to moral, political, and religious judgments—using the word "religious" in the broad sense found in anthropologists' discussion these days. (*Rhetoric* 419)

These realizations lead Booth to embrace feminism and other political issues more explicitly in *The Company We Keep: An Ethics of Fiction* (1989). Booth remains ultimately liberal, not embracing any radical critique, but his rhetorical approach leads him to recognize that social and political concerns are integral to literature. More importantly, he argues that literature makes arguments—political, ethical—to individual readers and larger communities in a variety of ways; his focus may be on the textual portion of that argument, but he indicates that wider context nevertheless.

Booth is not, however, the only one. If context haunts even the most stridently abstract narratologists, then the effects of those narratives in and on those contexts will also occasionally demand notice. For instance, Chatman takes issues with Booth's use of "moral," arguing that "acceptance of [an implied author's] universe is aesthetic, not ethical"; according to Chatman, we should not confound "the 'implied author,' a structural principle, with a certain historical figure whom we may or may not admire morally, politically, or personally" (149). Chatman wants to divorce the "implied author's rhetorical effort" from external concerns; the implied author's only goal "is to make the whole package, story and discourse . . . interesting, acceptable, self-consistent, and artful" (226–27). But in discussing his own critical argument, Chatman admits that "persuasiveness itself is a profoundly conventional notion, a reflection of cultural and historical attitudes" (265). Even if it were possible to completely bracket off the author, as Chapman wishes, what is "interesting, acceptable, self-consistent, and artful" is the product of a text's "rhetorical effort"; it is not a given but rather the product of an argument, and its persuasion—aesthetic, ethical, political—is indeed rooted in culture and history.

The two fields also share an interest in the representation of consciousness in literature; again, this critical interest is distinct from that of the New Critics, poststructuralists, and even some Marxists.[10] As recent cognitive narratology has shown, the depiction of minds is ubiquitous in literature but difficult to explain. Literature may be written by humans for other humans within social structures and discourses, but the construction and depiction of minds is not a straightforward thing. While narrative consciousness is not identical to social agency, the concepts of variable perspective and different social positions of power are interdependent. In other words, both early narratologists and Asian Americanists were interested in exploring how literature and writing contribute to the construction of minds and subjects embedded in history.

Booth and Chatman both discuss point of view, diegetic levels, and other considerations that have to do with consciousness and perspective, but Dorrit Cohn's *Transparent Minds* is really the pioneering work in terms of "the presentation of consciousness in fiction" (9–10). Cohn argues for a more precise delineation of the strategies for depicting minds, proposing the concepts of psycho-narration, quoted monologue, and narrated monologue in place of previous schemas based on modes of direct/indirect discourse. Cohn points out how the tradition of (primarily realist) fiction that naturalizes our knowledge of minds belies the actual difficulty of knowing other minds; her analysis of literary techniques thereby estranges what minds are and how they can be known. For instance, in psycho-narration—third-person narrators narrating the inner consciousness of a character—Cohn discusses the effects of "a vocal authorial narrator, unable to refrain from embedding his character's private thoughts in his own generalizations about human nature" (22). In cases of such "pronouncedly authorial narration," the narrator uses "the inner life of an individual character" as a "sound-board for general truths about human nature" (23). In novels by Balzac and Fielding, Cohn notes a kind of implicit

10. Even psychoanalysis after the linguistic turn is less interested in minds and agents than in discursively writ subjects.

struggle between overt authorial narrator and character: "even as th
draws the reader's attention away from the individual fictional chi
fixes it on his own articulate self: a discursive intelligence who com
with the reader about his character—behind his character's back" (25). By
drawing attention to the different and possibly contentious sources of information, Cohn's distinction between the narrator who prominently intrudes
and the effaced narrator who quietly reports opens the door to a correlation
of narration with hegemony:

> The narrator's superior knowledge of the character's inner life and his supe-
> rior ability to present it and assess. To some degree this superiority is implied
> in all psycho-narration, even where there is greater cohesion between the
> narrating and the figural consciousness. But the stronger the authorial cast,
> the more emphatic the cognitive privilege of the narrator. (29)

Asian Americanist criticism is centrally concerned with this struggle for
"cognitive privilege"—in particular, *which* minds have been seen to be legible or inscrutable and how "minds" (i.e., subjectivity, agency, identity) have
been defined. "Fifty Years of Our Whole Voice," the famed introduction of
Aiiieeeee!, is concerned with claiming subjectivity, mind, and voice for Asian
Americans, but particularly for men and the working class. But the feminist
collective that edited *Asian Women* points out two further problems that historically confront Asian American women. First is the very access—de jure or
de facto—to writing, affected by class, race, *and* gender; the editors note that
the common response to their requests for contributions was, "Oh, not me.
I can't write" (Asian Women's Coalition 4). Hisaye Yamamoto's "Seventeen
Syllables" is a poignant testament to the particular challenges faced by Asian
American women trying to write. Second is the presumed legibility of their
minds by others; for instance, the editors describe being met with derision by
Asian American men, who "somehow assumed to know everything about the
women's liberation movement, without ever bothering to do serious reading
or bothering to have serious discussion about the multiplicity of perspectives
and politics in the movement" (5).

The collection includes poetry, short fiction, visual art, personal reflections, and political tracts, covering a number of diverse topics: Japanese
internment, life in a political commune, racism and sexual exploitation by
the U.S. military, the Indochinese Women's Conference of 1971, women in
Iran, service and factory labor, interviews with Congresswoman Patsy Mink
(Hawaii) and revolutionary labor organizer Grace Lee Boggs, and even an
unfortunate essay about the socialist utopia of North Korea. Ellen Higa, an

Asian American student at Yale, notes, "People try to define me in their terms and have difficulty accepting me for what I am. . . . How is it that an Asian woman is differently idealized from a white woman or is she? Whether I as an Asian woman am expected more to conform to feminine ideals, I'm not sure" (Asian Women's Coalition 59–60). The one essay that focuses solely on traditionally literary concerns, "Women in Modern Japanese Literature," by Carolyn Yee, concludes that "Japan's literary failure [is] to deal with her women as humans capable of self-determination"; women are "Buddhas, snakes, or contrasted with the environment" (30). Although Cohn is concerned with fiction, we might put the project of *Asian Women* in her terms: *Asian Women* seeks to articulate all the characters that have hitherto been evaluated and circumscribed by the authorial narration of white supremacy and patriarchy.

My comparative consideration here of early scholarship in narratology and Asian Americanist literary criticism is just the tip of the critical iceberg. Sometimes explicitly, sometimes implicitly, contemporary criticism often assumes these earlier texts in both fields to be naively empiricist, essentialist, and/or otherwise intellectually narrow. Part of my argument is that examining these early texts together can provide useful insights for critics today, an era partially marked by an exhaustion with poststructuralism, as well as help us reassess the potential common ground between narratology and Asian American literary studies.

CHAPTER 2

Narrative Form, Ideal Readerships, and Oscar "Zeta" Acosta's *The Autobiography of a Brown Buffalo*

CHRISTOPHER GONZÁLEZ

SOME OF THE best known and most widely studied works of Latina/o literature feature narrators that adopt memoirist or (auto)biographer positions.[1] Pre- and early twentieth-century Latinas/os helped establish this strong tradition of documentary writing, from the accounts of fifteenth-century witnesses to colonization and exploration such as Fray Bartolomé de las Casas and Álvar Núñez Cabeza de Vaca; to the memoirs of Juan Seguín, who fought alongside Texas legends Sam Houston and Stephen F. Austin; to Puerto Rican–born Arthur A. Schomburg and his tireless efforts to reconcile his Hispanic and African heritages; and many others. The urge to document Latina/o experiences reached full bloom following World War II with works by Bernardo Vega, Ernesto Galarza, Luis Leal, Américo Paredes, César Chavez, Piri Thomas, Tomás Rivera, Richard Rodriguez, Esmeralda Santiago, Luis Alberto Urrea, and Luis J. Rodriguez, among others. Even works of Latina/o-authored fiction—conjurations of sheer imagination—in the mid- to late twentieth century continued to use a narrative style that emphasized the *documenting of experience*. Many Latina/o writers use narrators that filter their life experiences through the sieve of narrative, often to create a record that documents

---

1. I give tremendous thanks to the editors of the "Theory and Interpretation of Narrative" series, James Phelan, Peter Rabinowitz, and Robyn Warhol, for their generous patience and guidance in the shaping of this essay. James Phelan in particular gave me crucial insight concerning the irony and fictionality of life writing that was invaluable.

particular experiences to relate them for a reader's consumption. These narratives display a compulsion to document the experientiality of the Latina/o self.

In Latina/o literature, such devotion to first-person narration arises, in part, from an oral tradition and folkloric forms such as the *corrido* and the *testimonio*.[2] That Latina/o life writers structure their narratives around a framework of liminality allows them to cast their experience as a person from a marginalized community. These authors, in designing their narrative blueprints, create storyworlds that are carefully constructed with a particular readership in mind. In considering the relationship between the text and reader, this essay uses Oscar "Zeta" Acosta's *The Autobiography of a Brown Buffalo* (1972) as its case study. Acosta's narrator is uniquely positioned because it is an authorial counterself[3]—a shadow of the biographical author unambiguously enmeshed in the project of writing and documenting his own life through the very book we hold in our hand when we read it. What is key here, however, is that while this text purports to be an example of reportage, of life writing, Acosta ironizes the narrator, giving the veneer of fictionality to the book. Such an ironized narrative stance that flirts with fiction—a device used in such works as Norman Mailer's *Armies of the Night,* Frank McCourt's *Angela's Ashes,* Dave Egger's *A Heartbreaking Work of Staggering Genius,* and certainly Hunter S. Thompson's *Fear and Loathing in Las Vegas*—reflects a long tradition in literature. Yet an irreverent narrative attitude toward such a politically charged historical context of the Chicano movement certainly did not endear Acosta to many Chicana/o readers. The readers' inability—or unwillingness—to recognize Acosta's ironizing narrator contributed to the lukewarm reception *The Autobiography of a Brown Buffalo* received upon its publication, and it highlights the constraints of audience expectation.

Within *Autobiography,* two tellers are at work—Acosta the author who creates a version of himself that functions as the protagonist, who is also himself a writer. Many readers often wish to conflate the autobiographical author with the character narrator who claims to be the person writing the text we read. But that conflation misses an implied layer of the narrative communication, one from Acosta the author to his audience about his former self. Readers who are able to recognize this distinction between author and character narrator are attuned to this layer and thus are able to recognize that the

---

2. For more on the oral literary of Mexican-descended peoples, see Américo Paredes's seminal study *With His Pistol in His Hand: A Border Ballad and Its Hero.*

3. I am using the term "counterself" and its variants rather than the more standardized "implied author." Counterself, in my opinion, reflects more accurately the affinity the inscribed persona has with the biological author rather than the persona suggested by the narrative text. The authorial counterself is a near duplicate, obtrusive version of the biological author.

text is not simple reportage, an account of what happened when, but rather a creative construction in which Acosta the author uses multiple techniques to re-present his former self, warts and all. But because so much of the communication is done by implication, it presents an extremely rigorous challenge to its audience.

Because *Autobiography* announces itself as a document written by a subjective author, issues related to unreliability, selectivity of narrated events, and the constructedness of the text (artifice within artifice) all encroach upon and influence the reader's attempt to reconstruct the storyworld. Unfortunately for Acosta, his book is so like life writing, readers have treated it unproblematically as such for much of its publication history. *Autobiography* is treated more like an autobiography than a novel, when it actually has closer affinities with the postmodernist novel—a form not really seen again in Latina/o literature until after the turn of the twenty-first century.

Simply put, I am concerned with how Acosta's *Autobiography* challenges the reader and how such challenges have resonated in the development of Latina/o literature over four decades. This positions reading situations not only in terms of the author-text-reader relationship but also as reading the text within the context of history, as Hans Robert Jauss's horizon of expectation maintains. The passage of time has also influenced the development and reception of Latino/a literature. In *Toward an Aesthetic of Reception,* Jauss lays out the horizon of expectations as a means of arguing for the fluidity of a text's interpretation over the course of time:

> A literary work, even when it appears to be new, does not present itself as something absolutely new in an informational vacuum, but predisposes its audience to a very specific kind of reception by announcements, overt and covert signals, familiar characteristics, or implicit allusions. (23)

If, as Jauss maintains, readers must be within a text's horizon of expectations in order be in a position to interpret the text properly (what I would call reconstructing the storyworld), then what I mentioned above regarding the disparity between the ideal readership and the actual readership in large measure rests on the horizon of expectations. In *Aesthetic Experience and Literary Hermeneutics,* Jauss further articulates this phenomenon:

> In the analysis of the experience of the reader or the "community of readers" of a given historical period, both sides of the text-reader relation (i.e., effect as the element that is conditioned by the text and reception as the element of concretization of meaning that is conditioned by the addressee) must be dis-

tinguished, worked out, and mediated if one wishes to see how expectation and experience mesh and whether an element of new significance emerges. These two horizons are the literary one, the one the work brings with it on the one hand, and that of his everyday world which the reader of a given society brings with him on the other. (xxxii)

While Jauss works out an excellent paradigm of expectation concerning the vectors of the literary and the experiential, his binary model does not account for a trajectory of identity within his horizon. Jauss's invocation of reader experience has a direct effect on the Latina/o literary tradition and its development. He maintains that reader experience shapes reader expectation, which is another way of saying that reader experience helps shape a reader's evaluative measure of narrative aesthetic. If Jauss's contention is in fact the case, then it is easy to understand why authors of Latina/o narratives have had such a difficult time in establishing the freedom to create works that differ in significant ways from the expectations of audiences whose limited experience with Latina/o identity and culture has unduly shaped an understanding of what to expect from Latina/o literature. One wonders why it is so difficult for such works to find a readership willing to engage with it without the constraints of stereotypical expectations for what Latino/a literature ought to be.

To begin with, these challenges in publishing Latina/o literature directly reflect the constraints with which an author must contend when creating a narrative. While all authors must confront various challenges when writing, Latina/o writers, like other historically marginalized groups in the United States, must resolve the tension that manifests in the expression of narrative from within identity positions that do not align with the hegemonic storytelling conventions of American literature.

My focus here is made more complex by the seemingly antithetical positions taken by Latina/o studies and what it values in the literature produced by Latina/o authors—that is, predominantly ideopolitical concerns, and a vast majority of narrative theorists who do not engage Latina/o literature as a means of exploring the many permutations of narrative discourse.[4] Latina/o studies scholars often do not foreground formal concerns, and likewise narrative theorists generally tend to explore narratives not written by Latinas/

---

4. As early as 1982, scholar of Chicano literature Juan Bruce-Novoa advocated for a more formalist approach to complement the proliferation of culturally based studies of Chicano narrative and poetry that was to come. In his introduction to *Chicano Poetry: A Response to Chaos*, Bruce-Novoa writes, "The exact relationship between political activism and Chicano literature is yet to be properly evaluated, however; I leave the task to social scientists trained to do it. This study concerns itself with literary texts, those which form the heart of Chicano literature during its first decade and a half" (3).

os. Sue J. Kim makes a similar observation in her essay in this volume concerning the gulf between cultural and narratological engagements with Asian American literature, describing the view many scholars hold of narratology as a "structuralist enterprise," in contrast to the position held by Asian American studies that "race, history and politics are inextricable from literature" (13 in this volume). And, like Kim, I advocate for more interaction between the two scholarly camps, particularly by attending to earlier moments within the arc of literary narrative production of, in the case of this essay, Latina/o literature.

For most of their history, ethnic literatures of the United States have often been viewed by scholars, book sellers, and audiences through the lens of the author's identity. Because the public comes to expect that, say, a Latino author like Tomás Rivera would write about the Chicano migrant experience, there is the tendency to adopt an a priori way of looking at all literature produced by Latinos. Inherent in this position is the central concern of my essay: namely, that a priori ways of viewing Latina/o literature have tangible effects on the production and reception (enthusiastic or tepid) of Latina/o works. Overwrought interpretations of Latina/o authors and their implied authors at times become an a priori mode of engaging with a text that holds what is found in the narrative in the light of the author or author construct.

My approach to Latino/a narratives, then, attends to the text itself and its relation to its intended narrative target. I suggest that engaging with Latina/o literature itself rather than the identity position of the person who writes—the textual features and uses of narrative techniques in creating storyworlds for hospitable readerships—allows us to understand how the Latina/o literary tradition has developed vis-à-vis an ever-shifting reading demographic. If we are to understand how Latina/o literature has developed, we must also adopt an a posteriori approach to examining this corpus, by letting the corpus itself indicate the parameters of inquiry—the rules of interpretive engagement—via the ideal readership.[5]

David Herman's formulation of how storyworlds are created by authors and how readers take the narrated storyworld and reconstruct it in their minds helps illuminate the problem many Latina/o authors face when readers encounter their narratives. Herman establishes the advantages of thinking in terms of a storyworld in *Story Logic*:

---

5. I do not mean to suggest that my adopted approach allows me unique access to the text itself. On the contrary, a critic who examines, say, historical or political dimensions of the text may also allow such an investigation to be generated from the text itself. However, a standard criticism of more formalist approaches to ethnic literature is that they do not consider the social, historical, or political valences that are ingrained in such works.

> For one thing, the term *storyworld* better captures what might be called the ecology of narrative interpretation. [. . .] More generally, *storyworld* points to the way interpreters of narrative reconstruct a sequence of states, events, and actions not just additively or incrementally but integratively or "ecologically"; [. . .] the importance of such processing strategies in narrative contexts is part of what motivates my shift from story to *storyworld*. (14)

Both Blake Wilder and Deborah Noel have essays in this volume that rely on Herman's articulation of the processes of "storying the world" and "worlding the story" from his 2013 *Storytelling and the Sciences of the Mind.* "Worlding the story" is the process of storyworld reconstruction within the mind of the reader based on the inscribed text or narrative blueprint. On the other hand, "storying the world" is indicative of the cognitive changes that occur within readers after having read a narrative that causes them to see their world anew and perhaps from a fresh, but potentially altered, view and sense-making of the world.

If, as Herman suggests, narrative storyworlds are mentally projected, richly textured environments along dimensions of space and time, then it stands to reason that Latina/o narratives are much more than articulations of identity or explorations of themes of marginalization. The inscribed storyworld, as a dynamic construct bound only by the limitations of the author's imagination, ought to have the freedom to expand in ways its author sees fit. However, the reconstruction of a storyworld is effectively limited by what a readership can recreate in its mind. Herman's description of what goes into the creation of a storyworld (i.e., an ecology), denotes a highly complex process. Any narrative device employed by the author that exacerbates the complexity of the story-world and the reconstruction of its ecology in the audience's mind will prove to be a significant challenge, if not a downright obstacle. It is precisely the difficulty in reconstructing the storyworld of Acosta's autobiography that reveals how established expectations for given narratives can impede the development of historically marginalized literary traditions.

Undoubtedly, Oscar "Zeta" Acosta remains an enigmatic figure in Latino/a letters. Despite the concerted recovery of Acosta's work by Frederick Luis Aldama, Ilan Stavans, Manuel Luis Martinez, Ramón Saldívar, and others, Acosta looms like a phantom of the Latina/o imagination—more myth than actual person. Due largely to his notorious disappearance in June of 1974 (presumably in Mexico), his two works of life writing, *The Autobiography of a Brown Buffalo* and *The Revolt of the Cockroach People,* along with a handful of short stories, now speak for Acosta in his absence. Perhaps this is a fitting legacy to the self-knighted "Chicano lawyer" who was both a brown Gargantua and a countercultural Beat figure with a license to practice law. His legacy in Latino/a letters is curious. For someone who was a participant in several of the key historical moments of the Chicano movement, with relationships with the movement's central figures—one of the few writers who unabashedly incorporated these landmark events in Chicano history into his storyworlds[6]—his books were largely dismissed by Anglo readers at the time of their publication, and perhaps more surprising, by the Chicana/o community itself. Little has changed in the intervening forty years.

For instance, in Manuel M. Martín-Rodríguez's 2003 study, *Life in Search of Readers: Reading (in) Chicano/a Literature,* Acosta does not garner a single passing reference despite the study's concern with the historical trajectory of Chicano/a literature and its interaction with readers. I am indebted to Martín-Rodríguez's study, for it lays out much of the history surrounding how Chicano/a literature has evolved a readership over time—thus providing insights invaluable to my study. My point is not to unfairly criticize Martín-Rodríguez for not addressing the gaping lacuna where Acosta ought to be. That he omits Acosta in his study of how Chicano/a authors and their writings have shaped their readership indicates the little impression Acosta's books had on contemporaneous and subsequent audiences. Acosta's troubled relationship with his readership (or lack thereof) is an intriguing incongruity.

Stavans notes that Acosta wrote a novel when he was thirty-three that "no publisher accepted and only one or two acknowledged receiving" (*Bandido* 7), a manuscript that remains lost. Though he had much to write about, Acosta struggled to find an audience, even after his two irreverent, ideopolitically charged books were published. Further, if one views *Autobiography* or *Revolt* as social documents of protest, ones that speak or "write back" to power, Acosta's books should have been runaway best sellers. In both books, Acosta makes a move to unite Chicanos as a political force via his narratives. Further, one would think there would be some measure of pride within the Chicana/o community regarding Acosta's efforts, as there was with the exaltation of Rudolfo "Corky" Gonzales's epic poem "Yo Soy Joaquín."[7] While Gonzales's poem was printed at a furious rate to keep up with a grassroots distribution, performed widely in Luis Valdez's Teatro Campesino, Acosta's *Autobiography* languished,

6. *The Revolt of the Cockroach People* centers on Acosta, aka Buffalo Zeta Brown, and the landmark "Trial of the St. Basil Twenty-One." Unlike the meditative tone of self-discovery that infuses *The Autobiography of a Brown Buffalo,* the political struggles of Chicanos dominates *Revolt.* Despite this, *Revolt* is arguably even more critically ignored than is *Autobiography.*

7. The *Norton Anthology of Latino Literature* claims that "Yo Soy Joaquín" "came to define the Movement; Latino historians consider it a Chicano epic. In the 1970s, *I Am Joaquín* sold over 100,000 copies, becoming the first Chicano best seller. While the book's importance was mainly political, it also has influenced some contemporary writers" (Stavans, *Norton* 787).

and his notoriety, according to Stavans, is nonexistent both in Mexico and the United States (*Bandido* 10–11). Acosta, Stavans posits, "opted for literature as a redeeming act, the written word as a way of knowledge and salvation" (11). Undaunted by publishing rejections and a failed political campaign for sheriff of Los Angeles County, Acosta was irreverent and defiant of the power structure that had taken so much from his people; he did not fit within the confines of other people's expectations. As he states near the end of *Autobiography*:

> Ladies and gentleman . . . my name is Oscar Acosta. My father is an Indian from the mountains of Durango. Although I cannot speak his language . . . you see, Spanish is the language of our conquerors. English is the language of our conquerors. . . . No one ever asked me or my brother if we wanted to be American citizens. We are all citizens by default. They stole our land and made us half-slaves. They destroyed our gods and made us bow down to a dead man who's been strung up for 2000 years. . . . Now what we need is, first to give ourselves a new name. We need a new identity. A name and a language all our own. . . . So I propose that we call ourselves . . . what's this you don't want me to attack our own religion? Well, all right . . . I propose we call ourselves the Brown Buffalo people. . . . No, it's not an Indian name, for Christ sake . . . don't you get it? The buffalo, see? Yes, the animal that everyone slaughtered. Sure, both the cowboys and the Indians are out to get him . . . and, because we do have roots in our Mexican past, our Aztec ancestry, that's where we get the *brown* from. (198)

This passage, an imagined speech of Oscar's[8] call to political action and solidarity, is what might be called in political parlance "red meat"—rhetoric designed to fuel the motivations and subsequent actions of a political base. His speech is also the culmination of Oscar's meanderings within the narrative, one that gives him a purpose in life: "I merely want to do what is right," he states (198). Here Acosta, as the historical person, intertwines his rhetorical message with the flippant, ironical narrative voice that dominates the book. It is as if a vital message gets lost in the transmission, all because of the level of seriousness, or lack thereof, the author chooses to endow his narrative persona. On face value, Acosta's books seemed destined to be as widely distributed and read as Gonzales's poem among Chicanos, if no one else. They were politically charged and irreverent at the height of the Chicano movement. Instead, *Autobiography* reached publishing purgatory quickly, falling out of print by the late 1970s.

---

8. Henceforth, I will designate the biological author as Acosta and the character narrator as Oscar.

With a motivated and mobile Chicano base, fueled by
tices, discrimination, and the injustice of serving their ⟨
military action only to be treated as less than citizens at h⟨
cal situation was primed to establish Acosta's works as utter ⟨
Chicano spirit, independence, and imagination. In fact, becau
political message and support of the Brown Power movement, ⟨ ⟨phy
was arguably better positioned to find a receptive readership tnan another
Chicano novel also published in 1972: Rudolfo Anaya's *Bless Me, Ultima*. However, the comparative reception of the two works is striking. Anaya's novel is
unequivocally proclaimed as the Chicano masterpiece that proved harbinger
to the so-called Chicano Renaissance. It has never been out of print, and as of
2016 *Bless Me, Ultima* holds the distinction as perhaps the most widely taught
Chicano work in high schools and universities across the United States.

For reasons that no scholar has yet attempted to discern, a ready-made
audience comprising real individuals primed to engage with *Autobiography*
failed to respond as Acosta's ideal readership, and instead turned to Anaya's
folkloric coming-of-age story with zeal. Acosta's text targets a radical, like-
minded audience, while Anaya's text invites a readership that senses the
slipping away of tradition and yearns to recoup it through nostalgic reminis-
cence.[9] This apparent disjunction in audience reception has less to do with
the historical sociopolitical moment than it does with the narrative design of
Acosta's novel.

Autobiography is one of the first Latino/a narratives to break with a linear narrative structure. Unlike earlier examples of ethnic American autobiographies such as *The Autobiography of Malcolm X* by Malcolm X and Alex
Haley, *Down These Mean Streets* by Piri Thomas, *A Wake in Ybor City* by José
Yglesias, and *Barrio Boy* by Ernesto Galarza, which feature an account of the
protagonist's life from early childhood to young adult, *Autobiography* eschews
linear temporality. If, as Frederick Luis Aldama notes, "to be 'recognized,' the
racial and ethnic Other has had to convince his or her audience of the reality of his or her experience and, thus, adhere to narrating codes that do not
call attention to the gap between mimesis and reality" (*Postethnic Narrative
Criticism* 48), it is unsurprising that such autobiographies seek to chronicle
the protagonist's life as experienced. This type of narrative has become a part

9. To be clear, I am not arguing that *Bless Me, Ultima* and *Autobiography of a Brown Buffalo* seek the same readership. They clearly do not. What I am arguing is that the readership
each text seeks was available in 1972. But for reasons that remain unknown, *Autobiography*
essentially went unnoticed. Acosta's novel seems to be an example of the Zen koan: If a tree falls
in the woods and no one is around, does it make a sound? In this case, if no readership notices
the *Autobiography*, will it be read? The evidence suggests that whatever sound *Autobiography*
did make was slight at best.

a larger tradition in Latino/a literature wherein the narrator chronicles the autobiographer's life in chronological order, from childhood to adulthood. Through the temporal instabilities presented in Acosta's text, *Autobiography* breaks from this established tradition, along with many other characteristics that distinguish it from other ethnic autobiographies.

But I reiterate here that, despite its title and use of the autobiographical narrative trope, *Autobiography* is a work of fiction. Aldama makes this point clear in *Postethnic Narrative Criticism* by distinguishing the biological Acosta from the character Oscar depicted within the storyworld and by identifying "Acosta's use of magicorealism to reform the genre of autobiography" (47). This subversion of the autobiographical genre and its conventions is a risk that Acosta takes in his narrative blueprint, one whose potential payoff is based in the reader's ability to recognize both the conventions of autobiography and that Acosta is manipulating these conventions in the creation of his storyworld.

Rather than begin his "autobiography" with his childhood, as is conventional of autobiographies, Oscar delays revealing this time in his life until the second paragraph of chapter 2: "Although I was born in El Paso, Texas, I am actually a small town kid" (71). Instead, he begins his narrative on July 1, 1967, gazing at his naked body in the mirror, establishing his body as a central image for the rest of his autobiography. The opening passage presents Oscar in a vulnerable position—not one of childhood but rather one of adult self-doubt and depression. The result is an increased pathos and uncertainty.

At first it appears that Oscar is confiding in someone as he takes an inventory of his body while gazing into a mirror: "I should lay off those Snicker bars, those liverwurst sandwiches with gobs of mayonnaise and those God-damned caramel sundaes. But look, if I suck it in just a wee bit more, push that bellybutton up against the back; can you see what will surely come to pass if you but rid yourself of this extra flesh?" (11). The first part of the second sentence quoted here seems to invite the reader to match Oscar's gaze—to see what he sees. Yet, as the second part of the sentence reveals, Oscar is addressing himself, rebuking himself for his poor body image and how he has the power to change it if he motivates himself enough to do so. Already in this opening, Oscar signals multiple audiences. When he narrates in first person, his observations are directed to an unacknowledged narratee, as in this passage: "Every morning of my life I have seen that brown belly from every angle. It has not changed that I can remember. I was always a fat kid" (11). Here, Oscar is in traditional autobiographical mode. But as I have already indicated, there are moments when at least two separate audiences are acknowledged. The first of these is the reader of his autobiography, whom Oscar often calls upon to consider and judge certain actions or consequences in his own life. These readers are revealed in invitations such as, "See that man with the insignificant eyes drawn back, lips thinned down tight?" (12). This question is not simply rhetorical; Oscar is addressing the reader of his autobiography. Indeed, there are at least two audiences inscribed in the text—Acosta's narratee and Acosta himself. But there is also an audience, never directly but always indirectly addressed: Acosta the author's idealized readers.

For not the first time in *Autobiography,* Acosta recounts the recognition of heartbreak that often comes during the transition from childhood to adulthood. While in high school, he falls in love with a girl named Alice. To his astonishment, Alice reciprocates. As Oscar reveals to his narratee, there are many barriers to his union with Alice: their age, their difference in religion, and their disparity in ethnicity. The crucial moment comes when Alice lets her parents know about Oscar. After the weekend is over, he eagerly waits for Alice at school on Monday. "She didn't come to school that day . . . an automobile accident? A polio attack? Perhaps she got gored by one of those fucking bulls I've seen in their field" (116). Rather than mask his anxiety, his humor emphasizes his torment. When a letter arrives for him, he begins to understand the significance of his relationship with Alice:

> It was my family name. When she told her mother that name of her new boyfriend, the old bag said no dice. Never. Forget it. And she was never to speak to me again. In fact, she made her write the letter so that she wouldn't have to explain the situation to me in person.
>
> So goodbye, my love and please don't say hello to me in studyhall. Was that it? What a fool, I thought. There's no problem in a name change. Hell, if she can change her religion, why can't I change my name? I was unaware of my tears when my mother asked me if I was still sick. I asked her what she thought of my changing my name.
>
> "I think Oscar's a nice name," she said.
>
> "No. Not Oscar."
>
> "But you never use your holy name."
>
> "No, ma, I don't mean Thomas either."
>
> She stopped patting the dough for the tortillas and stared at me right in the face. "You'll go to hell if you change your family name. And your dad will probably hang you again." (116–17)

Oscar's use of an ironic tone to convey what must have been an emotionally wrenching moment in his youth risks conveying that this moment was not formative or significant to the man who now narrates *Autobiography.* The narration is reminiscent of someone talking at ease with a dear friend. The tone is not only casual, it is also self-deprecating. But the idealized reader also reads the prejudicial treatment of certain areas of white culture, as well as religious intolerance, at the heart of Acosta's experience. The difference between experience and narration is front and center here, as is necessary to recognize this difference in reading stances.

Marci L. Carrasquillo has highlighted Acosta's problematic attempt at self-actualization, stating that his "significant epiphany about the nature and complexity of identity does not lead Acosta to understand the gendered aspects of his 'choice'" (78). Here Carrasquillo cites Oscar's revelation that he is "a Chicano by ancestry and a Brown Buffalo by choice" (*Autobiography* 199). Carrasquillo contends that Acosta does not go far enough in constructing "the larger, radical identity project" (80) his protagonist works to achieve, that Acosta fails by not breaking from the grip of patriarchy both in Chicano culture and in white male America. While I concur with Carrasquillo in the male-as-master-of-his-own-destiny sentiment in *Autobiography,* I maintain that this is not necessarily as severe a shortcoming as Carrasquillo would have it for at least several reasons. First, if *Autobiography* is seen as a social document and historical artifact written by someone with immediate dealings with the Chicano and Brown Power movements, then Oscar's attitude toward women is historically accurate, albeit problematic. But *Autobiography* is not a social document; it is a work of fiction. This issue stresses Aldama's contention that Acosta uses a willful blend of realist and non-realist narrative techniques by using "jumps in time and space, [. . .] distinguish[ing] between author and narrator who is 'designing' his past as a story that is governed by fictive, rather than factually based, mimetic codes" (*Postethnic Narrative Criticism* 50). When Carrasquillo notes that Acosta "does not mitigate the larger problem of gender in his narratives" (80), she foists a retrograde constraint on *Autobiography* that does not enlighten our understanding of Acosta's novel. Put another way, just because Acosta (or any author) does not take his or her narrative in one predetermined direction or another does not affirm that the larger project (in this case, identity formation) is undermined; it does not uphold the notion that the project is fatally flawed. Instead of arriving at an appreciation of the novel that takes Oscar for the limited, flawed character he is, Carrasquillo concentrates on what he, and thereby the narrative, lacks. Acosta, who has demonstrated his ability to stretch beyond the bounds of realism even within a genre form (autobiography) that has a serious affinity to realism, could easily have recast Oscar as a valiant defender of the emergent rise of feminism in the Chicano community (a fact that feminist theorists would have trouble with in its own right—that is, a male champion of feminism, especially with Gloria Anzaldúa just around the figurative corner). But instead, Acosta ironizes Oscar's experiences through moments of self-deprecation, depictions of hallucinatory experiences, and delusions of grandeur. Irony is the engine that drives *Autobiography*. Here is Oscar's chapter 5 description of Fior d'Italia, a restaurant he, Casey, Maryjane, and Bertha have traveled to:

> I tip-toe into another world of fat-red carpets, violet tablecloths, dazzling chandeliers, white camellias, red roses and purple spider-mums. Young olive trees and casual green elephant ears are potted along the sides. There are pink brick walls to separate the parties and in the center of the dining room is a fountain spouting yellow suits and black glasses; old women with powder blue, short hair; young women with shivering gowns; furs of dead animals, diamonds from the caves of deepest Africa, rubies from the eyes of Asian dieties [*sic*]. Soft yellow lights, simple music from Mantovani, big black cigars, champagne, truffles, crepes suzettes, squab, wild rice, sweetbreads, saltimbocca, mushrooms and scampi alla casalinga . . . yes, sir, just another joint. Your Wing Lee's in the sky. Just like Trader JJ's! (60)

In describing Fior d'Italia, Oscar piles on exaggeration after exaggeration until it becomes a teetering mountain of irony. His adjectival description works sarcastically to cast the restaurant as even more pompous than it probably is. Yet there is a clear but subversive take on class inequality with his focus on the young women who bear treasures from imperial and colonial conquests of continental Asia and Africa. And as he reaches the crescendo of wonders of an alien lifestyle—"another world" where they listen to Mantovani rather than Procol Harem and eat expensive truffles and drink fine champagne—his narrative tone takes on that of the common man with his, "yes, sir, just another joint." It is clear that it is not just another joint, and by claiming that it is, Acosta, via his narrator, mocks the disparity between himself and the clientele of Fior d'Italia. The fine dining venue, he quips, is no different than the places of business he normally visits. It takes reading past the ironic, mock-heroic narrative voice to view the disenfranchised position in which he recognizes himself and thus his Chicano heritage. It is another instance in which the narrator-narratee communication (the ironic description of Fior d'Italia) and the critique of class and wealth (author-ideal audience) is apparent.

However, Carrasquillo's dissatisfaction with Acosta (i.e., that he did not go far enough to undermine entrenched patriarchy) speaks to my larger point about challenging reading situations. For readers with an affinity for feminist thinking, or even for those who advocate for a gentler treatment in Acosta's text of the equality and respect that should be afforded to all peoples regardless of gender, race, ethnicity, and so on, Oscar is an inscribed author with suspect norms and values that ought to be denounced. Yet this characteristic (some would say flaw) is complicated by moments in the text when he becomes a sympathetic figure, as, for example, when he recalls his humiliation at the hands of Junior Ellis. The ideal readership recognizes Oscar's character imperfections, noticing that tongue is often squarely in cheek when Oscar narrates, a result of the narrative's saturation in irony. I aver that Acosta renders Oscar in exactly this ironical fashion to demonstrate the complexity of the self to begin with. One of the strengths of *Autobiography* is its ability to allow the reader within the space of Oscar's ironic mind, troubled though it may be. The result is the ever-present ebb and flow of the potential for empathy for Oscar: there is the urge to help Oscar, while we recoil from his attitudes and treatment of women and race.

In reality, despite Oscar's narrative attempt at reunification with his people, except for a few luminaries such as Juan Bruce-Novoa and Rolando Hinojosa-Smith, who were among the first to laud Acosta's efforts, Chicanos have disregarded Acosta's writings. Despite his passion for Chicanos and Chicana/o causes, Acosta could never find the readership he so desired. Ilan Stavans recounts two separate conversations he had with Sandra Cisneros and Rudolfo Anaya regarding Acosta's writings. What Stavans recounts is a painful indictment of the pervasive disregard for Acosta's narratives:

> [Cisneros] was washing her hair when I asked her about Zeta. "What am I going to tell you, Ilan? *Tu sabes,* I really have nothing to say. I have his books, sure. But I've never read them, not entirely. His writings never spoke to me. I never found anything to identify with in them." I inquired about Zeta's feminine fetishism. "I don't know," she replied. "That's an ongoing problem in Chicano letters. I guess I would only read him if I was in jail!" (*Bandido* 116)

That Cisneros, an ambassador for Chicana feminism, would so casually disregard Acosta's writing as not having "anything to identify with," despite her admission of not having carefully read Acosta's texts, is stunning. Cisneros's remarks reflect in miniature the Chicano community's general reception to Acosta's work—the unwelcomed presence of irony in serious matters. But it is Rudolfo Anaya's comments to Stavans that best encapsulate Acosta's inability to find a zealous readership to align with his ideal readership. Stavans writes:

> Anaya, another classic Chicano writer, never met [Acosta]. "I read his work when it first came out," he writes in his correspondence, "and even taught

it in my Chicano literature classes. The students like *The Revolt of the Cock-roach People,* but had a harder time with his other book [*Autobiography,*] even though it spoke to the problem of lost identity. Zeta put a different slant, a zing, to our literature, and the tragedy of his disappearance is that it cut short his development. He had a lot to share, and it was cut short." (*Bandido* 116)

Unlike Cisneros, Anaya at least recognized that Acosta had "put a different slant" on Chicana/o literature. He intuited that Acosta was on a trajectory to continue his development as a writer and saw in his work something of merit. It seems these two writers, Anaya and Acosta, who published two different but equally important novels in 1972, recognized *Autobiography* as having something significant to say while failing to find the readership it so desperately sought.

With all of the above in mind, it is crucial to emphasize that narrative experimentation by Latino/a authors is not a recent phenomenon in Latino/a literature; it is just that such early examples of narrative innovation initially experienced a limited reception and inhospitable readerships. Many of these more daring narratives have only recently found engaged, willing readerships.[10] To be sure, early Latino/a authors who wanted to explore the complexities of narrative form—complexities Anglo American modernist writers were exploring fifty years earlier—were limited both by publishing and marketing expectations and by the lack of a receptive, willing readership. Secondly, the wider reception and attention garnered by more recently published Latino/a texts indicate a development or change in readership since the late 1960s. What ultimately marks Latino/a literature's maturation is not its successive narrative innovations but rather its creation and education of a willing readership. I assert that willing readers do not opt out of engaging with a storyworld simply because the narrative does not fit with prior expectations about how the text is likely to be structured or styled—a prior expectation based, in this case, on the ethnic identity or even linguistic choices of an author. In short, a willing readership strives to align neatly with the ideal readership.

This essay is only a brief foray into the rich terrain of Latina/o narrative studies that remains largely understudied.[11] While there are many aspects of

---

10. Some narratively challenging Latina/o texts such as Isabella Ríos's *Victuum* and Oscar "Zeta" Acosta's *The Autobiography of a Brown Buffalo* have suffered from a failed initial reception. But in a larger sense, Latina/o literature has often struggled with the issue of finding a readership. One has only to look Arte Público Press's "Recovering the U.S. Hispanic Literary Project"—an initiative to bring back into print works of Latino/a literature that have fallen out of print—as an example of the difficulty Latinas/os have in writing for readers who often have narrow expectations for Latina/o literature.

11. Notable exceptions to the dearth of scholars interested in the poetics of Latina/o narrative are Juan Bruce-Novoa, Ramón Saldívar, Patrick Hamilton, and Frederick Luis Aldama.

Latina/o narratives that might greatly expand our understanding of narrative writ large, my aim here is to propose a model for understanding how story-worlds invite readers to take up the task of not just understanding Latina/o narratives but also actually participating in the creation of these richly textured worlds as a hospitable, ideal readership might. My reason for concentrating on the reception end of the narrative and the reconstructed storyworld is that often in Latina/o literary scholarship, the narrative design itself is viewed the way some view the package of something purchased—as a necessary means of conveyance for its contents, but little more than that. In order for works of Latina/o or any minority literature to go beyond a localized readership and gain wider exposure, they must cultivate their own hospitable readerships by continually seeking to challenge publisher and reader expectations—even if it means, as it did for Oscar "Zeta" Acosta, that one's work does not find a contemporary audience.

CHAPTER 3

Narrative Disidentification

Beginnings in Toni Morrison's Song of Solomon

CATHERINE ROMAGNOLO

OVER THE LAST several decades, many scholars of narrative theory have called for what has been termed a "critical race narratology." Frederick Aldama's *Analyzing World Fiction* (2011) boldly began to move the field in that direction, "making us aware simultaneously both of the range of world fiction out there and of the myriad methodologies necessary for ferreting out those texts' complexities" (Nericcio 270). And yet, six years after the release of that volume, the consideration of social identity categories still appears to reside on the margins of the field of narratology. The work of decentering a narratological criticism that assumes a white, male, heterosexual, Euro-American subject still remains unfinished. I hope in this essay to advance this destabilizing move, and to explore what a "critical race narratology" might look like. My aim is not to lay out in broad strokes what such a reading practice would entail, but instead to provide a specific example of such a practice.

Because until recently narrative beginnings have received relatively little attention from scholars of narrative theory, they are particularly ripe for analysis in the mode being called for by the editors of this volume.[1] Indeed, two other contributors to this volume, Blake Wilder and Sterling Lecater Bland Jr., tacitly acknowledge the importance of beginnings by opening their own essays with discussions of the opening lines of James Baldwin's "Going to Meet

---

1. Since the publication of Brian Richardson's essay collection, *Narrative Beginnings*, attention to this topic has been deservedly renewed.

the Man" and Ralph Ellison's *Invisible Man,* respectively. Bland's reading of Ellison's narration emphasizes the importance of the opening pages in setting the stage for the fragmented narrative production of racialized identity, while Wilder's essay suggests the key role the opening of a narrative plays both in creating a narrative "world" of uncertainty and in the construction of social subjectivity through narrative worlds.

As my colleagues in this volume demonstrate, beginnings invoke the power of authority, authorship, and tradition, the very ideas upon which the narratives of racism and nationalism have heavily relied. While a number of critical race and ethnic studies scholars have explored the significance of beginnings and origins on the *story* level of fictional narratives, as of yet, there are few in-depth studies of the ways in which *formal* narrative beginnings play out in relation to these stories.

Beginnings play a role in both narrative content and form. They are addressed as concepts within narratives (what I term "conceptual beginnings"), and they are formal features within narratives (what I term "formal beginnings"), as in the opening pages of a text or chapter (discursive beginnings), the beginning of a plot (causal beginning), and the earliest chronological moment in a narrative (chronological beginning).[2] Their dual role as both story and discourse transcends the boundaries sometimes drawn between form and content and prompts us to examine the links that connect them.

As initiating moments in a text, formal beginnings have a symbolic primacy among the elements of narrative. They call into being writer and reader subject positions; they mark and participate in the production of what Susan Lanser calls "discursive authority"—the "intellectual credibility, ideological validity, and aesthetic value claimed by or conferred upon a work, author, narrator, character, or textual practice" (*Fictions of Authority* 6). As Sally Robinson claims in *Engendering the Subject,* "the subjectivities of writers, readers, and even texts themselves . . . are not products, but rather effects that emerge in the process of reading [and writing]" (13). Narrative beginnings are an ideologically embedded part of this process. Formal beginnings signify the emergence of a narrative and thereby the interpellation of the author as a writing subject and the reader as a reading subject. Formal beginnings mark the appropriation of the authority to speak and the authority to write. It is this authority with which writers of color have been contending over the past two centuries.

2. My book, *Opening Acts: Feminist Beginnings in Twentieth-Century U.S. Women's Fiction* (2015), as well as my article "Recessive Origins in Alvarez's *Garcia Girls*: A Feminist Theory of Narrative Beginnings" in *Beginnings,* edited by Brian Richardson, offer more extensive definitions of these categories.

As Edward Said makes clear, narrative beginnings have historically acquired a tendency to tacitly reinforce "traditional notions of origin, end, unity, and truth" (Clayton 43). But, when read in tandem with narrative content, in particular in co-signification with conceptual beginnings, this tendency is often undermined, even subverted. The act of beginning (reading or writing) a narrative and the formal beginnings *of* that narrative are informed by conventions of the past and will be transformed in unpredictable ways by conventions of the future. These norms have historically excluded minoritized subjects from fully assuming the power and agency of writing subjects. But, this historicity is the very place where agency and the possibility for the subversion of norms, of hierarchies, inheres. The diachronic nature of narrative communication makes space for change; in Judith Butler's words, it "opens up the possibility for a counter-speech, a kind of talking back" (*Excitable Speech* 15). Narrative beginnings contain within them the seeds of their own disruption.

Toni Morrison's novel *Song of Solomon* exemplifies the power of narrative beginnings and the ways in which writers of color may exploit that power. Utilizing both the conceptualization of beginnings *in* and the formal beginnings *of* her narrative, Morrison undermines conventional master narratives of identity and authenticity. Drawing attention to the role the concept of beginnings plays in the production of these constructions, she deploys formal beginnings to destabilize the ground upon which these narratives stand. She strategically intervenes in conventional narrative constructions of collective and individual origins that often provide the scaffolding for restrictive notions of social identity, and she disrupts the reinscription of hierarchically gendered and racialized conceptions of authority and agency.

This essay analyzes these interventions, with the hope that such an investigation will help move the field of narrative theory toward a critical race narratology. Examining form, content, and ideology as mutually constitutive is not merely an option when studying minoritized writers, it is essential—integral to a full understanding of the work their texts perform. As my reading will suggest, narrative elements such as beginnings can signify in vastly different ways for writers of color who have not had the luxury of assuming narrative authority and agency. The field of narratology, in general, continues to overlook this absolutely central piece of the puzzle, and I believe that one does a disservice to ignore the identificatory variables that are integral to the production of texts by writers of color. The intersection between a systematic formalist approach that considers ideology and social/historical context and a thematic, political, sociological reading that fully and systematically considers form is where the field of narratology must move.

Song of Solomon was published in 1977, a time in which opposing ideologies of race competed for prominence. As Michael Omi and Howard Winant explain, the late 1960s and '70s were characterized by "a sharp decline" and loss of "vitality and coherence" within movements advocating black power and black nationalism (95). Public discourse such as that which surrounded the Moynihan Report, a 1965 study of African American family structures, attempted to articulate and reestablish a racialized hierarchy. Working to counter alternative discourses circulated by movements for black liberation, pseudo-intellectual rhetoric characterized life in black communities as a "'tangle of pathology . . . capable of perpetuating itself without assistance from the white world,' claiming that 'at the heart of the deterioration of the fabric of Negro society is the deterioration of the Negro family'" (Watkins 218–19). Alternatively, the discourse of black nationalism and the recovery of African American historical, literary, and spiritual origins that provided support for claims of authentic black identity found public and popular expression in cultural products such as the novel and television series *Roots,* by Alex Haley. *Roots,* described as "a symbol of success for black Americans yearning to trace their heritage," popularized the notion implicit in the ideology of black nationalism that a recovery of origins represented the key to authentic powerful black identity (Mills 4). This authentic identity, however, was most often conceptualized as male, a fact that historically led to the occlusion of the particularity of black women's experiences. As Susan Farrell explains,

> [the movement was presented] as a struggle to attain manhood, but a manhood that . . . was based largely on the standards embraced by middle-class American whites. Focusing primarily on racial oppression, many male leaders in the movement failed to recognize the specificity of female oppression, what has been called the "double bind" faced by women of color. Along with this failure came a related problem—a refusal to interrogate gender roles as they were played out in the movement. (137)

Responding to these circulating discourses, *Song of Solomon* explicitly rejects a white supremacist worldview while simultaneously interrogating ideologies of authenticity implicit in movements for black liberation. In particular, Morrison addresses the impulse toward recovering origins (geographic, historical, mythical, racial). While acknowledging this recovery as empowering, Morrison also questions the danger in such claims of authenticity, particularly for female subjects. Positing instead a more contingent notion of identity, Morrison suggests a subject position akin to what José Muñoz calls

"disidentification."[3] Morrison's novel opens up the possibility of "a disiden-
tifying subject," a subject who is "unable"—or perhaps unwilling—"to fully
identify . . . [because] of the ideological restrictions implicit in an identificatory site" (*Disidentifications* 7). This notion counters a history of blackness
as constructed by the dominant white culture as well as essentialist notions
of identity posited by black nationalist movements. Morrison's conception of
subjectivity is enacted through resistance to and negotiation of "the conditions of (im)possibility that dominant culture generates" (6). It is subjectivity
produced "at the point of contact between essential understandings of self
(fixed dispositions) and socially constructed narratives of self" (6). This conception is one that is fluid, not static; it is not normatively gendered, and it
does not posit a restrictive essentialist conception of blackness in opposition
to its socially constructed inferiority. The words of Pilate seem to express well
Morrison's disidentification:

> There're five or six kinds of black. Some silky, some woolly. Some just empty.
> Some like fingers. And it don't stay still. It moves and changes from one kind
> of black to another. Saying something is pitch black is like saying something
> is green. What kind of green? Green like my bottles? Green like a grasshop-
> per? Green like a cucumber, lettuce, or green like the sky is just before it
> breaks loose to storm? Well, night black is the same way. May as well be a
> rainbow. (Morrison, *Song* 40–41)

Pilate's notion of blackness, like Norma Alarcón's notion of "identity-in-dif-
ference," describes a changeable, never static blackness, blackness as a "site of
emergence" (129).

The novel's main action spans the time from 1931 to 1963 and traces the
return of the main character, Milkman, to his family's origins in the southern
United States, where he encounters narratives of family history and ancestors. Milkman's journey has received significant attention from critics, the
vast majority reading it through the lens of the quest narrative. Primarily,
they interpret Milkman's quest as a search for communal and individual identity. The goal of this quest is, according to many critics, achieved through
the recovery of shared mythological and historical origins, and it is launched
within the context of symbolic and material violence perpetrated on blacks by
the dominant white culture. According to critics such as Theodore O. Mason,
the central quest of the novel "insists on the significance of shared history

---

3. See *Disidentifications* by José Muñoz.

communicated by shared stories, shared traditions, and shared experience" (383). Similarly, Susan Willis asserts that "Milkman comes to realize that only by knowing the past can he hope to have a future" (93), and Valerie Smith claims that Milkman's incorporation of "both his familial and his personal history into his sense of the present . . . repairs his feelings of fragmentation . . . and the coherence of his own life" (726).

According to these critics, *Song of Solomon* suggests that this recovery of origins is the key to African American selfhood in a white-dominated society. And many of these critics connect this quest to a classical mythic quest. As Catherine Carr Lee explains: "To be sure, Morrison's novel reflects archetypal initiation patterns found throughout Western literature" (43).[4] Lee suggests that Morrison revises and subverts this master narrative through the specificity of her African American protagonist. Many critics, however, simplify the work of Milkman's quest by reading it either through the lens of Western literary and mythic traditions or as a straightforward valorization of a black identity predicated upon a notion of recovering authentic origins. Morrison's examination of a past that is still palpably present at the time she is writing certainly rejects the white supremacy opposed by movements for black liberation, but it also questions the restrictive nature of claims for an authentic black identity and the narratives of origin upon which these claims rest. Through a reading of the novel that constellates ideological facets of *Song of Solomon* with its narratological elements, especially narrative beginnings, a more complex understanding of origins and their problematic relationship to the construction of individual and collective subjectivities emerges. Morrison's novel does not deny the importance of history and origins to a sense of self and community, but she never allows this contingent notion of subjectivity to solidify into an essential blackness.

The opening of Morrison's first chapter (the discursive beginning) simultaneously raises and disrupts the notion of a hero's birth.[5] The onset of labor for Ruth, Milkman's mother, is infused with symbolic significance. Set against a backdrop of red (rose petals), white (snow), and blue (Smith's wings), and marked by a singing woman (Milkman's Aunt Pilate) who predicts Milkman's impending birth, this opening invokes a sense of Milkman as the Western, American hero and ties the novel's opening to the notion of "natural" begin-

---

4. For discussions of *Song of Solomon* as a quest or initiation narrative, see Barthold, Josie Campbell, Harris, Royster, and V. Smith.

5. I define "discursive beginnings" as the beginning of the text or the beginning of a chapter. Discursive beginnings belong to the discourse level of narrative; therefore, they are determined by *how* the story is presented as opposed to being *a part of* the story itself. The category of discursive beginnings, most often referred to as "openings," encompasses the opening lines and pages of a narrative text as well as all paratextual material.

nings, a term that A. D. Nuttall uses to describe non-narrative origins, such as birth. This connection between the opening of the novel and the "natural" beginning of Milkman's birth seems to naturalize Milkman's heroic and representational status.

The opening, however, is also marked by an ending—a death. For as Ruth enters into labor, Robert Smith, an insurance agent and member of the community, having announced his intention to "fly from Mercy [Hospital] to the other side of Lake Superior at three o'clock," leaps to his death. In an inversion of a natural beginning, then, Morrison destabilizes the naturalizing effect this kind of opening might have, while simultaneously undermining her protagonist's heroic status. Moreover, Pilate's presence as the singing woman may go unnoticed at first, but the power of her predictive voice foreshadows the importance of her character to Morrison's subversion of the hero quest. What we will come to see as Pilate's radical subjectivity overshadows, in a sense, Milkman's status as hero. Morrison's appropriation of the mythic quest narrative "resists, demystifies, and deconstructs the universalizing ruse of the dominant culture" (Muñoz, *Disidentifications* 25). Morrison raises the specter of the Western heroic myth, acknowledging its power, but simultaneously undermining it.

Smith's attempted flight not only marks Milkman's birth with loss, it also immediately invokes the legend of flying Africans, a narrative whose origins stand in opposition to the Western masculine hero myth. As La Vinia Delois Jennings explains, Morrison invokes "an African tribal ancestral legacy, the oral stories and songs of Sneed, Delegal, Grant, and others that reclaim the belief that Africans could truly fly" (116). The invocation of this alternative tradition destabilizes the Western white tradition, appropriating its symbols and undermining its prominence. Morrison "[re]constructs the encoded message" of Western mythology "in a fashion that both exposes the encoded message's universalizing and exclusionary machinations and recircuits its workings to account for, include, and empower minority identities and identifications" (Muñoz, *Disidentifications* 31). As Morrison herself tells us:

> Myths get forgotten. Or they may not have been looked at carefully. . . . If [the flying myth in *Song of Solomon*] means Icarus to some readers, fine. . . . But my meaning is specific: it is about black people who could fly. That was always part of the folklore of my life. ("The Language Must Not Sweat" 122)

In this quotation, Morrison does not deny the connection of flying in her novel to the myth of Icarus. Instead, she implies that this mythology is far less important than, perhaps even supplanted by, the Afrocentric myth of flying Africans she wishes to tell.

Similarly, if we examine the symbols that accompany Milkman's birth, we see that the red, white, and blue of the scene operate not only as U.S. nationalistic symbols but as ones that place into question the nation and tradition they evoke. Like the myth of Icarus, the Western myth of American freedom is "occupied" by Morrison's alternative subversive meaning. The red here might be seen to represent blood that mars the purity of the snow on the ground, staining notions of whiteness with the violence it enacts. The blue of Mr. Smith's wings could be said to evoke "the blues," both the sadness referred to by the phrase as well as the musical form, which draws its energy and content from the often-violent historical, material conditions of black subjects in the United States. Finally, the blackness of Mr. Smith's skin evokes the identity upon which this violence has been imposed. These symbols, which immediately call to mind the American mythology of freedom and equality, are mocked by the scene around them—a scene in which the lives of African Americans like Smith and Ruth are assigned questionable value.

Although Milkman is not conscious of being marked by loss at the opening of the novel and the origin of his life, his character seems unconsciously to register this loss. As the narrator tells us, Milkman loses all drive upon realizing he lacks the ability to fly:

> The next day a colored baby was born inside Mercy for the first time. Mr. Smith's blue silk wings must have left their mark, because when the little boy discovered, at four, the same thing Mr. Smith had learned earlier—that only birds and airplanes could fly—he lost all interest in himself. (9)

Milkman's lack is read by critics such as Valerie Smith and Chiara Spallino as signifying a loss of connection to his mythic past. His alienation from himself is read as representing northern African Americans' dislocation from the South, from their ancestors, and even further from Africa. But as Morrison tells us in "Unspeakable Things Unspoken," just as the "proto-myth" of Western fable is deeply suspect, the African myth and the lost origins it signifies are "contaminated," corrupted by an exclusively masculine perspective, by the occlusion of black women's experiences—experiences that Pilate speaks to from the very first chapter of the narrative.

As the novel opens, Ruth Dead begins labor and Mr. Smith contemplates his flight. Pilate begins to sing a song that will take on increasing significance as the novel progresses: "*O Sugarman done fly / O Sugarman done gone . . .*" (9). Opening the novel with this song indicates its place of importance at the origins of Morrison's narrative, for, as we later learn, this song documents the originary narrative of Milkman's ancestors. It marks Milkman's loss and the recovery of that loss through the recovery of its narrative knowledge and the ability for flight. But, as the song is revealed in its entirety, it also implies a loss that is more complex, and perhaps deeper, for those who are gendered female. This fact is made only more apparent by the fact that it is Pilate's voice through which the song is first given expression:

O Sugarman don't leave me here
Cotton balls to choke me
O Sugarman don't leave me here
Buckra's arms to yoke me. . . .

Sugarman done fly away
Sugarman done gone
Sugarman cut across the sky
Sugarman gone home. (49)

As we learn more words to the song, the image of flight and the loss associated with it take on a gendered valence. The song, spoken from a female perspective, suggests that while "Sugarman" has found "home" through his flight, this flight only marks further loss for the female speaker. For the black male subject, flying may represent recovered origins, an identity found, but for the black female subject, the loss is much more profound and irrecoverable, a gap that the myth in its original form can never fully fill. Indeed, the power of flight is gained at the expense of black female identity.

Milkman's ancestor Solomon, the "Sugarman" of the song, escaped the oppression of his life. In doing so, however, he left behind his wife Ryna and twenty-two children to mourn a loss made only more profound by their abandonment. Milkman's authentic identity, signified by the ability to fly, is similarly sought at the expense of the women in his life, especially Hagar and Pilate, who, it seems, must die in order for him to recover his origins. Hagar's death (from a broken heart?) and Pilate's death by a bullet meant for Milkman are direct results of Milkman's drive for identity. Milkman's quest is powerful, but it's exclusive. And ultimately, it silences the women who have helped him discover his authentic black masculine identity.

In discussing the chronology of *Song of Solomon,* Morrison describes a teleological structure, one that she associates with a masculine narrative:

The challenge of *Song of Solomon* was to manage what was for me a radical shift in imagination from a female locus to a male one. To get out of the house, to de- domesticate the landscape that had so far been the site of my work. To travel. To fly. In such an overtly, stereotypically male narrative, I thought that straightforward chronology would be more suitable than the kind of play with sequence and time I had employed in my previous novels. . . . Old-school heroic, but with other meanings. (xii)

While *Song of Solomon*'s chronology is certainly "straightforward" in comparison to earlier Morrison novels, one must ask what Morrison might mean by "other meanings." And how are those alternate meanings conveyed in what on its surface is a linear narrative?

The trajectory of *Song of Solomon* appears to develop in a linear, what might be called folkloric, fashion. That is, it seems at first to maintain "a one-to-one correspondence between the 'real' order of events that are being told and the order of the narrative" (Genette, "Time and Narrative" 133). It opens with the protagonist's birth and ends with either his flight, or death, depending upon one's interpretation. This conventional structure might be read as reinforcing a notion of Milkman's quest as natural, his movement toward finding his family's origins as progressive. But, such a seemingly closed structure leaves little room for contesting voices, little room for questioning Milkman's quest, its goal, or its consequences. When we, however, shift focus to the chronological *beginning,* the teleology of this straightforward structure is disrupted, and along with it, "disobedient" voices and perspectives, such as Pilate's, can break through.[6]

The chronological beginning of *Song of Solomon* is not easy to identify. While the novel opens with birth and ends in flight/death, the narrative, through analepses, continuously returns the reader to earlier and earlier temporal moments. These flashbacks break through the linear narrative and, while allowing the impression of linearity to remain intact, destabilize it from within, making it impossible to fully identify the origins Milkman seeks.

While these moments of flashback begin in what is presumed to be the truth of Milkman's family history, eventually the "facts" become corrupted, infused and confused with folklore, lies, misunderstandings, and misreadings. Each time the story of Milkman's past is told, the central narrative becomes more complex, taking us to a chronologically earlier moment, filling us in on details. For example, just prior to Milkman's journey, the narrator tells the story of his grandfather's death and the subsequent break between his father and Pilate, a moment Milkman invests with the significance of origins. At this moment, Milkman and the reader have no reason to doubt the truth of this

---

6. Chronological beginnings are the beginning of the story. They exist on the fabula level of the text (they are part of the *story itself*). They may be defined as the earliest narrated moments in a text.

narrative, and the third-person perspective only further reinforces its veracity. The story, however, is retold several times, each time changing, sometimes significantly. These retellings, several of them Pilate's, represent alternative truths competing with the patriarchal narrative for prominence. As Milkman travels south, he discovers chronologically earlier and earlier moments of his family's history. Finally, he uncovers the narrative of Solomon/Shalimar/Sugarman, the story of his flying ancestor, revealed to him first through Pilate's singing and later through a children's game. At first, each revised narrative seems to replace the original, to suggest a more authentic origin. But if we look more closely, it becomes apparent that their relationship to one another is more palimpsestic. They do not replace each other; contradictions remain, not to be resolved.

Despite these structural anomalies, numerous critics discuss *Song of Solomon* in terms of the mythic quest plot, a relentlessly linear paradigm. Morrison herself has, however, spoken against the danger that such readings might engender:

> Sotto (but not completely) is my own giggle (in Afro-American terms) of the proto-myth of the journey to manhood. Whenever characters are cloaked in Western fable, they are in deep trouble; but the African myth is also contaminated. (Morrison, "Unspeakable Things" 226)

While she does not deny her own use of this traditional plot, she also uses the term "contaminated" in her description of it. This contamination becomes apparent when examining the ways in which causal beginnings function in *Song of Solomon*. Through her manipulation of the classic plot structure of "the quest," Morrison highlights and undermines both the Western perspective of what she calls the "proto-myth" as well as the gendered perspective of Afrocentric mythology.

Elsewhere I have defined causal beginnings as "the beginning of the plot . . . the first cause of narrative action" (Romagnolo, *Opening Acts* xxvi). With that definition in mind, one might easily posit that the causal beginning of a quest plot is what Joseph Campbell refers to as the "call to adventure," or what Vladimir Propp calls "the second stage [in which] a sense of lack is identified, for example in the hero's family or within a community, whereby something is identified as lost or something becomes desirable for some reason" (Alberski 10, 14). This definition seems to point to Milkman's desire for the gold he believes to be hidden in a cave in Danville, Pennsylvania, the town in which his grandfather settled after leaving the South. As the force that seems initially to propel him to embark upon his journey south, Milkman himself believes this to be the reason for his quest:

> Suddenly, in the midst of his telling, Milkman wanted the gold. He wanted to get up right then and there and go get it. Run to where it was and snatch every grain of it from under the noses of the Butlers. (236)

But Milkman's reason for seeking the gold shifts several times, leaving the impression that Milkman himself does not really know what propels him:

> He thought he wanted it in the name of Macon Dead's Georgia peaches, in the name of Circe and her golden-eyed dogs, and especially in the name of Reverend Cooper and his old-timey friends who began to die before their facial hair was out. . . . He also thought he wanted it in the name of Guitar, to erase what looked like doubt in his face when Milkman left, the "I-know-you-gonna-fuck-up" look. There wasn't any gold, but now he knew that all the fine reasons for wanting it didn't mean a thing. The fact was he wanted the gold because it was gold and he wanted to own it. (257)

The fact that the "hero" himself is unsure of the cause of his quest fundamentally destabilizes the forward momentum of the quest plot. Shifting our focus from the goal of the quest to its cause, the prize of Milkman's quest seems to shift, become unstable, and ultimately dissolve. The reader is never quite sure whether the gold existed. We are not left with a concrete sense of what Milkman's quest seeks but of the instability of the origins that launched him.

Once Milkman's reasons for embarking on his journey-quest are destabilized, we must revise our thinking about the catalyst for the central action of the narrative (causal beginning). No longer can we as readers believe that the catalyst is Milkman's desire for gold. Instead, shifting to the Afrocentric flying narrative, we might consider the narrative's causal beginning to be Milkman's realization that he does not have the power to fly. Returning to the opening pages of the novel, it becomes clear that this loss marks his entire young life:

> When the little boy discovered, at four, the same thing Mr. Smith had learned earlier—that only birds and airplanes could fly—he lost all interest in himself. To have to live without that single gift saddened him and left his imagination so bereft that he appeared dull. (9)

Morrison's story does not hinge on the teleological paradigm of the quest, but on a less linear trajectory. For much of the novel, Milkman and the reader do not know what he seeks or why he seeks it. The jagged line of the plot takes us from an ambiguous causal beginning to an open ending. We never know whether Milkman launches into transcendent flight or dies in the arms of his "brother" Guitar.

Through the beginnings of her novel, Morrison unsettles the ground upon which traditional Western quest narrative stands—destabilizing its authority to tell the "whole" story and insisting on the specificity of her character's experiences as a black man. Morrison's novel does not, however, leave the Afrocentric foundation of her narrative uninterrogated. In tying the causal beginning to the closing, it becomes clear that the symbolic power of flight as bequeathed patrilineally is not entirely triumphant. Milkman's recovery of his ancestral past, and the flight that represents it, is a double-edged sword. It is marked by both transcendence and abandonment. This transcendence, Morrison makes clear, is gendered. The origins Milkman seeks are not universal. The black male identity affirmed by them comes at the expense of black female subjectivity.

But Morrison offers the reader an alternative to the type of flight practiced by Milkman's male ancestors. This flight is associated with the female Pilate, and it does not imply the recovery of an authentic identity through the Name of the Father, but a type of disidentification, aptly signified by Pilate's lack of a navel. Pilate, the narrator tells us, is "self-born." Her mother dies shortly before her birth, and miraculously, she finds her way into this world completely unaided. She is marked as self-born by the uninterrupted smoothness of her abdomen. Because she lacks the symbol of connection to her origins, she is shunned wherever she settles:

> It isolated her. Already without family, she was further isolated from her people . . . [and] every other resource was denied her: partnership in marriage, confessional friendship, and communal religion. Men frowned, women whispered and shoved their children behind them. (148)

Her marginal status has forced her to remain outside of traditional racialized and gendered identities, a position she eventually embraces: "When she realized what her situation in the world was and would probably always be she threw away every assumption she had learned and began at zero" (149). In the end, the reader comes to understand that Pilate is the most powerful character in the text. And, it is her disidentificatory subjectivity that empowers her. Pilate's strength comes not from a recovery of authentic origins, but from an acceptance of the absence by which they are marked. Just after Pilate's death, Milkman thinks: "Now he knew why he loved her so. Without ever leaving the ground, she could fly" (336). The paradox of being able to fly without leaving the ground represents the contradiction revealed through an examination of beginnings in Morrison's text. *Song of Solomon* posits a subjectivity that acknowledges the power of origins and the strong masculine identity predicated upon them, but it also has a clear sense of the dangers inherent in such a bounded notion of identity.

Reading *Song of Solomon* with attention to both formal and ideological variables casts the complexity of Morrison's work into stark relief. The form of the novel must be understood as integral to an apprehension of its construction of a disidentificatory black subject, an understanding that can only be gained through the bringing together of narratology and critical race theory. The hope of this essay is that our struggle with "fixed dispositions . . . [and] socially constituted definitions" and Morrison's resistance to these constructions might allow us, along with Milkman, to light upon a disidentificatory alternative (Muñoz, *Disidentifications* 6).

CHAPTER 4

Narrative Process and Cultural Identity in Leslie Marmon Silko's *Ceremony*

STEPHEN SPENCER

> He took a deep breath of cold mountain air: there were no boundaries.
>
> —Leslie Marmon Silko, *Ceremony*

WHEN Leslie Marmon Silko was still an emerging writer, Paula Gunn Allen in her influential book *The Sacred Hoop* called for a "feminist approach to the study and teaching of American Indian life and thought" to resist the domination by "paternalistic, male-dominated modes of consciousness" (222). Allen writes,

> Traditional peoples perceive their world in a unified-field fashion that is very different from the single-focus perception that generally characterizes western masculinist, monotheistic modes of perception . . . the demands of type and analysis are, after all, linear and fixed, while the requirements of tribal literatures are accretive and fluid. The one is unidimensional, monolithic, excluding, and chronological, while the other is multidimensional, achronological, and including. (244)

Since Allen's work, the relation between Native and Western forms, traditions, and voices in Silko's writing has been addressed by many scholars, including Arnold Krupat, Arturo J. Aldama, and Bernard Hirsch. Hirsch, for example, writes about Silko's incorporation of characteristics of the oral tradition in her writing and the challenges this poses. As Allen and Hirsch have pointed out, written narrative is static and fixed, not fluid and dynamic, and the characteristics of the oral tradition, such as the traditional stories in *Ceremony,* are not within a tribal cultural context, that is, within a particular place, time, and social context.

Despite the recognition that Silko's work, and the work of other contemporary Native American writers, is a complex blending of forms, traditions, and voices, literary critics have tended to emphasize the historical and cultural contexts surrounding *Ceremony*, rather than the complex interplay between the formal and contextual elements of the novel. As the editors of this volume point out in the introduction, this is the case for much work in race and ethnic studies. As Sue Kim argues in this collection, "Asian American literary criticism is interpretative, contextualist, extrinsic, and praxis-oriented; narrative theory is concerned with articulating a formal poetics and is formalist, intrinsic, and abstract" (15 in this volume). Such is the case in Native American literary criticism as well. For example, scholars have discussed *Ceremony* in relation to law, land rights, education, nationalism, and colonial history.[1] Without doubt, these sociohistorical contexts have impacted Native American identity in devastating and complex ways and are important for a full understanding of literature written by Native American writers; however, now that many texts by contemporary Native American writers have long literary histories, what seems timely at this point in the literary history and reception of *Ceremony* is a more comprehensive theoretical approach for understanding how such a multidimensional and multivoiced written narrative contributes to the broader cultural themes of the novel. As Hirsch argues, attaining harmony of the oral tradition and written word requires a more inclusive approach that takes into account the multiple language forms, implicit and explicit, that give a text meaning.

This collection seeks to achieve a more inclusive approach by putting narrative theory in conversation with contextual narrative criticism. Our shared interest in this collection, as Kim points out, is an exploration of "the ways in which fictional narratives operate within larger social structures as well as an investment in scrutiny of how minds and subjectivity work in and through narratives" (16 in this volume). In this essay, I put Allen's socio-contextual approach to texts by Native writers in conversation with the narrative theories of Mikhail Bakhtin and their extension to feminist theory by Susan Lanser to create a critical space in which to develop a deeper understanding of the ways the novel merges tribal and Western narrative forms, resists the constraints

---

1. See Cheyfitz for a discussion of Native American literature and the context of federal Indian law and independence, Akins for a discussion of *Ceremony* and the context of the schooling of American Indians, Gohrisch for a discussion of Silko's work as "transculturation," Bauerkemper for a discussion of Silko and the context of nationalist history, and Tripathy for a discussion of Silko and the context of postcolonialism and resistance.

of Western language and forms, and dissolves boundaries, both formal and contextual, in the telling of Tayo's multidimensional story. Aligning Allen's approach and narrative theory overcomes what might have been a tendency in the past to see race and ethnic studies and narratology as somehow mutually exclusive.

Despite the attempts of early narrative theorists, as Kim outlines in this collection, to shy away from acknowledging the importance of context, Bakhtin embraced it in his theoretical approach. Although his work was initially associated with Russian formalism and does not specifically address works by Native American writers, Bakhtin fully acknowledges the significance of sociohistorical contexts in the analysis of written narrative. Bakhtin's approach is useful in analyzing the multivocal nature of Tayo's story in *Ceremony* because for Bakhtin all language is an area of social conflict, and the polyvocality of discourse in a literary text may disrupt and subvert the authority of ideology as expressed in a single narrative voice. Allen echoes Bakhtin in her description of Western written discourse as "unidimensional, monolithic, excluding, and chronological" and in her description of tribal narratives as "multidimensional, achronological, and including" (244). Allen also echoes Bakhtin in her call for a theoretical approach that challenges the "linear and fixed" nature of type and Western textual analysis. Similarly, Bakhtin argues that all discourse is inherently hybrid, "a mixture of two social languages within the limits of a single utterance, an encounter, within the arena of an utterance, between two different linguistic consciousnesses, separated from one another by an epoch, by social differentiation or by some other factor" (qtd. in Holquist 358). Discourse for Bakhtin operates as text and context simultaneously, thus making contexts surrounding discourse as significant as the text, rendering a purely formal, linguistic, or stylistic analysis of a text insufficient for developing a full understanding of a text:

> Discourse lives, as it were, beyond itself, in a living impulse [*napravlennost'*] toward the object; if we detach ourselves completely from this impulse all we have left is the naked corpse of the word, from which we can learn nothing at all about the social situation or the fate of a given word in life. To study the word as such, ignoring the impulse that reaches out beyond it, is just as senseless as to study psychological experience outside the context of that real life toward which it was directed and by which it is determined. (qtd. in Holquist 292)

Such an understanding of the hybrid nature of discourse for Bakhtin is accomplished through an understanding of "heteroglossia," which he defines as "the dialogue of languages as it exists in a given era," including social, cultural, and ideological contexts surrounding the text (qtd. in Holquist 417).

Susan Lanser discusses heteroglossia in terms of "surface text" and "subtext." Like Bakhtin, she argues that the subtext includes cultural contexts and traditions, but like Allen, Lanser addresses the ways these contextual elements are "more pronounced" in texts by women and oppressed peoples ("Toward" 458). Lanser writes, "The surface text and subtext are strikingly different both in story and narration, and a narrative theory adequate for describing the whole will have to account for both and for the narrative frame that binds them" ("Toward" 456). In addition to formal and contextual knowledge of a text, Lanser adds a third category, which is "the most hidden text, the hardest to see," requiring a reader who has knowledge of both the textual and contextual ("Toward" 463). Lanser echoes Bakhtin's ideas about the three-dimensional nature of a text and the necessity of a multi-languaged consciousness for a full reading of a text. Lanser's narrative theory bridges the gap between "formal structures" and "the causes, ideologies, or social implications of particular narrative practices" (*Fictions* 4). Lanser's approach also echoes Allen's assumption that "language embodies the unspoken assumptions and orientations of the culture it belongs to" (225). For Allen, a feminist theoretical approach helps us understand the "complex interplay of factors," including oppression, colonialism, and reclamation of traditions (223). Since, according to Lanser, "polyphony is more pronounced and more consequential in women's narratives and in the narratives of other dominated peoples" ("Toward" 458), it seems that an analysis of the narrative must account for and identify the multiple elements of heteroglossia. Critical analyses of *Ceremony* have tended to focus on the many sociohistorical contexts, such as oppression, colonialism, and traditions, that inform a reading of the novel. However, if we agree with Allen that language "embodies the unspoken assumptions and orientations of the culture it belongs to" and with Lanser that reading requires "knowledge of both the textual and contextual," *Ceremony*, as a text written by a woman writer who identifies as Laguna Pueblo, Anglo American, and Mexican American, writing a novel in English, certainly calls for a complex approach that analyzes the blending of forms, traditions, and voices in the novel. Bakhtin and Lanser provide a critical approach to *Ceremony* that goes beyond the limits of formal and postcolonial approaches to the novel and accomplishes what Allen hopes feminist theory, "when judiciously applied to the field," will do: "freeing the data for interpretation that is at least congruent with a tribal perceptual mode" (223).

Although *Ceremony* is a multidimensional and multivoiced narrative text written by a contemporary Native American writer, as the novel opens, the central character, Tayo, does not exist within what Allen would describe as a "tribal perceptual mode," but rather, his identity has already reached the culminating point of what Allen would describe as a linear, unidimensional narrative. As Blake Wilder writes in this collection, "Separate racial worlds influence aspects of narrative, but at the same time, it is narrative that creates those segregated worlds" (71 in this volume). Wilder analyzes the ways in which James Baldwin's story "Going to Meet the Man" constructs a white character's worldview, or perceptual mode, that seeks to maintain patriarchal power, the ways he "clings to the known narratives that reaffirm the power of white masculinity" (81 in this volume). Similarly, Silko uses a known narrative to construct Tayo's worldview, demonstrating how the Western narrative has constructed Tayo's identity; however, unlike the white character, Jesse, in Baldwin's story, as Silko's narrative proceeds, the narrative structure ultimately subverts and dismantles that known worldview. The worldview in which Tayo exists at the beginning of *Ceremony* has been constructed through a Western (white) narrative that began with his education as a child and continued through his experiences as a soldier in World War II. Rocky, Tayo's cousin and childhood friend, convinces Tayo to join the army to see the world, but they participate in some of the bloodiest battles in the Pacific, and Rocky is killed. Despite its power to shape his identity, Tayo cannot fully participate in this Western worldview and is unable to kill Japanese soldiers in the jungles of the Pacific because they look like his uncle, Josiah.

At the beginning of the novel, Tayo has returned from war, but his identity is still firmly bound and ensnared by the "known narrative" of the Western colonial worldview. The result is disharmony and illness, expressed through Tayo's physical and emotional sickness. As he recovers from post-traumatic stress disorder in a VA hospital in Los Angeles, he feels disconnected from family, cultural heritage, and community. He is unable to rest, because his "memories were tangled with the present" (Silko 6). The power of his present, as defined by the known narrative of a U.S. soldier returning from a foreign war, to ensnare him begins to diminish as a tribal narrative asserts itself, a process that had begun during the war. Before attending Indian school, Tayo "had believed in the [traditional] stories for a long time, until the teachers taught him not to believe in that kind of 'nonsense'" (Silko 19). Rocky, the all-state athlete and A-student, urges Tayo to reject the old ways and assimilate into the white world. Old Grandma does not scold Rocky for his rejection of tradition because she knows "what white people wanted in an Indian" (Silko 51). This desire to assimilate is a logical reaction to the Native position in the social hierarchy of American culture. Louis Owens writes, "The mask is one realized over centuries through Euro-America's construction of the 'Indian' Other. In order to be recognized, and to thus have a voice that is heard by those in control of power, the Native must step into that mask and *be* the Indian constructed by white America" ("As If an Indian Were Really an Indian" 17), and, I would say, the Indian constructed by a white American narrative. Tayo knows what white people think of the old ways and the stories. His science teacher calls them "superstition," and Tayo comes to believe "the science books explained the causes and effects" (Silko 94). In the military hospital as he recovers from the trauma of war, the language Tayo uses to describe himself is "white smoke," having "no consciousness of itself," fading "into the white world of their bed sheets and walls; it was sucked away by the words of doctors who tried to talk to the invisible scattered smoke" (Silko 14). Tayo sees himself as "white smoke" and "invisible scattered smoke" in a "white world." The words Tayo uses suggest the sterile and ephemeral nature of his identity that has been whitewashed like the hospital sheets and walls. Unable to understand the words of the doctors and unable to speak to them, Tayo "reached into his mouth and felt his own tongue; it was dry and dead, the carcass of a tiny rodent" (Silko 15). When the doctor tells Tayo he is sending him home, Tayo wants to scream at the doctor, "but the words choked him and he coughed up his own tears" (Silko 16). At this point in the narrative, a dialogue of languages seems to be trying to emerge through Tayo, but Tayo is unable to articulate a worldview beyond the one within which he is trapped.

When Tayo returns to his community, the elder storytellers help him begin to understand the ways that his identity has been constructed through a white worldview. They help him see that language is dialogic, that "all of creation suddenly had two names: an Indian name and a white name. Christianity separated people from themselves; it tried to crush the single clan name, encouraging each person to stand alone, because Jesus Christ would save only the individual soul" (Silko 68). When he returns to New Mexico, Tayo believes that his actions and illness have cursed the land, which has become dry and barren. Tayo's family calls on Ku'oosh, a tribal healer, to perform a healing ceremony. Ku'oosh soon understands that Tayo's illness requires a more powerful ceremony, and he sends Tayo to Betonie, a holy man who helps Tayo understand the true nature of his sickness and its larger implications for his community, Native American culture, and even the white world. As the narrative progresses, Tayo hears the traditional stories and begins to develop the multi-languaged consciousness necessary for moving beyond the white worldview to see discourse as what Bakhtin refers to as a "living impulse." Tayo must operate within "two different linguistic consciousnesses" (Bakhtin qtd. in Holquist 35), and as Tayo develops his consciousness, readers begin to see the social situation within which the words exist. As Tayo's ability to understand his story develops, the hybrid nature of language, as Bakhtin argues, becomes more apparent and begins to disrupt and subvert the authority of ideology as expressed in the surface narrative in which Tayo has existed.

As the narrative moves from the known Western narrative that has constructed Tayo's identity, the increasing dialogic nature of Tayo's story begins to resist the Western discourse and narrative that have shaped Tayo's identity early in the novel. Inside his head, Tayo begins to feel "the tension of little threads being pulled and how it was with tangled things, things tied together, and as he tried to pull them apart and rewind them into their places, they snagged and tangled even more" (Silko 7). Traditional stories from Tayo's past soon begin to intrude on and erode the Western narrative that demands assimilation and denial of his ancestral past. When Tayo is a soldier in the jungle, he recalls Josiah's story about the greenbottle fly helping people, but the flies crawling on Rocky's body enrage him and he curses them (Silko 102). At this point, he is unable to see the relevance of the traditional story in the context of the white man's war and the violence in the Pacific jungle. When Tayo is at the bar drinking with Emo and Leroy, Emo tells a story about soldiers during the war having a sexual encounter with white women. In the story, an Indian posing as an Italian has sex with two white women. The story appears in the novel in a traditional form, like other stories such as Reed Woman and Corn Woman, K'oo'ko, and Pa'caya'nyi, but the multiple sociolects of the story are apparent in language, context, and content. The story is not told in a Western narrative form, but in the form of a poem or perhaps a chant, with rhythm and repetition. Like the oral tradition, Emo performs the story for an audience, his bar buddies, who laugh loudly at the story and urge him to tell another one. The story is described as part of a repeated "ritual" in the bars that moves from cursing about lost land, to stories of sexual encounters with white women, to stories about the killing of Japanese soldiers, and ends with Emo displaying teeth taken from Japanese soldiers. Although the story is presented in a more traditional oral form, it is told in English and has a modern theme and context: a bar on 4th Avenue, U.S. army buddies drinking together, and sex with two white women in a car. Emo's story is described as part of a repeated ritual, but unlike traditional stories, the story does not teach, and as ritual it does not perform a healing function. In these examples, the meaning and function of traditional stories have been weakened by the contexts, language, and content of a Western worldview.

Another meaning of ritual, of course, is ceremony. The holy man, Ku'oosh, helps Tayo begin to understand that his story, and the story of his community, is a continuing, achronological ceremony that has been corrupted through white colonial versions of the past and present. Ku'oosh tells Tayo that the damage since the white people came may be irreparable. Ku'oosh's visit helps Tayo begin to realize that the old stories are fragile, susceptible to the foibles of even one person, like Emo, who might "tear away the delicate strands of the web, spilling the rays of sun into the sand, and the fragile world would be injured" (Silko 38). Once Tayo begins to recognize that his identity has been constructed by the complex processes of colonial history and discourse, he is able to begin the process of reconstructing his past and constructing a new ceremony. As Tayo moves from a bounded Western identity to a Native identity, his story begins to include more individuals, groups, forms, and cultural contexts that intermingle in what Bakhtin would call a dialogue of languages, a discourse that reaches out to become a living impulse. The text and context operate simultaneously, and Tayo's story becomes increasingly polyvocal and resistant to both the known Western narrative and Western narrative form.

Unlike Emo's story, which is presented in a traditional tribal form that does not resist the Western colonial narrative, the story "Thought-Woman, the Spider" presents language that Bakhtin would see as polyvocal discourse that disrupts and subverts the authority of ideology as expressed in a single narrative voice. "Thought-Woman, the Spider" opens the novel and imagery from the story reappears throughout. This traditional tale, according to Matthew Teorey, subverts traditional Western literary style by mixing oral and written storytelling that "guides the reader to a more harmonious, integrated self" and challenges traditional Western gender hierarchies through the restoration of the feminine side of Tayo's self (4). Teorey writes that the result is heteroglossia, "a fabric of interwoven voices, experiences, and meanings" that "ensnares male readers" in its web (4). Teorey argues that Tayo matures within a "feminist, Native worldview" (5). Teorey's analysis of this mixing of forms is mostly thematic and does not analyze how the array of voices and narrative strategies challenges conventional novel and narrative forms. Silko challenges conventional novel forms by weaving the images and symbols of this and other traditional stories throughout the narrative text of the novel. In the prologue to the novel, Silko writes,

> Thought-Woman, the spider,
>   named things and
>   as she named them
>   they appeared.
>
>   She is sitting in her room
>   thinking of a story now
>
>   I'm telling you the story
>   she is thinking. (1)

The words of Thought-Woman have the power to create, and the storyteller, perhaps the narrator transcribing her words, is telling the story. The narrator becomes the voice of the traditional stories and Tayo's story, establishing an awareness from the beginning of the novel that this is not a univocal, linear narrative, but one that merges traditional tribal voices and Western discourse and past and present. Through stories, Old Betonie, a Navajo medicine man, helps Tayo begin to see the importance of stories, and Tayo comes to see "a world made of stories, the long ago, time immemorial stories, as old Grandma called them. It was a world alive, always changing and moving" (Silko 95). The stories, to use Bakhtin's terminology, are living impulses that reach beyond the text to "that real life toward which it was directed and by which it is determined" (qtd. in Holquist 292). The stories are inclusive and dynamic, dissolving boundaries imposed by a Western worldview: past/present, words/oral tradition, individual/community, masculine/feminine. Night Swan also helps Tayo see his identity as multidimensional and his story, and the story of his community, as dynamic. She "encourages Tayo to embrace all sides of his identity, Native and white, masculine and feminine, which he can do only if he 'assume[s] the tongue and cosmography of Spider Woman' and reconnects 'to the enduring feminine principle inherent to Laguna cosmogony'" (Teorey 16). The "multi-languaged consciousness" that Lanser sees as necessary for "a full reading of a text" (*Fictions* 4) is important to an understanding of the significance of the tales of Thought-Woman. These tales give Tayo the cultural knowledge that will help him begin untangling the threads of colonial history and discourse that have ensnared him as a man and as a Native American living in a colonial context.

Old Betonie also helps Tayo untangle the threads of the colonial story and construct a new alternative story that is multivocal and dynamic. He explains why Tayo saw Josiah's face in the Japanese soldiers in the Philippines: "Thirty thousand years ago they were not strangers," Betonie tells Tayo. "You saw what the evil had done: you saw the witchery ranging as wide as this world" (Silko 124). Betonie helps Tayo understand that the process which has constructed his identity "has been going on for a long time" (Silko 125). Tayo "wanted to yell at the medicine man, to yell the things the white doctors had yelled at him," and he recognizes, at that moment, that his sickness is "part of something larger, and his cure would be found only in something great and inclusive of everything" (Silko 125–26). Tayo asks Betonie, "They took almost everything, didn't they?" (Silko 127). Betonie responds, "Indians wake up every morning of their lives to see the land which was stolen, still there, within reach, its theft being flaunted" (Silko 127). Betonie tells Tayo that deeds and papers are meaningless, that it is "the people who belong to the mountain" (Silko 128). When Tayo leaves Betonie, "he wanted to walk until he recognized himself again" (Silko 154). Tayo now understands why he is sick and that there are "transitions that had to be made to become whole again, in order to be the people our Mother would remember" (Silko 170). Tayo sees the colonial narrative as a lie, "the lie which they had wanted him to learn: only brown-skinned people were thieves; white people didn't steal, because they always had the money to buy whatever they wanted" (Silko 191). Tayo realizes that white people cannot see beyond the unidimensional, monolithic Western narrative, to see that they stole the land and themselves have been used and destroyed by the witchery.

The recognition Tayo gains initially causes him to hate white people and what they have done to the earth and to the animals. He wants to "kick the soft white bodies into the Atlantic Ocean . . . to scream to all of them that they were trespassers and thieves" (Silko 204). He realizes that the people have internalized the oppressor's story, in which they have been "taught to despise themselves" (Silko 204). However, a few people, Tayo realizes, understand that the lie is destroying white people faster than it is destroying Indian people. This aspect of the story is an example of what Lanser refers to as the third text, the most hidden, "evident only in the sterility of their [white people's] art, which continued to feed off the vitality of other cultures, and in the dissolution of their consciousness into dead objects: the plastic and neon, the concrete and steel" (Silko 204). The multiple voices of Ku'oosh, Betonie, and the traditional stories are necessary for Tayo's emerging understanding of the hidden aspects of his own story and the larger story of his community.

Once Tayo begins to recognize and understand the ways his identity has been determined by a Western story and discourse, he is able to begin constructing a new (his)story. Betonie helps Tayo understand that history is a matter of perspective. Betonie tells Tayo that people do not understand why he lives so close to the dirty town. He tells Tayo that his hogan was there first, long before the arrival of white people, and that "it is that town down there which is out of place" (Silko 118). In the center of *Ceremony,* Betonie tells Tayo the story of the origin of the white people and their witchery. The story is polyvocal, told by Betonie in a traditional Laguna form, but written in English, and including contemporary images and themes, referring to war, colonialism, pollution, disease, the search for gold and plutonium, nuclear testing, and nuclear destruction. The story takes the form of a chant, with rhythm and repetition. For example, the repetition of words creates a chant-like rhythm:

Killing killing killing killing. (Silko 136)

and

Whirling
whirling

whirling
whirling (Silko 138)

These lines, or variations of these lines, are also repeated throughout the tale:

Set in motion now
Set in motion . . .

In addition to using rhythm and repetition, this tale is collective and circular, merging the past and present. It is a continuing story that teaches Tayo what is wrong and why the community, now broadened to include both the Native and white worlds, is suffering. After Betonie tells this story, Tayo realizes that the actions of white ranchers, the National Forest, and the state have upset the balance of the world and "the people could expect droughts and harder days to come" (Silko 186).

Tayo's new awareness of history helps him to heal the pain of the past, construct a new definition of identity not bounded by colonial discourse, and ultimately create a new polyvocal and dynamic story. Rather than a monolithic, unidimensional narrative that has been an incomprehensible tangle of threads, Tayo now has a worldview that Allen might call a "unified-field" vision (Allen 244). Tayo cries in relief "at finally seeing the pattern, the way all the stories fit together—the old stories, the war stories, their stories—to become the story that was still being told" (Silko 246). Tayo experiences a moment of consciousness when he sees the irony of it all. When Grandma asks Tayo why people would make a thing like a nuclear bomb, Tayo says, "I don't know, Grandma," but the narrator writes, "But now he knew":

There was no end to it; it knew no boundaries; and he had arrived at the point of convergence where the fate of all living things, and even the earth, had been laid. From the jungles of his dreaming he recognized why the Japanese voices merged with Laguna voices, with Josiah's voice and Rocky's voice; the lines of cultures and worlds were drawn in flat dark lines on fine light sand, converging in the middle of witchery's final ceremonial sand painting. (Silko 245–46)

Tayo's unbounded worldview is reflected in the story's narrative, which draws on multiple and often competing influences, histories, voices, and identities to create an inclusive narrative. Silko opens the novel with a story of "Thought-Woman, the spider," and a story about "ceremony" and the power of words to shape reality. When Tayo is with Ts'eh, Silko writes that "the old memories were less than the constriction of a single throat muscle" (Silko 227). Ku'oosh

speaks in "the old dialect full of sentences that were involuted with explanations of their own origins, as if nothing the old man said were his own
but all had been said before and he was only there to repeat it" (Silko 34).
The word Ku'oosh uses to express "fragile" is "filled with the intricacies of a
continuing process" (Silko 35). Using Allen's terms, *Ceremony* is a narrative
about the "process of a shift in focus" (242). Tayo's story is not individual but
involves the interweaving of multiple voices, forms—both Native and Western—and cultural contexts. It is collective, not Tayo's or Ku'oosh's own, and
recursive, not linear. Readers unfamiliar with Native American storytelling
traditions may at first struggle to find meaning in tribal stories that resist the
traditional tropes and elements of Western narratives. In order to fully experience a narrative text, readers must, as Bakhtin argues, understand how narrative discourse lives beyond itself, or we risk learning "nothing at all about
the social situation or the fate of a given word in life" (qtd. in Holquist 292).
Inclusive tribal narratives, Allen writes, "are not easily 'read' by hierarchically
inclined westerners" (241). Allen describes tribal stories as forests in which
"all elements coexist, where each is integral to the being of the others" (241).
Traditional stories "work dynamically among clusters of loosely interconnected circles" rather than linear plots (241). Silko's use of traditional stories
and forms within the narrative constitutes what Lanser calls a "third mode,
communal voice," in which "narrative authority is invested in a definable community and textually inscribed either through multiple, mutually authorizing
voices or through the voice of a single individual who is manifestly autho-
rized by a community" (*Fictions* 21, emphasis original). The multiple voices
in *Ceremony* include Tayo, members of his family, Night Swan, Ku'oosh, Betonie, traditional stories, and war stories. The narrative of *Ceremony* becomes
polyvocal, moving, as Lanser might say, "away from individual protagonist
and personal plots" to form a communal voice (*Fictions* 22). The polyvocal
nature of *Ceremony* thus undermines Western narrative tropes such as the
quest motif and *bildungsroman*. Allen argues that Native American stories
resist such traditional Western narrative tropes, in that they have "no central
figure in the tale, though there is a central point. The point is concerned with
the proper process of a shift in focus, not the resolution of a conflict" (242).
Using Allen's terms, Tayo is not a "central figure," but he represents a "central point," that is, the "process of a shift in focus" (242). Tayo's shift in focus
occurs through a narrative that interweaves multiple voices and sociolects,
including written/oral, Western/Native, and male/female.

Tayo sees how, rather than being an individual story, a tangle of threads,
or a random set of stories and events, all of the elements of his experience
converge into a pattern, a unified whole that extends beyond his experience,

far into the past and into the distant future. When Tayo awakens after a sand painting ceremony, where "the world below and the sand paintings inside became the same that night," he looks out over the mountains and realizes "there were no boundaries" (Silko 145). By the end of the novel, the boundaries that define and confine Tayo have dissolved and he arrives "at a convergence of patterns; he could see them clearly now" (Silko 254). The people before him had seen the "mountains shift and rivers change course," and the story will go on "lasting until the fifth world ends, then maybe beyond" (Silko 254). Within the polyvocal narrative, Tayo, as a character, is able to transcend the boundaries of Western history and discourse. He is able to recount the past and historical events from the perspective of one who has been both inside colonial discourse as the marginalized colonial other and inside tribal discourse. Tayo's story is, as Allen writes, the "process of a shift in focus" involving a dialogue of languages (Bakhtin) within a narrative frame that binds them (Lanser). This narrative frame includes a contemporary Western novel form infused with multiple voices, traditional tribal stories, tribal stories that include contemporary contexts, and multiple ceremonies.

The dissolution of boundaries in *Ceremony* contributes to a reading of the novel as a dialogic and polyvocal narrative that involves a complex interplay of cultural contexts, language, literary forms, and narrative strategies. As Allen argues, "Language embodies the unspoken assumptions and orientations of the culture it belongs to" (225). For Allen, a feminist theoretical approach helps us understand the "complex interplay of factors," including oppression, colonialism, and reclamation of traditions (223) that inform our reading of *Ceremony*. As many critical analyses of *Ceremony* over a period of almost three decades since its publication have demonstrated, an understanding of these many sociohistorical contexts has informed and enriched our readings of the novel. Bakhtin's and Lanser's narrative theories further deepen our understanding of the complex interplay of both cultural factors and narrative elements of *Ceremony*. Putting Allen's approach to texts by Native writers in conversation with narrative theory does provide a more inclusive approach that dissolves the boundaries between ethnic studies and narratology.

CHAPTER 5

Black World / White World

Narrative Worldmaking in Jim Crow America

BLAKE WILDER

SEVEN YEARS AFTER the *Plessy v. Ferguson* decision formalized the doctrine of "separate but equal," W. E. B. Du Bois published *The Souls of Black Folk* (1903), an exploration of "the two worlds within and without the Veil" (xli–xlii). James Weldon Johnson also acknowledged separate racial worlds in *The Autobiography of an Ex-Colored Man* (1912), describing his "transition from one world into another; for [he] did indeed pass into another world" (20–21). This idea of segregated worlds would remain a potent symbol for authors throughout the Jim Crow period. Richard Wright dramatized the psychological effects of separate racial worlds in "The Man Who Lived Underground" (1942). Like the narrator of Ralph Ellison's *Invisible Man* (1952), the protagonist of Wright's story—who "hovered between the world aboveground and the world underground" (*Eight Men* 40)—allows the author to interrogate the incorporeal effects of Jim Crow segregation. Describing the origins of *Native Son* in "How Bigger Was Born" (1940), Wright expounds upon the existence of separate racial worlds:

> In Dixie there are two worlds, the white world and the black world, and they are physically separated. There are white schools and black schools, white churches and black churches, white businesses and black businesses, white graveyards and black graveyards, and, for all I know, a white God and a black God. (*Native* xi)

Moving from the physical segregations of Jim Crow to the abstract possibility of separate racialized Gods, Wright's commentary suggests that the material enforcement of segregation influenced the grand narratives of existence that individuals used to make sense of their place in the larger world around them.

Separate racial worlds influence aspects of narrative, but at the same time, it is narrative that creates those segregated worlds. In considering the two-way interaction between the material conditions of institutional racism and the worldmaking potential of narrative, this essay seeks to juxtapose critical race theory and narrative theory to the benefit of both strands of scholarship. Critical race theory insists we consider how power and racial privilege are materially determined within "a broader perspective that includes economics, history, context, group- and self-interest, and even feelings and the unconscious" (Delgado, *Critical Race Theory* 3), whereas narrative theory offers a framework for situating worldmaking within a broader matrix of narrative features. Critical race theorist Richard Delgado has called for counter-story-telling as a powerful tool to work against "the prevailing mindset by means of which members of the dominant group justify the world as it is" and which for many minority persons is "the principal instrument of their subordination" ("Storytelling" 2413). But insights from narrative theory suggest that the ability of counter-stories to contest "the world as it is" and overturn subordination is no simple matter. Using James Baldwin's 1965 story "Going to Meet the Man" as the occasion to delve into the "prevailing mindset" of Jim Crow America, this essay argues that the material reality of separate black and white worlds constrains the workings of narrative worldmaking for authors, readers, and characters alike. In doing so, this chapter utilizes David Herman's recent theoretical framework, which replaces the narrative-communication diagram with a model that equates the narrative choices of authors, narrators, readers, and characters in an effort "to foster a fuller, more open dialogue" (*Storytelling* xi) between narrative studies and a broad field of cognitive sciences. On the one hand, the tools of narrative theory enable a more detailed analysis of the power structures of the "prevailing mindset" of Jim Crow America. On the other hand, attending to the context of segregated worlds foregrounds the importance of considering a broad range of lived experiences as part of narrative analysis. Kenneth Warren has argued that African American literature is the corollary of "the social world defined by the system of Jim Crow segregation" (1). But as Nelson Goodman points out in his foundational text, *Ways of Worldmaking* (1978), worlds are made "from worlds already on hand" (6). Thinking about how the social world of Jim Crow is made "from worlds already on hand" draws on, but also benefits, both critical race theory and narrative theory.

I suggest that the idea of separate racial worlds as an intelligible signifier is itself a product of worldmaking, specifically of the worldmaking process that Goodman calls "composition," in which worlds are "consolidated by the application of labels . . . [and] temporally diverse events are brought together under a proper name" (7–8). In Charles Chesnutt's *The Conjure Woman* and *The Wife of His Youth,* both published in 1899 but composed of stories written in the early 1890s, "world" appears less than two dozen times and is used only in a singular, and usually colloquial, sense: "why in the world?" (*Conjure Tales* 165). In contrast, "world" appears more than a hundred times in *The Souls of Black Folk.* Although "world" appears frequently in the work of Paul Laurence Dunbar throughout the 1890s, expressing either a common poetic apostrophe or an indictment of racial injustice, it is always singular, such as in his famous "We Wear the Mask": "But let *the* world dream otherwise, / We wear the mask!" (167; emphasis added). Dunbar expresses a bitter isolation not from the *white* world but from *the* world itself. In contrast, Du Bois describes his childhood realization of racial difference as being "shut out from *their* world by a vast veil" (4; emphasis added). After *Plessy v. Ferguson* (1896), the existing practices of segregation could be grouped together under the idea of "separateness" as a now easily accessible worldview. In order to interrogate the ways in which narrative was integral to the creation and maintenance of a system of separate racial worlds, I explore James Baldwin's short story "Going to Meet the Man" (1965), a story published around the time that the civil rights movement and court cases such as *Boynton v. Virginia* (1960) began to undermine the institutional support of separate racial worlds. I argue that Baldwin depicts Jesse's narrative acts within the story as attempts to force order onto the disruptive social world around him through narrative worldmaking. In doing so, Baldwin draws attention to the blind spots of master narratives and implicitly suggests the collective benefit of moving beyond Jim Crow definitions of white masculinity.

The complex narrative levels of "Going to Meet the Man" provide a glimpse into the "prevailing mindset" of white patriarchy through Jesse's engagement with the world around him. But at the same time, Baldwin's narrative strategies showcase the necessary complications that counter-stories must overcome to be recognized as valid. This consideration of narrative structure as simultaneously relevant for Baldwin as author and Jesse as character draws on the framework that Herman posits in his recent work, *Storytelling and the Sciences of Mind* (2013). Herman's model streamlines narrative inquiry by focusing on *contexts* for interpretation, storytelling *actions, persons* who perform acts of telling, and defeasible *ascriptions* of communicative and other intentions to performers of narrative acts (17). In adopting the model that Herman proposes, I suggest that Baldwin and Jesse are both *persons* performing storytelling *actions* within the *context* of Jim Crow segregation. Subsequently, the possible *ascriptions* of communicative intention involved in the story can be discussed in terms of narrative worldmaking and separate racial worlds. Herman's work is also helpful in distinguishing "worlding the story" and "storying the world" as separate processes that can help foreground issues of worldmaking within narrative inquiry. "Worlding the story" is the process by which readers understand the imagined world of a story through textual cues and their own personal history, whereas "storying the world" is the process by which readers might reevaluate their understanding of the external world through insights found within storyworlds (Herman, *Storytelling* x–xi).

The beginning of "Going to Meet the Man" exploits readers' natural tendencies to "world the story" through the use of a restrained extradiegetic narrator who withholds information necessary to "world the story," prompting readers to engage in a hyperactive process of sense-making. Exposition is only revealed incrementally through the internal focalization of Jesse's thoughts and frustrations. A Southern, white deputy sheriff may seem like an odd protagonist for a story that critiques Jim Crow power structures, but focalizing the story through Jesse allows Baldwin to expose anxieties that motivated segregationist policies but remained unstated in public discourse. Arthenia Millican points out that Jesse parallels Lyle Britten, a fictional version of Emmett Till's murderers, who appears in Baldwin's *Blues for Mister Charlie* (1964), suggesting that Jesse, like Britten, was Baldwin's attempt to understand Till's murderers, who confessed to feeling compelled by social expectations to kill Till despite their own personal reluctance (171). Scholars commenting on the significance of Jesse's point of view present a muddled picture of the relationship between Jesse's perspective and the world around him by overemphasizing Jesse as a "warped, perverted" individual (Pratt 45). To simply call Jesse "warped" obscures the systemic and everyday structures that Baldwin was attempting to chart. Beyond the more obvious legal and economic systems of oppression, it is important to understand the role that worldmaking and separate racial worlds played in the perpetuation of racial violence in Jim Crow America. Setting aside ethical judgments about racism or patriarchy, Jesse's mind is no more warped than any other mind. He witnesses events in childhood that provide narrative models and a worldview that shape his subsequent understanding of the world. Baldwin's story takes the reader into Jesse's interior world, but Jesse's understanding of the world is an understanding of the white world only, creating conflicting versions of reality in the reader's understanding of the storyworld. Jesse honestly does not understand why African Americans want to change the status quo and views a push for civil rights as an unjustified infringement on his natural racial (and gender) privileges. By contrasting Jesse's confusion about the changing state of the world with the reader's growing awareness of Jesse's limited worldview over the course of the story, Baldwin implicates narrative structures in the maintenance of white patriarchal power. To accentuate the contrasting awareness at the close of the story, Baldwin begins the story by replicating Jesse's confusion for the reader.

The opening line—"'What's the matter?' she asked" (229)—presupposes a problem to be solved, a problem that has not yet been revealed. The immediate and abrupt presentation of a conflict, preceding any grounding details, transforms the "matter" into a defining characteristic of the storyworld itself. In one sense, the "matter" is very straightforward: Jesse is impotent. But such a conclusion overlooks the fact that Baldwin delays the direct statement of Jesse's "trouble getting it up" and other tangible details that allow the reader to "world the story" until after introducing vague anxieties about Jesse's job, the issue of race, and a threat of violence. Jesse's wife, Grace, implies that the cause of the "matter" is his "working too hard," but the nature of his work is not revealed. Jesse contrasts his feeling for Grace with "the image of a black girl that caused a distant excitement in him" (229), but the identity of this hypothetical black girl and how Jesse relates to her remain a mystery. A car drives by and Jesse reaches for his gun, but the reader is not told why. Although the reader can likely guess that the "matter" is impotence by this point, there are a range of other uncertainties that seem to be in some way significant. Eventually, Jesse's focalized reflection provides an assortment of substantiating facts that the reader can use to "world the story": "his watch said it was two in the morning," the car was "from out of state most likely, and they would be at the courthouse tomorrow," and

> he was a big, healthy man and he had never had any trouble sleeping. He wasn't old enough yet to have trouble getting it up—he was only forty-two. And he was a good man, a God-fearing man, he had tried to do his duty all his life, and he had been a deputy sheriff for several years. Nothing had ever bothered him before, certainly not getting it up. (230)

Here, Jesse reveals specifics about the time of night, his age, his job, and his understanding of his place in the world, but the abrupt ambiguity of the story's first line and the initial narrative withholding have already put the reader into a position of uncertainty that mirrors Jesse's own state of mind. By the time Jesse finally answers the opening question, the "matter" of impotence has been connected to a larger matrix of psychological and social disturbances. Through the formal uncertainty of the opening, Baldwin prompts the reader to make an initial uncertainty a part of the storyworld itself.

Herman's concept of "worlding the story" provides an excellent lens for understanding the opening of "Going to Meet the Man." But at the same time, the dynamics of the opening—the presupposed problem and the sustained uncertainty—foreground the importance of understanding how readers might "story the world." Two relevant, but divergent, theories illuminate the complexities of how individuals, like Jesse or even Baldwin's reader, might possibly revise their understanding of the world when confronted with new information. David Lewis delineates several linguistic "rules for accommodation of presupposition[s]" (340), suggesting that conversations will "evolve in such a way as is required in order to make whatever occurs count as" true (357). Marie-Laure Ryan identifies a "principle of minimal departure" governing the readerly habit of assuming storyworlds are identical to "reality" unless otherwise told (*Possible Worlds* 22), a dynamic that Deborah Noel discusses in her analysis of possible worlds in works by Judith Cofer and Junot Díaz elsewhere in this collection. The principle of minimal departure is, in some respects, the opposite process of accommodation, and the two offer alternate paths for readers to "story the world." Individuals encountering unprecedented ideas might accommodate their worldview to include new data, or they might interpret that data as a minimal departure unrelated to reality beyond the bounds of the storyworld. Considering these possible alternatives from a critical race perspective that incorporates "history, context, group- and self-interest, and even feelings and the unconscious" reveals that analyses of Herman's concept of "storying the world" need to account for multiple dynamics beyond the bounds of the text, such as what world models individuals might have available to them and how those models intersect with privilege and power. When confronted by a confidently assertive black man, will Jesse revise his understanding of blackness or will he view him as an aberration from the world that Jesse "knows" to be true, the world of unchallenged white power? When confronted by Jesse's tortured neurosis, will Baldwin's readers interrogate the structures of white patriarchy or will they interpret Jesse as an isolated phenomenon of a fictional storyworld? The separate racial worlds of Jim Crow America organized a wide range of material privileges by controlling which actions and identities were recognized as permissible. Foregrounding segregated worlds as an interpretative context illuminates "Going to Meet the Man" as both a critical response to the material conditions of a racist society and an interrogation of the worldmaking potential of narrative. Elsewhere, Christian Schmidt analyzes the racial dynamics of seeing "only what we have been trained to see" in Percival Everett's *I Am Not Sidney Poitier* (2009), which suggests that the narrative constraints of separate racial worlds might well outlast the historical era of segregation (93 in this volume).

After the opening scene of "Going to Meet the Man," the majority of the remaining narrative space comprises two discrete clusters of hypodiegetic narration and focalized reflection. The first cluster consists of the recent past and furthers the connections between the "matter" of impotence and social challenges to Jesse's understanding of the world. The second cluster, flashing back to Jesse's childhood, represents both the origin of his worldview and his attempt to restore social order through narrative order.

Presented as Jesse's intradiegetic narration to Grace, the first cluster is composed of three linked flashbacks that draw the reader fully into Jesse's white world perspective and extend the social dimensions of the "matter" as a context for interpreting both Jesse's impotence and his efforts to "story the world" in the second cluster. The first cluster moves to Jesse's activities torturing a protest leader in a jail cell earlier in the day, back several years to when Jesse (then a collector for a mail-order catalog) first met the leader as a boy, and then forward again to the present-day scene of torture in the jail, before finally returning to the narrative present of the bedroom. As Jesse begins to tell about his day, Grace is asleep (or intentionally unresponsive), and Jesse's utterances of direct address go unanswered. Conditioned by the opening to read more actively with attention to uncertainty, the reader is drawn into Grace's role as narratee by Jesse's style of direct address. Moving from internal reflection ("he had had trouble with one of them today") to explicit narration ("'There was this nigger today,' he said") (231), Jesse provides the kinds of details that are expected by a reader looking to "world the story": "This nigger's one of the ringleaders. We had trouble with him before. We had him out at the farm three or four times." Continuing, Jesse relates how the sheriff "Big Jim C. and his boys" attempted to disperse protestors trying to register to vote. All of these "worlding" details are context for Jesse's active role in the story: "I didn't see this nigger til I got to the jail. They were still singing and I was supposed to make them stop" (232). Already transported into the bedroom as implicit narratee, the narration pulls the reader further into the mind of Jesse, "whose previously stable world is daily changing around him" (Sylvander 121), and illustrates how "narratives are often launched in response to current worries, complaints, and conflicts." (Ochs and Capps 25). At the same time that Baldwin gives Jesse's narration an authentic voice, he carefully manages clues connecting the hypodiegetic cluster back to the narrative frame to highlight the relationship between sexual impotence and social disruption. Jesse's question to his sleeping wife ("you listening?") is paralleled in his interrogation of the ringleader ("you hear me?") (232). And the segue back to bedroom scene contrasts his impotence with the erection he gets while assaulting the ringleader: "to his bewilderment, his horror, beneath his own fingers, he felt himself violently stiffen—with no warning at all" (235). Frustrated in his desires to "pick up a black piece or arrest her" (230) or "to kill the nigger" (233), the juxtaposition of Jesse's unexpected erection in the jail with his unexpected lack of one in his own bed suggests that "what's the matter?" is Jesse's (perceived) social impotence as much as, if not more than, his sexual impotence.

The first hypodiegetic cluster and Jesse's internal reflections within the framing bedroom scenes link his sexual impotence to a tension between his version of the world, the white world, and the social reality of the 1960s that segregated the black world less and less. The progressive breakdown of rigidly segregated racial worlds can be seen in cases like *Boynton v. Virginia* (1960), which in overturning Bruce Boynton's conviction for trespassing, subjected local practices to federal jurisdiction without declaring any laws unconstitutional and paved the way for the efforts of the Freedom Riders in the summer of 1961. Jesse's struggle to understand experiences that were previously beyond the bounds of his (white) world is revealed by the contrast between his and the reader's interpretation of the storyworld. He genuinely believes that "they all liked him" (231) and that "there were still lots of good niggers around . . . [who] would thank him when this was over. In that way they had, the best of them, not quite looking him in the eye" (236). Jesse's equation of "goodness" and lack of eye contact highlights the challenge that comes from the ringleader, whose "one eye, barely open, [was] glaring like the eye of a cat in the dark" (233). In the scene of their first meeting, Jesse observes that "the eyes of the pickaninny . . . were charged with malevolence" (234). As he reflects on this challenge, rooted in a blackness that insists on recognition, Jesse notes that he "missed the ease of former years" and that "they had lost, probably forever, their old and easy connection with each other" (237, 238). Here, Jesse's use of the pronoun "they" shifts from describing a reductively imagined racial other to a community that he imagines himself as part of.

The connection that "they" previously had is particularly relevant to the issue of worldmaking and to the intentions of Jesse's storytelling actions in the second hypodiegetic cluster. Faced with Grace's silence in the opening scene, Jesse thinks, "it was all right. He knew he was not alone" (231). But he does not elaborate on this possible sense of community. After narrating the first cluster, Jesse states that "everyone felt this black suspicion" and reveals that "they" are "men much older than he, who had been responsible for law and order much longer than he . . . [and that] these men were his models, they had been friends to his father, and they had taught him what it meant to be a man" (236). Appearing thirty-one times in Jesse's short reflection, this use of "they" sometimes implies a "we" that includes Jesse and sometimes an antecedent "they" that Jesse emulates. It is the stories, "shared across a community, recounted and transmitted from one generation to another," that incorporate Jesse into the communal "we," by instilling "needs, obligations, desires, hopes, and ambitions" (Ritivoi 29). Given the context of Jim Crow culture, the "law and order" maintained by Jesse's model men implies a broad system of social, political, and economic privileges reserved for white men alone. The push for civil rights that are the "matter" in the first storytelling cluster represents a tension between Jesse's expected script of the white world narrative and his day-to-day encounters with a changing social world. The second hypodiegetic cluster not only shows the origin of Jesse's expectations about the white world but also represents his use of narrative order to reimpose the social order that is no longer guaranteed by virtue of his white masculinity alone. Jesse's use of narrative order in the second storytelling cluster to reestablish an unchallenged white masculinity as the central feature of the white world within Jim Crow society illustrates how "narrative activity attempts to resolve the discrepancy between what is expected and what has transpired" (Ochs and Capps 27).

The second hypodiegetic cluster shows Jesse "storying the world" using narrative and the remembered storyworld of his childhood to make sense of the social-sexual "matter" presented to the reader in the narrative frame and the first storytelling cluster. Significantly, the transition to the second cluster is controlled by the singing that Jesse "had been hearing . . . all his life" (235). The first cluster, which relates Jesse's failure to complete his assigned task "to make them stop [singing]" (232), ends with a bit dialogue that recalls the reader to the narrative present of the bedroom: "'All that singing they do' he said" (235). Unlike the immersive narration of the jail cell scene, this line is clearly spoken to Grace, and it is her continued silence that leads to Jesse's extended meditation on "they" and their loss of ease. Jesse's reflection in the present is abruptly interrupted by a line of song, set apart in italics for the reader, and explained only after the fact through a syntax that emphasizes uncertainty, paralleling the opening of the story itself: "out of the darkness of the room, out of nowhere the line came flying up at him" (239). Questioning whether he ever knew its true meaning, Jesse thinks back to the time when he first remembers hearing such singing, on the day he first witnessed a lynching. The second cluster is presented as Jesse's internal reflection rather than as verbalized narration but begins with the same sort of "worlding" details: "it had been night, as it was now" (239). The lack of an explicit narratee, such as Grace for the first cluster, reveals how Jesse's storytelling actions in the second cluster are deployed as a means to reframe his understanding of the world for himself. Although the singing is presented as a subconscious memory beyond Jesse's control, the intricate temporal ordering within the second hypodiegetic cluster reveals Jesse's control over the narrative.

Comprising four related episodes, the second cluster begins with a car ride returning from a lynching, moves to a bedroom scene later that night, and then jumps back to the early morning car ride that takes them to the lynching, before finally presenting the scene of the lynching itself. Millican points to the link between sexual potency and racial violence in this cluster, noting that "later, his father said that he anticipated a night of conjugal bliss after enjoying the lynching and the picnic" (173). Millican's use of "later" reveals a focus on the temporal chronology of the storyworld itself rather than the narrative presentation, which is, of course, under both Baldwin's and Jesse's narrative control. This second storytelling cluster first presents sexual potency in Jesse's "mother's moan, his father's sigh," in the sound of their rocking bed, and in "his father's breathing seem[ing] to fill the world" (241). The narrative jumps back to a scene of racial violence only after this scene of sexual success. The first half of "Going to Meet the Man," moving from bedroom to jail cell, contrasts Jesse's impotence with a social challenge from black men; the second cluster presents the successful sexual encounter before the scene of the lynching, connecting sexual potency with the lynching of a black man. In essence, the second cluster shows "what's *not* the matter." This arrangement also creates the transition from the castration and the death of the lynching victim directly back into the narrative present and the final bedroom scene, where Jesse finally achieves an erection and forces himself on his sleeping wife, telling her he is going to "do [her] like a nigger, just like a nigger" (249). This transition reverses the segue from erection to impotence that ended the first storytelling cluster. Thus, through a narrative order that restores the connection between sexual potency and racial domination, Jesse has succeeded, at least temporarily, in recreating the white world as he believes it to be. Jesse no longer hears "the sound of tires on the gravel road" in the last line of the story as the car "from out of state" headed to the courthouse, symbolizing social change and instability, but rather as the car leading both to the sexual dominance in the bedroom and the racial dominance of the lynching, symbolizing the unimpeded mobility of white masculinity. In the temporal arrangement of his childhood memories and his meditation about a stable Jim Crow world of white superiority, Jesse effectively "stories the world" of the narrative present, thus resolving the "matter" of his impotence.

Baldwin and Jesse, in the terms of Herman's model, are both *persons* performing storytelling *actions* within the *context* of Jim Crow segregation; however, the intention behind their narrative acts differs greatly. Jesse seeks to deny challenges to the stability of the separate racial worlds of Jim Crow America, challenges that undermine his sense of self as a naturally potent and powerful white man. But Baldwin, through his representation of Jesse's impotence and desperate attempt to restory his changing world, hopes to expose both the complicated intersection of race, gender, and sexuality in Jim Crow thinking and also the interplay between narrative, psychology, and prejudice. Through the use of a minimal extradiegetic narrator and substantial internal focalization, Baldwin strategically foregrounds Jesse's resistance to social change because, as he said elsewhere,

> any real change implies the breakup of the world as one has always known it, the loss of all that gave one an identity, the end of safety. And at such a moment, unable to see and not daring to imagine what the future will now bring forth, one clings to what one knew, or thought one knew; to what one possessed or dreamed that one possessed. (*Collected Essays* 209)

Jesse's successful erection at the end of the story signals his clinging to what he dreamed he possessed, but "the sound of tires on the gravel road" signifies that Jesse's temporary narrative reimposition of white world stability will not stop the wheels of change. Moreover, the disturbing juxtaposition of the remembered lynching with the successful erection and Jesse's apparent lack of awareness, at the end of the story and throughout, provides the impetus for readers to reconsider the foundations of their own worldview. Thus, Baldwin's depiction of white impotence and insecurity presents a counter-story that "offer[s] a respite from the linear, coercive discourse" (Delgado, "Storytelling" 2415) of the "rule-of-law model . . . that requires those who exercise government authority to conform strictly to the rules" (Massaro 2102). By using a third-person narration and allowing the intentions behind Jesse's storytelling actions to expose the injustices of Jim Crow segregation, Baldwin's implicit critique sidesteps the empathic fallacy—"the belief that one can change a narrative by merely offering another, better one" (Delgado, *Critical Race Theory* 28). The necessity of Baldwin's choice to present an implicit critique is illuminated by Jesse's understanding of the black man he tortures in the jail cell. The reader never knows the ringleader's name because Jesse only ever refers to him as "the nigger" or "boy." Baldwin's use of a restrained extradiegetic narrator who refrains from providing the black man's name foregrounds Jesse's inability to recognize the legitimacy of the civil rights leader's explicit speaking back to power and illustrates the asymmetries of narrative, which, according to Elinor Ochs and Lisa Capps, involve the "silencing of alternative stories [as] a form of linguistic oppression" (33) and "curtailing narrative rights of parties central to an event" (34). Elsewhere in this collection, Sterling Bland points out that the narrator of Ellison's *Invisible Man* similarly confronts the fact that "it is virtually impossible for people who have been written out of the public sphere to influence the direction of its conversation" (146 in this volume). Recognizing the silencing power of dominant narratives, Baldwin was able to create a counter-story that challenged white superiority by foregrounding Jesse's selfish desires for sexual potency and social power.

In addition to providing a counter-story to the narrative of white supremacy, "Going to Meet the Man" highlights the importance of trying to imagine possibilities beyond the bounds of your own worldview. Baldwin's choice to use an extradiegetic third-person narration that is closely focalized through Jesse's perspective enacts a sort of "interest convergence"—a term coined by Derrick Bell to explain how the decision to desegregate in *Brown v. Board of Education* (1954) was motivated by white interests in a global context as much as for reasons of racial justice. That is to say that knowing that white readers threatened by "the loss of all that gave one an identity" might very well cling to models of the world as they knew it, Baldwin uses Jesse's insecurity and brutality to make it clear that it is in everyone's interest to try to imagine a worldview that doesn't depend on racial domination for stability. Before Jesse resolves the "matter" of his impotence by reaching back to what he thought he knew, he actually contemplates the possibility that the world is broader than his knowledge of it. Reflecting on current social disruptions before attempting to "story the world" with the second storytelling cluster, Jesse realizes "he had never thought of their heaven or what God was, or could be, for them; God was the same for everyone, he supposed" (235). Echoing Wright's pondering about "a white God and a black God" (*Native* xi), Jesse's thoughts reveal the possibility that desegregation might extend beyond the legal and the physical to include the grand narratives of existence as well. But without alternative world models and faced with his own impotence, Jesse clings to the known narratives that reaffirm the power of white masculinity. The reluctance to consider someone else's point of view is fundamental to the makeup of segregated worlds, as "Of the Coming of John," the lynching story that closes Du Bois's 1903 work, *The Souls of Black Folk*, reveals: "And yet it was singular that few thought of two Johns,—for the black folk thought of one John, and he was black; and the white folk thought of another John, and he was white. And neither world thought the other world's thought, save with a vague unrest" (233). By using a restrained extradiegetic narrator to focalize Jesse's thoughts without commentary, Baldwin succeeds where Jesse fails. He is able to imagine a worldview not defined by separate racial worlds, and he exploits the productive power of unrest to do so.

CHAPTER 6

Postblack Unnatural Narrative—Or, Is the Implied Author of Percival Everett's *I Am Not Sidney Poitier* Black?

CHRISTIAN SCHMIDT

IN RECENT YEARS, a number of African American novels have developed new literary representations of blackness.[1] Contemporary authors such as Paul Beatty, Trey Ellis, Percival Everett, Mat Johnson, Alice Randall, and Danzy Senna have written fictional texts in which race continues to play a crucial role at the same time as these texts refuse to represent a single version of racial reality or to present race as the be-all and end-all of their fictional universes. Following art critic Thelma Golden, I call these narratives "postblack" as their art "is characterized by artists who [are] adamant about not being labeled as 'black' artists, though their work [is] steeped, in fact deeply interested, in redefining complex notions of blackness" (Golden 14).[2] This ambivalent stance toward race is crucial not only on a thematic level but also for the ways in which these novels create literary voices that refuse to be read as clearly raced,

---

1. I would like to thank the editors, especially Jennifer Ann Ho, for their truly incisive and extremely helpful comments on earlier drafts of this essay.

2. In many respects, my argument is related to Ramón Saldívar's recent theory of a "postrace aesthetic," yet diverges from his approach in important ways: I consciously employ the term "post*black*" and thus restrict the scope of my argument to African American literature. Furthermore, I am wary of using "post*race*," as it brings with it connotations of a complete transcendence of race, which is true neither in the real world nor in the diegetic worlds of these novels. Postblack fiction formulates a complicated, even contradictory relationship to blackness, a discourse that insists on blackness, albeit via the distance it takes from it. See my *Postblack Aesthetics* for an extended discussion of postblackness.

black voices. These texts resist the category "ethnic literature" in an attempt to be taken seriously as fiction rather than as sociological statements about race or as mimetic images of the real world filtered through the raced bodies of their flesh-and-blood authors. In this essay, I will focus on the formal playfulness and unnatural narration of Percival Everett's *I Am Not Sidney Poitier,* a novel that refuses to be read mimetically and thus also complicates (re-)constructions of a clearly raced implied author.

My approach to "minority" fiction is related to but distinct from what Richardson does in "U.S. Ethnic and Postcolonial Fiction." Whereas he focuses on the racial difference on which these narratives insist, by constructing a communal voice of the other through the use of we-narration, I read Percival Everett's first-person novel as an explicit refusal to speak "collective[ly]" for anybody and to be read as a communal counter-discourse. However, we, as readers, need to be aware of the existence of these "local counterpoetics" ("U.S. Ethic" 15) in order to judge the distance that Everett's novel self-consciously creates. After all, he is an author of perhaps the most visible racial minority writing in a heavily racialized literary and social landscape, yet we would not do justice to the complex character of his fiction if we let his race become the dominant lens through which the actual textual narrative is explicated and analyzed. In order to mark his distance from the category of "black author," Everett employs a wide variety of textual strategies to undermine authorial identity and to sever the mimetic link to the extratextual world of blackness. Most importantly, Everett's novel installs an implied author (IA) that refuses to be equated with its flesh-and-blood author (FBA) (or its character-narrator) and simultaneously refuses to be raced accordingly, which allows me to read the novel's implied author as a postblack entity that neither is clearly raced nor can be read mimetically. Since an implied author by definition is a disembodied narrative entity, the novel's postblack implied authorial agency self-consciously points to the gap between text and world and between raced reality and raced/unraced diegesis, as it highlights the oxymoronic and non-naturalizable nature of postblackness.

(UN)RACE-ING THE IMPLIED AUTHOR

In rhetorical approaches to narrative, the IA is conceived of as a textual entity created consciously by a text's author and, thus, responsible for the textual whole. Nelles pinpoints the relevant distinctions: "the historical author writes, the historical reader reads; the implied author means, the implied reader interprets; the narrator speaks, the narratee hears" ("Historical" 22).

The implied author is thus neither a real person nor simply the sum total of what the reader reconstructs from the text. Rather, it is an author's conscious creation as part of an intentional discourse with an implied readership that is supposed—and ideally able—to grasp this implied author's intentions. As Phelan defines the implied author in one of the most important reformulations of Booth's original concept, it is "*a streamlined version of the real author, an actual or purported subset of the real author's capacities, traits, attitudes, beliefs, values, and other properties that play an active role in the construction of the particular text*" (*Living to Tell about It* 45, emphasis original). When dealing with African American literature, the "streamlined version of the real author" quite often turns out to be a streamlined version of the real author *as representative* of the racial whole. Thus, the implied author of much of African American fiction is linked not only to its concrete FBA but also to a generalized idea of black authorship and a stereotypical version of the real black author imagined by the reader.[3] And here also lies the central importance of the category of the implied author for my purposes: if we agree that African American fiction tends to be read overly mimetically—even if the texts at hand are anything but mimetic—then it is paramount to focus on the ways in which Everett's novel complicates the relationship between fiction and reality by turning our attention to the category of the implied author who stands right at the cusp between text and world, between author and reader, and thus at the heart of the rhetorical act that is fiction.[4]

In my account, I follow Rabinowitz, who insists on the "*pragmatic* usefulness of the implied author" ("The Absence of Her Voice" 101, emphasis original) rather than calling for its essential necessity for all studies of narrative fiction. For him, the concept comes in handy for analyzing "fraudulent texts [. . .] that can be usefully illuminated by distinguishing the author from his or her projected self-image" (104–5). While Everett's novel is not a literary hoax whose authorship is in question, the issue of fraudulence is still crucial for a reading of the novel, as the very name of its character-narrator reveals him to be a fraud. By explicitly establishing the speaking I of the novel as a fraudulent character, the novel self-consciously questions both the reliability of its narrator and his equation with any extratextual person, be it Sidney

---

3. This stereotypical version need not be a negative or racist one, as much African American fiction is being celebrated for its truthful representation of issues pertaining to race and/or racism. This, however, already limits the expressive freedom of African American fiction to the extent that the only thing it is accorded liberty to speak about is the issue of race.

4. Interestingly enough, the race of implied authors has never been much of an issue. Nelles concedes that some might "attribute gender to implied authors" or maybe an "eye color" ("Hypothetical" 112), yet even though his example in the latter case is Toni Morrison, he does not mention whether or not readers also race those implied authors.

Poitier or Percival Everett. While not a liar in the literal sense, the narrator is as much a fraud as is the implied authorial agent, whose racial identity belies conventional expectations. The novel thus problematizes the subject of its enunciation and complicates the assignment of its rhetorical authority to any real person as it always already points to the gap that opens between I and Not I, black and not black. By using the analytical category of the IA, I can name that gap, as it stands in between the FBA and the text. What I call the novel's postblack IA, thus, is neither a concrete, raced person, nor just an effect to be inferred from the text. And while Percival Everett obviously is a black author, the novel's implied author speaks from a more ambivalent position and, as such a figure of ambivalence, sends up conventional notions of blackness. In Rabinowitz's words, then, the IA of Everett's novel can be read as a "double self-projection" (105) of its author, one who produces a "black" text and another who concurrently puts this very category in doubt. This tension between simultaneous attraction to and marking distance from traditional forms of literary blackness lies at the center of the postblack literary endeavor, and through this ambivalence of its IA, *I Am Not* metaphorically plays with the potential fraudulence of (black) authorship.

Even though I am convinced that we need to be wary of author-centered approaches to literature, it seems dishonest simply to disavow the author and authorial intent when reading and analyzing African American fiction. Obviously, the very category of African American fiction rules out entirely textual approaches, as the author's race is the defining membership criterion. And as the contributions by Li and Breger to this volume show, focusing on the role of the FBA in our readings of the respective novels yields important insights into the ways in which African American texts play with issues of racial identity. What this often means, however, is that our readings of African American texts end up supporting the assumptions we bring to them a priori. In this, the study of African American fiction often "falls prey" to what Alber et al. have described as a "mimetic reductionism" (1): namely, that we read novels as if they were statements by real people in our extratextual world of race.[5] In this context, Phelan has suggested a helpful taxonomy of "character functions" in first-person narration by differentiating between "mimetic," "thematic," and "synthetic" (*Living to Tell about It* 12–13) dimensions. For a variety of (mostly historical and political) reasons, African American characters routinely are

---

5. Hogan makes a similar observation when he points out that we distinguish between author, implied author, and narrator "only to the degree that they diverge. [. . .] In other words, a basic principle of discursive interpretation is that *the default assumption is congruence of narrator, implied author, and real author*" (*Narrative Discourse* 31, emphasis original). Even more so, I claim, when reading African American fiction.

read "as representations of possible people," thus highlighting the "mimetic" (and the "thematic") functions, whereas the "synthetic" realm, in which characters serve "as artificial constructs" (13), often is overlooked. Historically, discussions of African American literature have foregrounded the way in which fictional characters mirror real-world experiences of blackness rather than analyzing the narratives first and foremost as fictional constructs. When looking at earlier, perhaps more mimetic (or at least less unnatural) texts such as Ellison's *Invisible Man,* this makes perfect sense, as Bland's analysis in this collection convincingly shows. Contrary to this, however, Everett's novel invites such a "mimetic reductionism" as it simultaneously stresses and undermines this very similarity to an extratextual world. It thus also triggers what Richardson calls the "mimetic [. . .] impuls[e]" (in Herman et al. 103) even though *I Am Not* is an unnatural, and thus antimimetic, narrative. Defining unnatural narratives as texts that "problematize their own ontological status" (20), Richardson reminds us that "postmodern and other antimimetic authors [. . .] delight in collapsing established categories, and the triad of author, implied author, and narrator too has been a source of that delight" (52). In his criticism of mimetic approaches to literature, he urges us not to read all narratives as if narrators and characters were real people or to assume that "narrators are rather like human storytellers" (21). In the words of Nielsen, yielding to this "mimetic impulse" entails "naturalizing reading strategies" unfit for unnatural narratives. Readers of African American literature have been trained to employ such naturalizing strategies that allow them to relate the texts to the real world as if these novels were natural narratives and could be mapped mimetically onto the real world. They do so by constructing naturalized implied authors, who will automatically be raced black if the author is black, and then interpret the novel at hand accordingly. Everett's novel clearly plays with such naturalizations: by including the character Percival Everett—tantalizingly close to being an incarnation of the "career [implied] author" (Booth, *The Rhetoric of Fiction* 431) Percival Everett, as he has also written a novel entitled *Erasure—I Am Not* cleverly establishes a link to Everett's other "black" fictions, only to pull out the rug from under the authorial audience's feet by metaleptically complicating the ascription of the texts to this same (black) author.[6] Emanating from a postblack IA who refuses to write more traditional black fiction, however, *I Am Not* ultimately denies such a naturalizing reading of its narrative voice into a clearly race-able, natural person.

----

6. Moreover, while the career IA "Percival Everett" has a more or less clearly recognizable voice and tone (humorous, highly self-referential, irreverent, sardonic, etc.), he certainly has no easily discernible racial identity, given the fact that a large number of his texts do not deal with racial issues at all or do not emanate from a clearly raced authorial agent to begin with.

By claiming to present fictional doubles of this extratextual reality—through its inclusion of the doubles of Sidney Poitier and other celebrities, such as Ted Turner, Harry Belafonte, and Elizabeth Taylor; through its mirroring of existing fictional narratives taken from the filmic oeuvre of the not-quite-eponymous protagonist; and through including a character that shares the name of the author of the novel, Percival Everett—*I Am Not* almost dares its readers to read it mimetically. It does so by folding its diegetic world into the real world in a highly synthetic approach, in which the textual nature of this representation is highlighted at the same time as the mimetic impulse is triggered through real-world doubles. On the most basic level, the novel undermines the direct link from Everett (FBA) to Not Sidney Poitier by including a character with the name "Percival Everett" in the novel's diegesis *without* making this character a narrator. In fact, Everett remains a mere surface, rather than a truly round character, as none of the passages in which he appears are focalized through him, nor do we ever encounter him unless in direct relation to Not Sidney. Everett's novel's antimimetic narrative strategies thus undermine a reading of its implied authorial entity into the narrow frame of black authorship, as its IA cannot simply be equated with either real author or narrator. Since the narrator, both by name and by his own admission, is not even himself, let alone the IA, Everett's novel frustrates readerly attempts to construct a clearly raced IA by playing with the dominant "mimetic impulse" of its implied audience at the same time as it continuously offers invitations to race that very IA and to equate him with either Not Sidney or Percival Everett (FBA). Yet Not Sidney is not simply the mouthpiece of Everett (FBA), nor does Percival Everett (the character) fulfill that role. Rather, the novel relishes its complex play with author personae, ultimately undermining the idea of a coherent authorial voice. This ambivalent stance can productively be read as a postblack implied author standing at the center of the novel's rhetorical strategies.

DEAD RINGER FOR (NOT) SIDNEY: PERCIVAL EVERETT'S *I AM NOT SIDNEY POITIER*

The general premise and the running joke of Everett's comedy of misunderstandings is that its protagonist is named *Not* Sidney Poitier even though he is the spitting image of the famous actor. As Not Sidney, the first-person narrator, explains in the opening paragraph: "I am tall and dark and look for the world like Mr. Sidney Poitier, something my poor disturbed and now deceased mother could not have known when I was born, when she named me Not Sidney Poitier" (3). Yet the novel complicates this relationship between text and real world by underlining that his name, actually, has nothing to do with his famous namesake. Rather, Not Sidney's mother had chosen the name without reference to Sidney Poitier at all: "But her puzzled expression led me to believe that my name had nothing to do with the actor at all, that *Not Sidney* was simply a name she had created, with no consideration of the outside world" (7). The protagonist's very name—*the* central identifying mark of a person—inevitably and ineradicably links him to an outside measuring stick, and since Sidney Poitier is such an outstanding role model of African American achievement in the realm of popular media also links Not Sidney to this very discourse. Of course, the irony of all this is that Not Sidney turns out to look exactly like Poitier, so that the most arbitrary of signifiers—the name—comes to carry all the meaning until, in the very end, he *becomes* Sidney Poitier. The novel thus complicates the relationship between character and extratextual world, forcing its readers to make sense of how the two are connected. It is here that the novel marks its difference from earlier African American texts, such as Ellison's *Invisible Man,* as Bland's analysis of *Invisible Man* in this volume makes clear. Whereas Bland links the invisibility of the narrator more or less directly to the visibility of Ellison, the author, Everett's novel complicates such short-circuiting by way of its insistence on the titular Not, refusing to present any clear-cut extratextual mirror to the diegetic presence of the narrator. That is why I assign the rhetorical agency not to Everett (FBA) but rather to the IA of the novel, a disembodied entity that is neither Not Sidney nor Percival Everett. This critical gesture also allows me to insist more strongly on this IA's postblackness, a complicated, perhaps even oxymoronic state that mirrors the protagonist's simultaneously being Sidney and Not Sidney. Different from Bland's naturalizing reading of the narration of *Invisible Man,* my reading of Everett's thoroughly unnatural novel claims that it refuses to construct any coherent, let alone stable authorial identity at all. Rather, revolving around the negative Not, the novel destabilizes notions of narrative and/or authorial identity to the degree that the only quasi-stable identity left is the agency of the implied author. As a conscious creation of its author, and therefore outside the text, the IA is an intriguingly disembodied figure and as such ideally represents the contradictory premise of postblackness as simultaneously "embracing and rejecting" (Golden 14) the notion of black authorship and corresponding expectations of black literature.[7]

---

7. In a related argument, Breger's reading of Cole's *Open City* in this volume interrogates the "narratological significance of the un/marking of identity [. . .] categories" and investigates the ways in which the novel's "nonsovereign, polyvocal narrative worldmaking" mirrors our contemporary world's "multidirectional process of cultural appropriation" (162, 176 in this volume). Her essay intriguingly complicates readings of the novel in relation both to white/

Over the course of the novel, Not Sidney undertakes a picaresque journey through the netherworld of American racism and the filmic oeuvre of
his not-quite-namesake. In fact, the novel revolves around the reenactment
of these films and thus further distances the fictional world from reality, as it
incorporates mirror images of media images already mirrored on the silver
screen, until, at the very end, it is no longer clear what is original and what
is copy. As if this were not enough, Not Sidney repeatedly crosses paths with
Professor "Percival Everett," who mistakes him for "Harry Belafonte" (87).
Thus, the character who shares the novel's author's name mixes up two of
the most visible black on-screen personae of the 1950s and 1960s, almost as if
to say that it does not really matter which of the two Not Sidney resembles,
as long as he is a black actor look-alike. Having a non-narrating and non-
focalizing character perpetrate this outrageous mistake, however, complicates
readerly assumptions about authorial intent or implied authorship, as we no
longer can easily naturalize the narrative by according the narrative voice to
the author, as the direct link between autodiegetic narrator and author is sev-
ered by inserting a character with Everett's name in between them. And true
to form, the character Everett self-consciously acknowledges this by admitting, "I'm a fraud, a fake, a sham, a charlatan, a deceiver, a pretender, a crook"
(101).[8] Here, the novel almost dares its readers to equate Everett the character with Everett the author, playing with mimetic (mis)readings of literature
through our "frames of recognition"[9] based on what we know about (the race
of) a particular author. And in fact, the entire premise of the novel is so outrageous that it is (almost) impossible to take seriously anything that happens

Western intertexts and to non-Western call-and-response-type models. She thus severs the
direct link between narrative voice and extratextual authorial identity in a similar way to my
own analysis, even if she does not directly engage with the analytical category IA. In contrast
to this approach, Li focuses on the distinction between narrator and implied author in Ann
Petry's white-world novel *Country Place,* only to elide the distinction between FBA and IA in
the process. While I would argue that a stricter separation of these categories could add another
interesting dimension to Li's argument, she convincingly analyzes the ways in which the novel
contests whiteness as the unspoken norm through what she calls the narrator's "claim to narrative authority" (108 in this volume). Our individual approaches' differences notwithstanding,
this collection on critical race narratology hopefully contributes to an interlacing of the critical
vocabularies of African American studies and narratology that mutually enhance one another.

8. Ever since Booth's original definition, the IA has been used as the norm against which
to determine the (un)reliability of a narrator, an issue that is impossible to decide for Everett's
novel as both the narrator and the IA self-consciously defy unequivocal definitions of what they
"really" are.

9. In one of the few extended analyses of *I Am Not Sidney Poitier,* Demirtürk reads the
novel as a parody of the extant frames through which white people read and (fail to) recognize
black people. Contrary to my own reading, however, she pays little attention to the unnatural
narration of the novel.

within its pages. At least one critic of the novel has made this point, claiming that the joke of Not Sidney's name "gets old in a hurry" (Lingan par. 1) and that the novel fails because Everett does not "take his satire more seriously" (par. 9). Granted, the joke does get old in a hurry. Against Lingan, however, I argue that this structure *is* the central critique echoing throughout the novel. By refusing to point to a concrete target and by entirely dismissing the outside world of our lived reality, *I Am Not* abstains from formulating the criticism of race we expect to hear from a black implied author on a mimetic (mis)reading of the novel.

As a form of unnatural narration, *I Am Not* goes to great lengths to destroy the assumption that there is anything real represented in the text. The novel goes to equally great lengths, however, to imply such an assumption of extratextual reality by including real-life people—or, rather, fictional doubles of real-life people—in its cast of characters. Fittingly, *I Am Not* opens with a copyright disclaimer that points out this ambivalence: "*All characters depicted in this novel are completely fictitious, regardless of similarities to any extant parties and regardless of shared names. In fact, one might go as far as to say that any shared name is ample evidence that any fictitious character in this novel is NOT in any way a depiction of anyone living, dead, or imagined by anyone other than the author. This qualification applies, equally, to the character whose name is the same as the author's*" (n. pag., emphasis original). Printed on an otherwise empty page, this disclaimer is neither part of the usual front matter nor the standard copyright page but already has a somewhat dubious in-between status. Not quite paratext but not fully part of the narrative proper, these lines inevitably point readerly attention to the novel's very status *as* fiction. By highlighting the characters' synthetic rather than mimetic dimensions, the text also prompts the reader to look even more closely for possible mimetic mappings, as such an exaggerated denial cannot be taken at face value. This disclaimer further invokes authorial control over the text only to pull the rug out from under its own feet and effectively undermines authorial intention by implying its own inefficacy. Coming from the margins of the narrative proper, and thus neither explicitly from the real author nor from the narrator, this statement, which we had best accord to the novel's IA, addresses the "mimetic impulse" of its implied readers quite directly as it literally points at simplistic and, in this case, problematic mimetic readings.

Through its inclusion of a character of its author's name, the novel makes furthermore clear that Percival Everett is not the IA of the novel but just another literary character. By splitting Percival Everett into two discrete entities—author of and character in the novel—*I Am Not* complicates what Lanser has called "attaching."[10] Given that Percival Everett, on the diegetic level, is not a narrator but just another character seen and described from the outside, the novel makes it quite difficult for the reader to attach its discourse to its real-life author, as this would necessitate the cumbersome differentiation between "Everett, the author," and "Everett, the character." Presenting an author image in its pages through its depiction of Percival Everett, the novel deeply worries Booth's original definition of the implied author as the FBA's "second self," as this novel includes at least a third self as well. As Booth argues, "the writer should worry less about whether his *narrators* are realistic than about whether the *image he creates of himself,* his implied author, is one that his most intelligent and perceptive readers can admire" (*The Rhetoric of Fiction* 395, emphasis original). Everett's novel does everything it can to avoid creating such an ideal image, as the diegetically rendered image of Everett is anything but flattering. And by metaleptically playing with these distinctions, Everett's novel severs the link between Everett, the black author of the novel, and the characters rendered therein, thus also questioning the projection of the author's person (and his race) onto the text. In doing so, however, it at the same time installs an implied authorial entity that is clearly meant *not* to be an author image, let alone a flattering one.

As Not Sidney moves through movie after movie of his famous look-alike, the plot increasingly thickens when he has to identify a corpse that looks "exactly like [him], a fact that was apparently lost" (211) on everybody around him. This happens in Smuteye, Alabama, where Not is reenacting Sidney Poitier's role of Homer Smith in *Lilies of the Field.* Adding to the confusion is the fact that Not's dead look-alike, in turn, was killed while similarly enacting Homer Smith, effectively doubling Not's doubling of Sidney Poitier's character. Ironically, the only link between the dead person and Not is the simple fact that both are black—"You all look alike" (213), as Not Sidney is told by a police officer—and neither of them is known in Smuteye. Not is so real as to stand in oxymoronically for two of the most stereotypical roles expected of black characters: the dead victim and the default suspect of a murderous crime. The only thing that matters in this context is Not's blackness, to which he and his (literally) dead ringer are reduced through the mimetic misreading of their environment. What is stunning about the description of these events is the emotional distance with which Not narrates them, as he seems to be flabbergasted, rather than disgusted, by the ways in which he and his body are

---

10. In "The 'I' of the Beholder," Lanser has developed the suggestive terminology of "attached" versus "detached" first-person writing, where the former denotes statements that become connected to, and associated with, a particular speaker or, in fictional texts, character-narrators' statements that are taken to emanate from their real authors.

read throughout his encounters in Smuteye. The first-person narrative voice's complete lack of outrage throughout the novel seems to indicate that what is at stake is not so much a full-fledged attack on the "frames of" racial—or, rather, racist—"recognition," as Demirtürk argues, but a subtle smirk at the nonsensicality of these very frames through which all readers respond to the world. Reading the IA of the novel as postblack, I argue, explains this lack of outrage by complicating its assignment to a clearly raced black author, whom we can expect to protest such racist treatment only on a mimetic *mis*reading.

At the very end of the novel, Not finds himself in Los Angeles, waiting to be awarded the "Most Dignified Figure in American Culture" award at a ceremony in the Shrine Auditorium. Finally, he *is* "none other than Sidney Poitier" (234), as Liz Taylor announces in her laudation. At last, Not Sidney has become the famous actor, as it is only here that he enacts not one of Poitier's movie roles but, rather, a scene from the off-screen life of his famous namesake. Now, it is most certainly no longer possible to read Not Sidney mimetically as he has literally become two persons, Sidney and Not Sidney. Moreover, the final scene also reveals the novel as a truly unnatural narration in Richardson's sense, as it "transgress[es] the principle that a coherent and chronological *fabula* should underlie the *sjuzhet*" (Herman et al. 77). Even though only a few months of story time have passed, Not Sidney has aged by about fifty years as he now embodies a Sidney Poitier who, supposedly, is in his early seventies. The novel ends with Not's acceptance speech, directly addressed to his narratees and, by extension, to the novel's implied and real readers. In this speech, he echoes sentiments that any actor—or fictional character, for that matter—could utter at such an occasion: "'I have learned that my name is not my name. It seems you all know me and nothing could be further from the truth and yet you know me better than I know myself, perhaps better than I can know myself'" (234). Not feels like "a specimen" standing before the eyes of his audience, who see him not for the person he is but as a representative of something larger, *the* first black major movie star. Indeed, as a "specimen," he is anything but an individual, and all characters in the novel see in him only the fake, the doppelganger, and a representation of the mimetically real as they only see and respond to Sidney Poitier, even though he is Not.[11] Similarly, reading the novel *mimetically* we, as real readers, only see and hear a black author presenting a story of white misrecognition of black-

---

11. As such, they reveal themselves as "naïve readers" in Rose's sense of the term. In her reading of parody as meta-fiction, Rose argues that "the clash between the worlds of fiction and reality is shown on the example of [those] naïve readers, who, because they are unable to clearly distinguish the two worlds, cannot cope with either" (72). In "The Parody of Postblackness," I

ness, rather than acknowledging the contradictory complexity of a postblack IA who complicates traditional notions of literary blackness. Through its anti-mimetic, unnatural setup, *I Am Not Sidney Poitier* thus satirizes the "mimetic impulse" that lets us see only what we have been trained to see, and that is a text by a black author with a necessarily black implied author.

CONCLUSION

The crucial punch line of Everett's novel, of course, is that Not Sidney dwells in the very negation of any such category. As he states in the novel's final words, his epitaph should read: "I AM NOT MYSELF TODAY" (234). Insisting on the not, Not Sidney is a walking, talking disclaimer of all positive forms of (racial or authorial) identity ascription, and thus in some ways as "invisible" as Ellison's protagonist was. Rather than narrating a clearly defined—if "unstable" (Bland 146 in this volume)—identity, however, Everett's novel embraces the defiant Not of its protagonist's name in a gesture that disallows simple naturalizing and racializing readings. And just as much as Not Sidney and Percival Everett are and are not black artists in Golden's deliberately contradictory sense of the term, the novel's implied author also inhabits the ambivalent space of postblackness in which such simplistic racial ascriptions become as problematic as are mimetic readings of the IA as possessing an embodied racialized identity. To put this differently: "I am not myself today" may be spoken by the autodiegetic narrative voice of the novel but can clearly be traced back to the novel's IA, who cannot easily be raced and/or embodied.[12]

In yet another twist on Richardson's collapsing triad, *I Am Not* ends not only on an echo of the real life of actor Sidney Poitier in fictionally restaging one of the crowning moments of his Hollywood career. Everett's novel about Sidney Poitier's double also ends with the mirror image of Everett's own "crowning moment" as an author—namely, the climax of *Erasure*. By echoing that novel's final scene on the closing pages of *I Am Not,* it is almost as if Everett adds a metafictional comment on the criticism of his own oeuvre, thus folding critical readers and audiences into Richardson's collapsing categories. Moreover, by echoing *Erasure,* the novel's IA invites his authorial audience to

offer an extended reading of the novel as parody of *Erasure* and the ways in which postblack literature playfully engages with African American literature.

12. For an excellent analysis of the relation between first-person narrators and implied authors, see Lanser's "(Im)Plying the Author," in which she also suggests the analogy that the IA is "not [. . .] a body but [. . .] the clothes the body wears" (158).

include their knowledge of this previous novel into their reading of *I Am Not Sidney Poitier* and, thus, to read it as a critique of naturalizing assumptions about black (implied) authors (just like *Erasure*). Yet by installing a character in the novel who is the author of the diegetic *Erasure*, the later novel simultaneously problematizes these understandings as, by doing so, it ultimately undermines a stable notion of a career (implied) author Percival Everett, as he exists both inside and outside the novel. As readers of Percival Everett's fictional oeuvre have come to know, the stability of meaning is a fickle thing, and while the narrative voice (and the IA) of *I Am Not Sidney Poitier* certainly is in line with the career IA Percival Everett has constructed, that entity's race willfully remains vague, unstable, and, most pertinently, anything but clearly black. In this respect, the novel does all it can to refrain its authorial audience from naturalizing its IA into a clearly raced person, yet at the same time prods it to yield to the mimetic itch and do exactly that. As a creation of the black author Percival Everett, the implied author of *I Am Not Sidney Poitier* therefore inhabits the complex terrain of postblackness in Golden's formulation of the term. And, much like Not Sidney Poitier is and is not the figuratively and perhaps literally dead ringer of Sidney Poitier, the novel's IA is and is not the black author Percival Everett—he is Not Percival Everett, if you will—but rather a postblack agent that refuses to tally with conventional ideas of black authorship.

CHAPTER 7

The Presumptions of Whiteness in Ann Petry's *Country Place*

STEPHANIE LI

ANN PETRY published *Country Place* (1947) one year after her best-selling first novel, *The Street* (1946). Often compared to Richard Wright's *Native Son* (1940), *The Street* focuses on Lutie Johnson, a single mother desperate to provide for her son amid rampant sexism and racism. Critics hailed Petry as a dynamic new literary voice whose emphasis on the plight of women offered a key correction to the protest writing of most mid-twentieth-century black writers. That year Petry was featured in *Ebony* as a sophisticated up-and-coming celebrity author. Not surprisingly, critics responded with special vitriol to the seemingly apolitical *Country Place* and its nearly all-white cast. Writing in *New Masses*, José Yglesias dismissed it as the stuff of a "woman's magazine" or "lending library fare," no more than "formulas" and "banalities" (18). David Littlejohn suggested "reading the novel, skipping the plot" as if the book best served as a warning to black writers who dared to experiment with such dubious subject matter (155). A number or prominent black writers of the time, including Richard Wright, Zora Neale Hurston, Chester Himes, and James Baldwin, published their own white life novels, that is, texts that focus primarily on white characters. Like *Country Place,* these texts were largely excoriated when first published and have since fallen into obscurity because they challenge conventional definitions of black literature. Petry's novel, like other postwar white life narratives, speaks to anxieties about a newly integrated America while demonstrating a desire to move beyond the strictures of protest literature.

With its focus on domestic dramas and small-town life, *Country Place* involves deceptively prosaic themes and characters. However, its conventional subject matter belies a remarkably radical approach to narrative and race. Petry's understudied and currently out of print novel has confused readers and critics because it upends expectations not only of who can tell white stories, but more importantly, of how white stories are told at all. Scholars remain divided on one of the novel's most basic characteristics: who is telling the story. Hilary Holladay and John C. Charles understand the text to have two narrators, an unnamed omniscient narrator and Doc Fraser.[1] Noting the many intimate details that the druggist could not possibly know, Holladay understands the presence of the omniscient narrator as a way for Petry to "subvert(s) Doc's claims to narrative control" (24). While my analysis of *Country Place* shares Holladay's close attention to Petry's multilayered narration, I identify Doc Fraser as the narrator of the entire novel.[2] I base this interpretation, in part, on the fact that the novel does not distinguish between chapters narrated by Doc Fraser and those by the supposed omniscient narrator; in fact, some chapters begin in the first person but devolve into the third person during events that the druggist admits he did not witness. He makes frequent mention of his supposedly "accurate" accounts despite having little or no firsthand evidence to substantiate such claims. The novel willfully confuses readers by withholding information about who is narrating various sections of the text. I take this conscientious obfuscation as revealing rather than simply careless or inartful.

Petry's novel is best understood through insights provided by narrative theorists Jonathan Culler, James Phelan, and Henrik Slov Nielsen. By emphasizing distinctions between the narrator and the implied author, we may recognize the novel's deft critique of the false entitlements of whiteness. Doc Fraser's frequent masking of his subjective storytelling reveals his fundamentally racialized desire to possess the stories of others. *Country Place* is a study in what George Yancy terms "the omniscient pretensions of whiteness" (13). This is the voice of whiteness and its presumed authority. Petry's discursively sophisticated novel affirms Culler's contention that omniscience is best understood as a manufactured conceit. He explains, "the power to decide what will be the case in this world is a product of a conventional performative power

---

1. "The Presumptions of Whiteness in Ann Petry's *Country Place*" appeared in modified version in chapter 3 of *Playing in the White: Black Writers, White Subjects* (Oxford UP, 2015), which was entitled "Whiteness and Narrative Authority in Ann Petry's *Country Place*" and appeared on pages 95–128. It is reproduced by permission of Oxford University Press.
Citing Holladay, Charles writes, "an omniscient narrator controls seventeen of the twenty-five chapters . . . [and] the remainder is told primarily from the perspective of Doc Fraser" (77).

2. Laura Dubek and Emily Bernard also share this interpretation of the novel.

of language" ("Omniscience" 24). The novel presents whiteness as intimately linked to the "conventional performative power of language." *Country Place* demonstrates how such totalizing narrative presumptions depend upon a predatory, voyeuristic gaze that derives its power from the unearned privileges afforded to white masculinity. This seeming omniscience has significant limitations as it is derived from a patriarchal perspective that maligns women and proves unable to account for black subjectivity. Doc Fraser's narrative perspective typifies Nielsen's notion of the "impersonal voice," which includes information that the "'narrating I' cannot possibly know" (133). The druggist's claim to such knowledge demonstrates what Ruediger Heinze calls "a dual voice . . . where one belongs to the character function and the other to the narratorial function" (287). In *Country Place,* these two functions merge as the character of Doc Fraser is best defined by his totalizing approach to narrative power.

The long-neglected *Country Place* has a complicated plot. Johnnie Roane returns from four years in the army to discover that his wife, Glory, has become infatuated with the town rake, Ed Barrell. Meanwhile, Glory's mother, Lil, who is married to the scion of the Gramby family, Mearns, plots her mother-in-law's death so that she may inherit her husband's fortune. In a series of manipulative setups, the Weasel, the intrusive town cabdriver and narrative foil to Doc Fraser, allows Mrs. Gramby and Mrs. Roane to learn of Glory's affair with Ed while also discovering that Ed was once involved with Lil. The Weasel confronts Mrs. Gramby with this information. Lil then attempts to murder Mrs. Gramby by inducing a diabetic shock, but the older woman survives. Meanwhile, the Portuguese immigrant Portalucca, the Grambys' gardener, woos Neola, the household's African American maid. At the end of the novel, Mrs. Gramby changes her will, bequeathing her stately mansion to her three servants and cutting Lil out entirely. As she exits her lawyer's office, she falls down the stairs, taking Ed with her. Both die in the accident, leaving the multiethnic collective of Portalucca, Neola, and the Italian Gramby cook to inherit the town's most prestigious property.[3]

COUNTRY PLACE'S "MEDIUM"

Doc Fraser begins *Country Place* by asserting:

> I have always believed that, when a man writes a record of a series of events,
> he should begin by giving certain information about himself: his age, where

---

3. All of the characters in the novel except for Portalucca, Neola, and the Grambys' cook are white Americans.

he was born, whether he be short or tall or fat or thin. This information offers a clue as to how much of what a man writes is to be accepted as truth, and how much should be discarded as being the result of personal bias. (1)

Doc Fraser's recognition that every story is colored by its teller suggests his own broad-minded objectivity. However, his casual reference to "a man" reveals his dangerous conflation of universality with masculinity. By admitting his identity and even his prejudices, Doc Fraser urges readers to trust his version of events, for though not unbiased, as no story can be, it will at least be free of manipulative conceits. Thus in a gesture of high-minded honesty, he adds,

I hasten to tell you that I am a bachelor; and a medium kind of man— medium tall, medium fat, medium old (I am sixty-five), and medium bald. I am neither a pessimist nor an optimist. I think I have what might be called a medium temperament. (1)

Doc Fraser presents himself as a medium "medium," so resolutely in the middle of human diversity as to be the embodiment of social norms. But while Doc Fraser may be "a medium kind of man" by virtue of his height, weight, and age—qualities that do little to illuminate his character or approach to others—he is hardly representative of the townspeople of Lennox. Doc Fraser is unique in owning and operating his own business, and unlike the other characters in *Country Place,* he is without close friends or associates. Doc Fraser simplistically assumes the position of a medium because he is medium. However, Petry's play on this word exposes the problem of conflating some vague notion of representativeness with narrative authority. Doc Fraser's "medium" or average qualities have no bearing on his storytelling abilities. Rather, in taking on the responsibility of telling the town's history, the druggist sharply distinguishes himself from others. To be a narrating "medium" is to cease to be a typical or "medium kind of man." Moreover, as Dubek notes, Doc Fraser normalizes his patriarchal views by identifying himself as "medium." In this way, he "speaks in this novel to a postwar white America anxious for a return to 'normalcy'" (68). Dubek's quotation marks around the word "normalcy" highlights how this quality is as much a social construction as the racial categories that shape Doc Fraser's worldview.

Doc Fraser's opening description of himself omits one of the most critical aspects of his identity: not merely his name, but the fact that the narrator of this black-authored text is white. However, Petry's sly refusal to specify the race of her narrator neatly confirms his whiteness. As Toni Morrison has observed, American literature has long depended upon the presumptions of whiteness.[4] By mimicking the entitlements of white narrative authority, Petry undermines Doc Fraser's reliability since one of the most obvious and most significant qualities about this character remains unspoken and ignored. He does not disclose his whiteness because he does not recognize it as a key component of his identity, so deeply engrained in his sense of self it is invisible to him. In this way, Petry locates the power of whiteness in its silence and the assumption that whiteness equates with universality or medium-ness.[5] Precisely because it remains unexpressed, whiteness establishes the narrative frame of the entire text. The obvious differences between Petry and Doc Fraser highlight the distinction between the novel's implied author and its narrator.[6] Phelan reminds us that "character narration is an art of indirection, one in which the same text simultaneously communicates two different purposes to two different audiences" (*Living to Tell about It* 7). As such, there are two principal narratives in *Country Place*: one told by Doc Fraser and the other by Petry or the implied author.[7] Doc Fraser purports to tell us a historical account of Lennox during a strong hurricane. However, by drawing our attention to Doc Fraser's unreliability and his manipulative exchanges with the Weasel, Petry offers a very different story about the town's transformation and its anxious narrator.

Doc Fraser presents himself as dependably sober and even-tempered. As the town druggist, he dispenses medicines and homemade fountain syrups, balancing remedies with slight indulgences, seemingly moderate in all things. However, his candid introduction poses a striking contrast to the story that follows. Beginning with the second chapter, the novel adopts a largely omniscient perspective. From this point of view, Doc Fraser freely narrates the inner thoughts of various Lennox residents and relates intimate encounters

---

4. In *Playing in the Dark,* Morrison writes, "the readers of virtually all of American fiction have been positioned as white" (xii).

5. Grace Elizabeth Hale affirms this conception of whiteness, writing, "Central to the meaning of whiteness is a broad, collective American silence. The denial of white as a racial identity, the denial that whiteness has a history, allows the quiet, the blankness, to stand as the norm" (xi).

6. Phelan describes the implied author as "the agent responsible for bringing the text into existence" (*Living* 45).

7. Phelan acknowledges that "for many practical purposes, insisting on a distinction between the author and the implied author is multiplying entities beyond necessity" but explains "that including the implied author in our general theoretical model of narrative communication allows for greater clarity, precision, and comprehensibility" (*Living* 45–46). As *Country Place* does not involve the kind of multiple authorial versions (hoaxes, ghost-written works, and collaborative works) that for Phelan demands a distinction between the author and the implied author, I conflate these labels in my analysis.

that occur behind closed doors. Though he admits to being "an eyewitness" neither to the first significant event in the text, Johnnie Roane's return to Lennox, nor to all that transpires later at the Roane family home, Doc Fraser assures readers that his intimacy with those in contact with Johnnie guarantees the truth of his story: "Over the years I have acquired an intimate, detailed knowledge of all of them." Thus he offers what he believes "to be a true account" (8). Such comments demand that we read the novel not as split between two narrators but as derived from a single subjective voice. Doc Fraser figures his narrative authority, like his racial identity, as beyond question, while the implied author urges readers to question his presumptions. Critics have mistaken the druggist's version of events as unimpeachable truth, too quickly dismissing his opening confession of bias as evidence that the narrative that follows is ultimately trustworthy.

In addition to not mentioning his whiteness, Doc Fraser also fails to name himself in his self-introduction. Readers do not learn exactly who is telling this story until nearly one hundred pages into the novel. This absence works to erase Doc Fraser's subjective narration of the events that follow. Although he uses the narrating "I" in the novel's first section, by not explicitly identifying himself, he naturalizes the disappearance of his "I" in subsequent sections. Having not known Doc Fraser's name to begin with, readers may not immediately notice his apparent absence later on. After his brief personal opening, Doc Fraser effectively disappears (at one point in the novel he even refers to himself in the third person), offering instead a novel that mimics the perspective of an external, disembodied observer, a figure closer to God than to man.[8] Joyce A. Joyce, among other critics, finds the narrative discontinuities in *Country Place* to be "an obvious inconsistency in Petry's use of narrative point of view" (103). However, they are better read not as amateurish disruptions, but rather as deliberate constructions that reveal the necessarily strained process of consolidating narrative power.[9] Doc Fraser's awkward shifts in point of view underscore his desperate and ultimately failed desire to contain and possess the story of Lennox.

---

8. In tracing the origin of omniscience in literature, Culler observes, "The basis of 'omniscience' appears to be the frequently articulated analogy between God and the author: the author creates the world of the novel as God created our world, and just as the world holds no secrets for God, so the novelist knows everything that is to be known about the world of the novel" ("Omniscience" 23). Culler rejects the charade of omniscience in part because it is derived from something of which "we have only rumor and speculation to go on" (25).

9. Reviewing *Country Place* in the *New York Times,* Richard Sullivan characterizes the novel's narration as a "technical defect" that confuses what may be "the objective re-creation of actual fact" and "the subjective re-creation of what the alleged narrator imagines the fact to have been" (12).

Despite his assurances concerning the truth of his story, Doc Fraser admits to "having a prejudice against women," noting that women make "no effort to control (their) emotions" (1–2). Implicitly defining himself against the emotional volatility of women, Doc Fraser appears to offer a rational, seemingly objective perspective untainted by female outbursts. Bernard explains that "within his very prejudices are irrational contradictions and his awareness of them" (100). These contradictions are especially important because much of *Country Place* depends upon the actions and emotional responses of women; their failure to "control their emotions" provides the druggist with his narrative. Moreover, although Doc Fraser does not know Glory, Johnnie's wife, personally, he claims that having observed her actions "for so long a period," he "can tell you with a fair degree of accuracy what she thinks about when she wakes up in the morning" (6). The power of his white male gaze alone affirms the authority of his voice. Although Doc Fraser recognizes that any story is influenced by the prejudices of its teller, he ignores the tension produced by his scorn for women. Through his presumed omniscience, he authorizes both his misogyny and his racial entitlements.

Doc Fraser derives much of his narrative power from his position within the marketplace, a position that marks his racial and gender privilege. He inherited the drugstore from his father, who in turn inherited it from his father; racialized patriarchy, not talent or hard work, is primarily responsible for his wealth and livelihood. His wealth aptly illustrates George Lipsitz's claim that "whiteness has cash value" (vii). Notably, Doc Fraser is a bachelor with no children. Just as the text works to undermine his narrative authority, the absence of a son or daughter who might inherit the family business affirms the druggist's impotence and waning symbolic authority. Doc Fraser assumes that because the residents of Lennox are his "customers," he knows them intimately and can identify what most deeply motivates them. However, this logic equally applies to the Weasel, who, in chauffeuring most of the novel's characters, has occasion to interact with all of them. Doc Fraser's assertion that he "is in a better position to write the record of what took place here than almost anyone else" (4) must thus be read alongside an ongoing competition between the two men for narrative control. Doc Fraser presents himself as the more dependable authority of the town largely because of his higher class status.

DOC FRASER AND THE WEASEL

Holladay aptly characterizes *Country Place* as a study in narrative control centered on the competitive storytelling of Doc Fraser and the Weasel, but she does not explicitly link this tension to the narrative authority assumed by whiteness.[10] The uneasy exchange of information between the Weasel and Doc Fraser reveals the sordid underpinnings required to manufacture narrative control. Despite Doc Fraser's fair-minded assurances, he struggles intensely to possess and express the story of his fellow townspeople. His simultaneous reliance on and repudiation of the Weasel reflects his quiet exploitation of a social other as well as his anxious claim to a more refined form of whiteness. While the working-class Weasel crudely enters into the minds of others, Doc Fraser stages his narrative interventions from afar. Though he barely interacts with the novel's main characters, the druggist takes broad license in narrating their lives and most intimate thoughts. However, as Holladay notes, Doc Fraser's version of events depends entirely upon the Weasel; though the former scorns the cabdriver's rumor mongering and manipulations, he needs these details and plot accelerations to construct his narrative.

The creepy cabdriver and the well-respected druggist seem to have very little in common. However, they are in fact united by a number of key details. Both are bachelors who carefully scrutinize the lives of others. As single men, they are unencumbered by the demands and encroachments of a wife. While the various husbands of the novel struggle to control their partners, Doc Fraser and the Weasel are free to influence the lives of others without such "womanly" interference. Both are also white men who harbor prejudices; while Doc Fraser largely disdains women, the Weasel expresses anti-Semitic views and a fear of immigrants. The Weasel's concern with explicitly delineating the boundaries of whiteness reflects his own class insecurities. Unlike the professionally well-established Doc Fraser, he has more to fear from competing immigrant workers. However, the druggist also evinces class-based concerns. Instead of targeting Jews and immigrants, however, he focuses his disdain on the lower-class Weasel, carefully if more subtly enumerating their differences. Unlike the cabdriver, he is a well-educated gentleman who does not prod others for information. In contrast to the Weasel, who is figured as physically repellant, Doc Fraser is a clean, reliable town citizen who listens more than he speaks. As the epitome of civilized dignity and quiet authority, he is the very model of idealized whiteness.

Although Doc Fraser and the Weasel exemplify two differing approaches to narrative control, both are necessary to produce the illusion of omniscience.

---

10. Noting the ways in which the Weasel orchestrates key events in the text, Holladay identifies the town cabdriver as the book's "author," who is "closer in spirit to the novel's omniscient narrator than Doc" (25). However, while Holladay ultimately argues that Doc Fraser is upstaged by the intrusive Weasel, I read the druggist's veneer of omniscience as his ultimate claim to narrative authority.

The Weasel deliberately orchestrates the revelation of various scandals, teasing his customers with loaded questions and strategic allusions. He drives Mrs. Gramby and Mrs. Roane to Obit's Heights knowing that Glory and Ed will likely be there entwined in each other's arms. More insidiously, he steals a love note from Ed's wallet, which he later learns was written by Lil, and then passes the note to her husband, Mrs. Gramby's son, Mearns. Doc Fraser does not describe himself soliciting these details from the Weasel, but the novel depends upon the Weasel's discoveries and manipulations. The druggist needs the repellent cabdriver to tell the story of Lennox even as he distances himself from such scandalous revelations.

As codependent story creators, Doc Fraser and the Weasel demonstrate how the feigned omniscience of whiteness operates as a manufactured fiction. Doc Fraser needs the details and plot accelerations offered by the Weasel, while the cabdriver needs the druggist's social authority. Doc Fraser adopts the respectable, trusted voice of the novel, but the Weasel's underhanded intrusions lay the foundation of this purportedly unbiased account. His unattractive manner and working-class background might be easily read as a kind of racial coding that positions him as black and Doc Fraser as white. However, Petry's description of these twinned storytellers resists such a simplistic interpretation. Rather, *Country Place* presents both Doc Fraser and the Weasel as beneficiaries to the entitlements of whiteness. The Weasel's intrusive manner with others is unimaginable for a nonwhite character. Moreover, he repeatedly displays resentment toward characters like Lil and Rosenberg, Mrs. Gramby's Jewish lawyer, who have moved beyond his own class status. He seethes not with racial hatred (he is largely indifferent to Neola, the novel's only black character), but with anger that others, especially European immigrants, have prospered more than he. In this way, Petry offers a nuanced and heterogeneous description of whiteness inflected by notions of class, citizenship, and migration. It is not defined by monolithic privilege but instead fosters a sense of entitlement that can be either frustrated or fulfilled.

Like Doc Fraser, the Weasel's true name is not disclosed when he is first introduced. After telling Johnnie his actual name, he notes in phrasing that affirms his lower-class status, "There ain't three people 'round here who remembers it" (14). Like Doc Fraser, who is sometimes called Pop, the Weasel has a nickname that reflects his relationship to others and, perhaps more importantly, to storytelling. Even Mrs. Gramby observes how the Weasel "had an uncanny and disconcerting way of following one's train of thoughts," as if he were a burrowing rodent in one's own mind (87). "Pop" confirms the patriarchal position that Doc Fraser aspires to attain as the town's narrator. The fitting nicknames reflect the shared desire of both men for control over the lives of others. While Pop assumes a fatherly perspective that enforces traditional gender and class roles, the cabdriver ferrets out stories through invasive questions and inappropriate asides.

Doc Fraser emphasizes the physical appropriateness of the Weasel's nickname when he describes him through the observations of Johnnie. Having just stepped off the train in Lennox, the returning veteran approaches the Weasel's car: "Johnnie saw his sharp ferret's face, the close-set eyes, an out-of-shape cap turned backward on his head" (7). A few pages later, Johnnie again notes "the sharp face, the small, close-together, beady eyes" (14). The nearly verbatim repetition of the Weasel's physical appearance reflects the constrained purpose of Doc Fraser's narration. The druggist does not aim to expand upon his characters' qualities and perspectives; rather, he seeks to limit each character to a handful of conventional attributes. Dubek observes that Doc Fraser's imagination has "been (mis)informed by dominant and conservative ideologies of gender, race, and class" such that he only reifies preexisting prejudices (66). This strategy of containment works to consolidate Doc Fraser's narrative authority even as it reveals a remarkably unimaginative and even apprehensive point of view. Doc Fraser is more concerned with assigning specific roles to his characters than he is with exploring a more complex set of motivations. Consistent with the restrictive aims of omniscience, he works to classify and label his subjects, not to interrogate their latent drives or elucidate their contradictions.

The difference between how Doc Fraser and the Weasel interact with others and then construct stories from these encounters is best exemplified by their opposing approaches to Johnnie Roane. The plot of the novel begins with the young man's unannounced return to Lennox after four years serving in World War II. Doc Fraser acknowledges that he "did not see Johnnie Roane when he got off the train at Lennox. Nor was I an eyewitness to what happened afterward." However, he assures readers that he received the story "in such detail" from the Weasel that he "might just as well have been standing on the station platform when Johnnie got off the train, and have looked inside his head as well" (66). However, while Doc Fraser limits himself to "looking" inside the head of Johnnie, the Weasel is depicted as a far more intrusive presence. On the ride to his parents' home, Johnnie chafes at the very presence of the Weasel, feeling that the cabdriver is pressing upon him: "his sly way of looking at you so that you weren't quite aware of it at first, but before you knew it his glance was inside you, feeling its way around" (15). Johnnie even feels that the cabdriver is invading his body when the Weasel speaks about town life: "Listening to The Weasel was like having a dirty hand paw through your personal belongings, leaving them in confusion; and so soiled that after the first look you were disgusted and tempted to throw them away, for they had changed" (18). Unlike Doc Fraser, who only "looks" inside Johnnie's mind, the Weasel appears to dirty its contents in a kind of mental and emotional assault.

However, in some respects, the druggist's narration is even more invasive than the Weasel's insistent questions and comments. Doc Fraser takes enormous liberties in describing Johnnie's thoughts. He references childhood memories that return to Johnnie as the young veteran looks at the town's Catholic church and even recounts what Glory wrote in letters to him while he was away. These details have no evidentiary basis but instead reflect the mundane observations Doc Fraser believes Glory would make: "She wrote that she missed him and that the weather was cold or the weather was hot or that it had rained or snowed."[11] Johnnie notes of the letters, "If you looked at them sharply, trying to analyze them, they didn't say anything." If Glory's letters indeed say nothing, it is because Doc Fraser cannot imagine what meaning they might actually convey. Johnnie's observation that "She never said anything really personal" applies just as well to Doc Fraser's inability to access Glory's mind (17).

The details Doc Fraser fabricates for Glory's letters are ultimately trivial when compared to how the druggist narrates Johnnie's reunion with his wife. In one of the most disturbing scenes of the novel, Doc Fraser describes Johnnie raping Glory after she shrinks from his advances on his first night home. Although Glory is infatuated with Ed and no longer in love with Johnnie, there is no evidence to suggest that such a violent encounter actually occurred. Doc Fraser explains that he bases his account on his close friendship with Mrs. Roane, who may have told him that she and her husband heard Glory scream that night. According to Doc Fraser's description, this scream occurs well after the rape, when Glory and Johnnie are speaking in bed. This illogical sequence of events is further muddled by Glory telling Mr. Roane that she screamed because a window fell on her hand. Although Johnnie feels dirtied by the Weasel's presence in the cab, Doc Fraser does far more to dirty the young man's narrative. He presents Johnnie as a brutal rapist who tries to strangle his wife, projecting his own hatred of women onto the returning veteran. While readers may recognize how Doc Fraser corrupts and soils Johnnie's experiences, it is important to note that he may not perceive his narrative this way. As Dubek observes, "Doc presents the rape as the result of Johnnie simply exercising his rights as a husband and a veteran of a war that promised him 'glory' in exchange for his faithful duty to his country" (71).

11. Doc Fraser's very limited interaction with the Roane family affirms that he has no direct access to the letters Glory wrote.

By narrating events from a seemingly omniscient perspective, Doc Fraser gives credence to this version, and in fact many critics of *Country Place* assume that the druggist is a reliable narrator. Bernard Bell notes that Doc Fraser "immediately establishes his reliability" and characterizes the druggist's distaste for women as no more than a "petty prejudice" that apparently has no bearing on the novel's point of view (110). Dubek's description of the novel as "parody" offers a more nuanced reading as she argues that Petry uses her novel to respond directly to "postwar white family narratives" like William Wyler's acclaimed 1946 film *The Best Years of Our Lives* (74). However, Petry's parody extends beyond such popular domestic dramas. She effectively parodies the very construction of omniscience and the ways in which white narrative authority betrays its biases even when such biases are fully admitted. By revealing Doc Fraser's prejudice against women in the first chapter of the novel, Petry challenges readers to discern how such chauvinism later manifests in his storytelling. His illusion of omniscience serves to universalize the notion that misogyny is natural. However, in her role as the implied author, Petry here exposes the ways in which such prejudice is as constructed and tenuous as Doc Fraser's narrative authority.

Doc Fraser appears to be so removed from the immediacy of the Weasel's irritating presence that in one scene he even references himself in the third person. The episode involves an encounter between the Weasel and Lil at the drugstore. Annoyed at how Lil demands that she be called "Mrs. Gramby," the Weasel scoffs, replying that he remembers when she used to wet her pants in the first grade. Following the crude comment, "Doc Fraser looked like he wanted to laugh, but he remembered his dignity" (106). To maintain his "dignity," the druggist must do more than stifle a laugh; he must mask his own first-person narration. "Dignity" here signifies as a justification for his charade of omniscience; Doc Fraser cannot expose his true response and laugh because he must remain a detached observer. His peculiar reference to himself creates the illusion that the scene is being filtered through the Weasel's perspective, as if Doc Fraser truly has free access to the minds of others. Moreover, by not responding to the exchange between the Weasel and Lil, the druggist places himself above such petty class squabbles. Because of the business he has inherited, he operates from a more secure social position.

This scene's odd perspective also highlights the Weasel's inability to control the narrative that follows. Frustrated by his failure to decode the love letter he stole from Ed, the Weasel tries to agitate Limpy, the taxi ticket seller, and thereby assert a modicum of control. He tells Limpy that he heard his wife has not been well, mentioning that "she was buying a bottle of Lydia Pinkham's down in the drugstore yesterday" (115). Although Lydia Pinkham tablets continue to be sold today to alleviate menstrual and menopausal pains, when Limpy asks what they are for, the Weasel states he "always figured it was to bring their passion back" (116). The Weasel's erroneous understanding of the purpose of Pinkham tablets emphasizes Doc Fraser's expertise since, as a druggist, he would certainly be familiar with them. Moreover, the Weasel does not admit to having seen Limpy's wife buy the Pinkham tablets; he only "heard your wife ain't so well" (116). Presumably, the Weasel heard about this purchase from Doc Fraser, suggesting that the two habitually exchange information. Petry thus affirms that the Weasel is not alone in spreading gossip about others.

The Weasel eventually learns that the love letter was written by Glory's mother, Lil, who is married to the wealthy Mearns Gramby. He makes this realization while Doc Fraser is updating his scrapbook of prescriptions. However, because the Weasel has not told Doc Fraser about the stolen letter, the latter is not aware of what causes the cabdriver to leave in such a giddy hurry. Given the previous chapter's focus on the Weasel's encounter with Ed, readers understand that Ed had an affair with Lil. As the narrator of the novel, Doc Fraser has provided his audience with knowledge that he does not yet possess within the chronology of the story. This bizarre sequencing seems to undermine Doc Fraser's narrative authority as the Weasel leaves without telling him what he has discovered nor what he intends to do with this information. Afraid of what scandal the Weasel may unleash, Doc Fraser threatens to run him out of town. But the Weasel immediately calls his bluff, "What s'matter, Doc? . . . I thought I was one of your best friends. What would you be running me out of town for? And come to think of it, just how would you go about getting me run out?" (136).

Although the Weasel indicts Doc Fraser for his impotence, the druggist finds another means of seeking retribution. Aware that his threat was indeed empty, for despite his pretensions, he has little influence in such matters, Doc Fraser seeks revenge the only way he can: through storytelling and the manipulation of information. He recounts for readers the Weasel's private scandal, the cabdriver's impregnation of a mentally disabled fifteen-year-old girl. Remarking on the Weasel's confession about this affair, Doc Fraser notes: "He gave me certain information about himself, in confidence, and I have never yet been able to bring myself to violate that confidence" (137). However, his subsequent description of how the Weasel seduced a summer worker from the State Farm and then convinced her that Superman was the father of her child violates the very confidence Doc Fraser references. This recounting of the Weasel's sordid history is a blatant attempt by the druggist to reestablish himself as the text's true narrative authority and moral center. But just as his avowed misogyny forces readers to question his depiction of female characters, the dissonance between Doc Fraser's claim to keeping the Weasel's confidence, followed by his immediate violation of that trust, exposes "the double communication involved in unreliable narration" (Phelan, *Living* 50). These inconsistencies demand reappraisal of Doc Fraser's claim to authority and reveal the nuanced workings of the implied author.

By exposing her narrator's hypocrisy and his inability to keep the Weasel's confidence, Petry reveals the hollow foundation at the core of Doc Fraser's claim to narrative authority. He is a man who cannot be trusted, neither as the guardian of private stories nor as the teller of public ones. In his attempt to describe the history of Lennox over a series of tumultuous days, Doc Fraser offers a troubling portrait of a town wrought by melodrama and filled with anxious, scheming people. Despite his best attempts to depict himself above such petty disputes and competitive jostling for power, Doc Fraser proves to be just as manipulative and small-minded as his other white neighbors. His racial and gender privilege do little to separate him from the desperate men and women he describes. If not a medium medium, he is at least a fitting one.

CHAPTER 8

"One Silence Had Led to Another"

Strategic Paralipsis and a Non-Normative Narrator in Bitter in the Mouth

PATRICK E. HORN

MONIQUE TRUONG'S 2010 novel *Bitter in the Mouth* presents the story of Linda (Linh-Dao Nguyen) Hammerick, a Vietnamese American girl adopted by a white family at age seven after her parents died in a fire, as told by herself. Linda is subsequently raised in the small southern town of Boiling Springs, North Carolina, where she has an uneasy and sometimes hostile relationship with her adoptive mother, DeAnne. Linda's adoptive father, Thomas, a respected lawyer in the community, dies of an apparent heart attack after being discovered having sex with his young black female secretary, and the only member of Linda's adoptive family with whom she has a healthy and enduring relationship is her gay great-uncle, known by family members as Baby Harper. At age eleven, Linda is raped by a high school student whom DeAnne had hired to mow the grass, but she never tells her adoptive parents about the rape. Before Linda graduates as valedictorian of Boiling Springs High School and matriculates at Yale, her (white) best friend Kelly becomes pregnant with the child of Linda's (white) neighbor and romantic interest, Wade Harris, and Kelly goes to live with her (white) aunt in Rock Hill, South Carolina, to prevent the Boiling Springs community from discovering her out-of-wedlock pregnancy.

But much of the plot information summarized above is withheld from readers for a significant portion of the novel. The narrator recounts Linda's season of adolescent sexual exploration before revealing that she was raped as a child. Likewise, crucial information about several characters' identities is conveyed much later than one might expect. Not until page 158 does the narrative disclose that Linda's actual name is Linh-Dao, that she is Asian American, or that she was adopted. The circumstances regarding her adoptive father's infidelity with his secretary and his sudden death are not divulged until page 129, and the race of his secretary is not mentioned until page 170. Baby Harper's sexual orientation is hinted at but not confirmed until page 152, and we learn (along with Linda) that Wade is the father of Kelly's child on page 262. In the novel's closing pages, Linda recounts learning (as an adult) how she had come to live with the Hammerick family, and she realizes that her childhood presence had been a constant reminder to DeAnne that Thomas had been in love with Linda's mother before her death.

Truong's novel employs a great deal of what Gérard Genette calls "paralipsis," or "infractionary omission" of information of which the narrator is aware (*Narrative Discourse* 95).[1] The strategy is quite common in literary narratives: "narrative always says less than it knows, but it often makes known more than it says" (98). Genette notes that key information about the plot that will unfold is often withheld at the beginning of literary narratives, particularly in novels of "intrigue or adventure" (190). This device is to some extent an unavoidable aspect of all narratives, which, as Aristotle and many others have noted, necessarily consist of a beginning, a middle, and an end (VII: 13–15). And yet, certain narratives intentionally withhold significant facts, beyond mere variations in the temporal sequence of the plot. For example, one might argue that *Bitter in the Mouth* merely relates the event of Linda's adoption out of order—after events that transpired later in the fictive sequence, or *erzählte Zeit* (33). Genette identifies this type of narrative anachrony—or "discordance between the two orderings of story and narrative"—as "analepsis," or "any evocation after the fact of an event that took place earlier" (36, 40). But because the information about Linda's identity as an adoptee and as a racial minority pertains to all events in the story, I argue that its initial omission is more than a simple anachrony: paralipsis rather than mere analepsis.[2] Particularly given the context of the protagonist's childhood in a small town in the U.S. South during the 1970s and 1980s, Linda's racial identity is perhaps the most salient fact about her, and its omission seems "infractionary"—not in the sense of a moral or civic transgression, but rather as an intentional withholding of information likely to significantly influence readers' comprehension of and

---

1. We should be careful to distinguish paralipsis, or the infractionary omission of information, from prolepsis, which Genette defines as the "narrating or evoking in advance an event that will take place later" (40).

2. The end of Truong's novel does engage in such an evocation of former events, and it therefore constitutes what Genette calls "analepsis on paralipsis" (*Narrative Discourse* 53).

personal responses to her story. The fact that Linda's narratee is not identified as someone who knows her apart from the story, placing the actual reader in the same position as the narratee, only strengthens this sense of "infractionary" withholding.[3]

The withheld information takes on greater significance through Linda's conversation with Leo, her partner for eight years, which she recounts in the second half of the novel:

> When we first met, I tried to tell Leo about my childhood in Boiling Springs. He said that these experiences meant that I did know what it was like *being* Asian in the South. For a soon-to-be psychiatrist, he wasn't a very good listener. No, Leo, I knew what it was like *being* hated in the South. (173, emphasis original)

This passage makes it clear that for (the adult narrator) Linda, Asian American identity and the experience of "being hated in the South" were closely linked, if not corollary, and could be easily mistaken for each other by a poor listener. In a separate autobiographical essay, Truong has described her own childhood in similar terms. Boiling Springs Elementary School, she explains, "had one Asian child in its enrollment, only one child who was different from the rest. Her name was Monique Truong. . . . They rewarded me for introducing them to multiculturalism with a daily barrage of name-calling . . . *Jap* and *Chink* were favorites" ("American Like Me" 2–3). When Truong's mother brought an ornate, three-tiered cake to school for her eighth birthday, Truong writes, the exotic cake seemed to signify her "now cemented status as the freak of Boiling Springs Elementary" (para. 9). In this small Southern town in the late twentieth century, with the Vietnam War still fresh in America's collective memory, Asian American identity was still regarded by many as "freakish" and foreign, and Truong was repeatedly reminded of that fact. Yet in a region in which racial identity had for so long been considered as a white/black binary with an obvious and chronic power differential, Truong (like Linda) represented a confounding variable.

Leslie Bow has described the position of Asian Americans in the U.S. South as an "unspoken in-between" (230). The logic of Jim Crow did not adequately account for nonwhite, nonblack Others, whose very presence challenged its dichotomous logic. As Bow poignantly puts it, "where did the Asian

---

3. Readers' sense of surprise at Linda's identity may be muted because of their knowledge of Truong's Vietnamese American ethnicity, particularly if they assume that a novel's narrator will share the racial/ethnic/sexual identity of the author. Of course, many novels and their narrators do not follow this pattern or support this assumption.

sit on the segregated bus?" (1). Truong's novel also demonstrates how the fields of narratology and ethnic literary studies can find common ground, despite their conventional oppositions. As Sue J. Kim writes, Asian American literary criticism emerged primarily out of an "interpretative, contextualist, extrinsic, and praxis-oriented" mode, while narrative theory was traditionally "formalist, intrinsic, and abstract" (15 in this volume). *Bitter in the Mouth* presents us with an opportunity to bring these historically opposed critical lenses to bear on a single text, and I hope this essay will demonstrate how fruitful that common ground can be. I argue that Truong's omission of key information about Linda's identity as an adoptee and as a racial minority constitutes an intentional and "infractionary" omission; that this omission is likely to influence readers' identification with Linda in important ways; that the delaying of "estranging" information about characters is likely to incline readers to identify more closely with them; and that the unusual nature of Linda's narrative—including the fact that her "mother" turns out to be an adoptive mother of a different race—may result in other estrangements, as readers are initially unprepared to contextualize Linda's unexplained antipathy for her "mother" and other family members. The upshot of all this is that while the racial and ethnic identities of readers and characters may influence readers' responses to specific characters, they are not necessarily the strongest or most salient factors at work in the reader/narrator/character relationship.

•

In her groundbreaking critical study *Playing in the Dark: Whiteness and the Literary Imagination* (1993), Toni Morrison wrote that "until very recently, and regardless of the race of the author, the readers of virtually all of American fiction have been positioned as white" (xii). Related to this assumption that implied readers are white is the often unacknowledged convention that American literary characters whose race is not explicitly stated are also implied or assumed to be white.[4] As Morrison writes of a character in Hemingway's *To Have and Have Not,* "Eddy is white, and we know he is because nobody says so" (72). Therefore, Truong's delayed identification of Linda's racial identity seems to play on the unwritten rules of American literature. If readers assume,

---

4. According to Wolfgang Iser, a text's "implied reader" is established through the nebulous interactions between the "prestructuring of the potential meaning by the text" and "the reader's actualization of this potential," which results in the production of "literary meaning" (xii). Perhaps a more practical definition of an implied reader might be the set of ways in which a text presumes a reader will comprehend its "meaning" and therefore guides actual readers to do so.

early in the novel, that Linda Hammerick from Boiling Springs, North Carolina, is white, it is for precisely this reason: because nobody says so (or otherwise). And with the revelation that Linda is in fact an adopted Vietnamese American immigrant, everything changes. But why—Truong's novel seems to ask—must this be so?

Of course, not all readers will or should assume that all "unmarked" characters are white. If Linda's story was set in Vietnam, it would be a logical assumption that she was Vietnamese—at least, if she did not indicate otherwise. Likewise, if the story depicted an African American community like Zora Neale Hurston's hometown of Eatonville, Florida, it would be intuitive to assume that an unmarked character was black. But because Linda's story is set in a predominantly white Southern town and her "family" is white, it seems natural to assume that she is as well, for better or for worse.

The "infractionary" or transgressive omission of Linda's racial identity is especially likely to influence readers' identification with her character because Linda serves as the autodiegetic narrator of her story. As Genette explains, a homodiegetic narrator is one who also appears as a character in her story, and homodiegetic narrators who double as the protagonist or "star" of the narrative can be described as autodiegetic (*Narrative Discourse* 244–45). As readers, we have no choice but to credit or blame Linda with the facts that she chooses to share with us or to withhold from us: there is no additional narrator who serves as a filter or intermediary. Genette notes that many narratives featuring such paralipses begin by employing "external focalization"—or "vision from without"—in which characters' thoughts and feelings are unknown because narrative events are related by a heterodiegetic, or external, narrator who is "absent from the story" (*Narrative Discourse Revisited* 65; *Narrative Discourse* 244). This narrative positioning, with the suggestion of either the third-person narrator's limited knowledge of narrative events (how could they have known?) or with the implication that the omniscient third-person narrator wishes to tell a more compelling story (wait for it!), does not bear as directly on the reader's identification with characters in the story that proceeds. But *Bitter in the Mouth* begins and remains internally focalized through its first-person, autodiegetic narrator, Linda, who (like all narrators) chooses to tell or not to tell certain things (including her identity as an adopted Asian American child) as she recounts past events.

Susan Lanser has intriguingly pondered the narratological and psychological effects of literary texts narrated by non-gendered speakers. In her critical assessment of Jeanette Winterson's *Written on the Body,* Lanser writes that the novel "leads me to recognize that sex is a common if not constant element of narrative *so long as we include its absence as a narratological variable*" ("Sexing the Narrative" 87, emphasis original). She notes that "while the narrator's sex is normally unmarked in heterodiegetic texts, sex *is* an explicit element of most homodiegetic, and virtually all autodiegetic, narratives of length" (87, emphasis original). In other words, when the narrator is identifiable as a particular character in his or her story, and especially when that character happens to be the protagonist, it is unusual for the text to avoid or delay identifying the narrator/character's gender. Lanser argues that "the primary omission of sex itself would seem to constitute what Genette has called a *paralipsis*: the under-reporting of information conventional to a particular narrator or focalizer" (88, emphasis original). The "primary omission" of racial or ethnic identity is a parallel move: a paralipsis that strategically engages readers' expectations, presumptions, and stereotypes. Like *Written on the Body*, *Bitter in the Mouth* employs strategic paralipses that play on readers' preconceived notions of who an "unmarked" narrator or character is or should be. Just as characters of unstated race in American literature are often presumed to be white, narrators of unstated sex are often assumed to be male and heterosexual. Lanser suggests that unidentified narrators are often granted "the normative authority of the male narrator" and therefore considered more reliable (88). But what happens for us as readers when assumptions of "normative" identity are challenged by narrators who turn out to be non-normative? Are they rendered "unreliable" by virtue of their failure or unwillingness to self-reveal as non-normative? Or does their delayed identification call us to be more open-minded as readers and less presumptuous of what constitutes a "normal" narrator?

Linda's silences about these identity categories also figure U.S. Southerners' traditional unwillingness to discuss issues of race, ethnicity, class, gender, and sexuality in "mixed company"; these subjects are often considered to fall beyond the pale of polite conversation (though they are certainly not absent from vernacular discourse) in Boiling Springs. Narrator Linda muses that "there were two kinds of absences: the void and the missing. The void was the person, place, or thing that was never there in the first place. The missing existed but was no longer present" (161). I would argue that cultural silences about these identity categories constitute a third kind of absence: things that are *always there* but rarely acknowledged—the absent presence of the taboo. As Linda looks back on her adoptive parents' difficult relationship, she realizes that "one silence had led to another, and eventually the silences became the life preservers dotting the dangerous ocean between them" (281). Even within the private, domestic space of the Hammerick household, some subjects are believed to be best avoided, and Linda's history constitutes one such absent presence.

Linda begins her story in a confidential, personal voice. The first line of the novel informs the reader, "I fell in love with my great-uncle Harper because he taught me how to dance," and the narrator goes on to say, "I'm not ashamed to admit that I have tried to find him in the male bodies that I lie next to" (3–4). She then relates her (adoptive) grandmother's dying words—"What I know about you, little girl, would break you in two"—to which the teenage Linda replies, simply, abruptly, and elegantly, "Bitch" (5). These disclosures seem to establish the narrator as truthful and unfiltered: she does not appear to hold back or gloss over her private sexual life or her troubled relationships with family members. And revealing that she called her dying grandmother a "bitch" to her face establishes Linda the narrator, like Linda the character, as a person who will say anything, regardless of how others may judge her. This does not seem like a reticent or "unreliable" narrator—unstable, perhaps, but seemingly willing to tell it all.

Linda is equally forthcoming about another form of personal difference, a condition that she eventually learns is called "auditory-gustatory synesthesia" (218). To Linda, words have distinctive flavors, and she spends a significant amount of effort (both as a narrator and as a character) explaining her condition. For example, a sentence that she recites in fourth grade becomes fixed in her memory because of its strange pairings: "Wright*Frenchfries* brothers' first*Pepto-Bismol* flight*cantaloupe* was on December*vanillaicecream* seventeenth*ketchup*, 19*whitebread*03" (116). Thankfully, the novel is not entirely narrated in this fashion; it is only spoken dialogue that triggers what Linda calls her "incomings," and she frequently spares readers from full transcriptions. The flavors of words often seem counterintuitive, and they remind us that words themselves are arbitrary names that humans have assigned to the creatures, objects, and ideas that people our worlds. As a child, Linda attempts to explain to DeAnne that "God*walnut* tastes like a walnut*hamsteaksugar-cured*. The word*licorice* God*walnut*, I mean*raisin* . . ." (107). DeAnne replies to this comment, as usual, by telling Linda not to talk like a crazy person. But Linda's example demonstrates the peculiarity of her condition—and of language in general. It is not only odd and interesting to think of God (or the word "God") tasting like a walnut, but also to note that the word "walnut," to Linda, tastes like ham. Considering Linda's sentence, one can imagine an endless parade from flavor to flavor: in order to explain how one word tastes, she must trigger another incoming, for few words are "flavorless" or taste like whatever they signify. And why should the word "word," or words in general, taste like licorice? Linda's synesthesia is reminiscent of the startling (and ostensibly synesthetic) irrationality of Gertrude Stein's modernist poetry collection *Tender Buttons*, which attempts to convey the essence of "Roast Beef" through lines such as "In the inside there is sleeping, in the outside there is reddening, in the morning there is meaning, in the evening there is feeling" and "please be the beef, please beef, pleasure is not wailing. Please beef, please be carved clear, please be a case of consideration" (19, 22). Seemingly channeling Stein, Linda muses, "I had to disregard the meanings of the words if I wanted to enjoy what the words could offer me" (74).

One answer to the question of why words signify specific concepts or sensory experiences is that there is simply no reason. As Saussure reminds us, the designation of certain words in any language, or the linkages between sounds and ideas, is completely subjective; words have no natural essence or source. "Not only are the two areas which are linguistically linked [sounds and ideas] vague and amorphous in themselves," according to Saussure's *Course in General Linguistics,* "but the process which selects one particular sound-sequence to correspond to one particular idea is entirely arbitrary" (111). This often seems to be the case with Linda's synesthesia as well, although it is difficult not to speculate about the possible relationships between words and flavors. The word "Mom" tastes to Linda like chocolate milk, "Jesus" like fried chicken, "Dolly Parton" like Sweet'N Low, and "matricide" like peach cobbler (107, 238, 78, and 102). The synesthetic flavors of these words stand in contrast to the flavorless casseroles that DeAnne regularly cooks, and the pleasant flavor of the word "matricide," which Linda admits is a "guilty pleasure," seems less than random, given her difficult relationship with her adoptive mother (102–3). Multiple cultural and experiential connections between "Jesus" and fried chicken, "Mom" and chocolate milk, and "Dolly Parton" and Sweet'N Low may also suggest themselves, whether or not one hails from a small Southern town. Does Linda stop calling DeAnne "Mom" because her adoptive mother doesn't serve enough chocolate milk? And should we believe Linda when she claims that she "long[ed] for the word . . . 'matricide,'" but that "food and taste metaphors . . . shed their figurative qualities," retaining only flavors? Is it possible to enjoy the word "matricide" (as a tasty bite of peach cobbler) without wishing harm to one's mother, at least on some level? The relationships between words and flavors in Linda's synesthesia sometimes belie comparisons to Saussure's claims about the arbitrariness of the linguistic sign.

Linda's synesthesia serves various purposes in the novel, both symbolic and plot-related. First, it makes conversation difficult for her, further estranging her from friends and family. Even when Linda wishes to engage in conversation as an adult, she sometimes finds it necessary to sip liquor or to smoke cigarettes in order to lessen the effects of her "incomings." The condition therefore renders literal the metaphor of "painful conversations," and as a result Linda turns to behaviors some people adopt as coping mechanisms for stressful or traumatic experiences. The condition also emphasizes Linda's identity as a cultural outsider. At Boiling Springs High School, she finds social acceptance only when "outside smoking with the stoners . . . charmed by their shared exclusion" (100). And this social group gestures back to Linda's little-discussed identity as an adopted Asian American immigrant in a culturally insular society, which may be the more proximate cause of her exclusion. "I was Boo Radley, not hidden away but in plain sight," she recalls (171). Linda's synesthesia, which her family, friends, and neighbors do not understand or share, gestures toward the strange, exotic, foreign flavor that she represents to Boiling Springs and to the Hammerick family.

●

A 2012 study by psychology scholars Geoff F. Kaufman and Lisa K. Libby examined readers' levels of "experience-taking," which they define as "the imaginative process of spontaneously assuming the identity of a character in a narrative and simulating that character's thoughts, emotions, behaviors, goals, and traits as if they were one's own" (1). The study analyzed the extent to which readers assumed the identity of "outgroup" members in literary narratives, operationalized in two separate experiments as an African American character and a homosexual character. (The investigators did not discuss the race, gender, or sexual orientation of their experimental subjects, rendering assumptions of "outgroup" status problematic.) Nevertheless, the study found that the timing of the revelation of these identity categories played an important role in determining whether or not readers significantly assumed the characters' identities. Kaufman and Libby concluded that "revealing a character's stigmatized group identity . . . later versus earlier in a story was an effective technique for overcoming the barrier to experience-taking that non-shared group membership typically creates" (15). The study also found that "as a result of this experience-taking with the outgroup member, readers of the late-revelation were less likely to judge the character stereotypically, and these readers expressed more favorable attitudes toward the character's group" (15). This study is intriguing because it empirically indicates what many students and scholars of literature may already suspect, based on our own individual, subjective reading experiences: once we "get to know" literary characters intimately, it becomes more difficult to judge them harshly or stereotypically, or to extract ourselves from already-forged imaginative identifications.

Truong's novel puts this tenet to the test. The revelations that Linda is actually Linh-Dao and that Baby Harper is gay come well after readers have begun the process of "getting to know" both characters quite intimately. As a result, readers who may have found these identity categories estranging or who may have turned quickly to stereotypes in order to understand Linda and Baby Harper will have already come to terms with them through different heuristic processes. In this sense, the novel seems designed to elicit readerly empathy or "experience-taking" that early perceptions of non-normativity might have thwarted. Of course, every reader's experience of a literary text will be different, as many reader-response theorists have observed. But as James Phelan stipulates, "[our] experiences as [readers] . . . are responsible to the text as it has been constructed by an author who guides us to experience it in one way rather than another" (*Experiencing Fiction* ix). *Bitter in the Mouth* guides us to experience Linda's story in certain ways, strategically delaying revelations of non-normative identity.

Kaufman and Libby's study indicates that delayed revelations of non-normative identity tend to promote increased identification (at least by so-called normative readers) with the characters in question. But narratives are analogous to highly complicated equations, and omitting pivotal variables in those equations' early stages may have surprising results. The argument lurking behind my argument about this novel is that few social scientists adequately grasp the incredible complexity that human narratives encompass, and therefore literary scholars offer a unique set of skills as we strive to understand the many layers of literary narratives and reader responses, which mirror and signal the complexity of the human brain.

Despite Kaufman and Libby's intriguing findings, it would be a mistake to conclude that Truong's novel inspires greater empathy for Linda or for Baby Harper simply because their non-normative status is not immediately conveyed to readers. The facts that Linda is an adopted Asian American immigrant and that Baby Harper is gay are only two variables in the highly complex equation that constitutes Linda's narrative. And the absence of this information leads to other gaps in understanding. For example, we learn at the end of the novel that DeAnne felt pressured into accepting her husband's adoption of the orphan of another woman whom he had loved. This information helps to explain DeAnne's absences and silences for much of the early narrative of Linda's childhood with the Hammerick family. Moreover, we learn midway through the novel that Linda had been raped by Bobby, a disturbed teenager with whom DeAnne had flirted before leaving Linda alone with him. For this perceived failure on DeAnne's part, Linda comes to hate her adoptive mother, but this explanation is not available to readers for much of the novel, and it is unclear if DeAnne ever learns about the rape. Amid the final revelations about Linda's adoption, DeAnne informs Linda that "I had turned to Iris for comfort, though [I] knew that there would be little there but truth." Narrating, Linda muses, "And you also turned to Bobby. This thought didn't keep me from reaching over the kitchen table and holding on to [DeAnne's] hands"

(281). In other words, this paralipsis is never clearly redressed or corrected, at least from DeAnne's perspective.

Moreover, the missing information toward the beginning of the novel may incline readers to find the two Lindas (narrator and character) quick to judge DeAnne, and her judgments needlessly harsh. For example, Linda is heavy-handed in her criticism of her "mother's" cooking:

> Considering what came into and out of my mother's kitchen—the unneces-sary canned vegetables, the shaken and baked, the hamburger helpmeets, and so on—the food at our table was always punishment. . . . The nightly cross that I had to bear was dependably one of the following casseroles: chicken à la king, tuna noodle, [or] beefy macaroni. . . . Variety meant never having the same casserole two nights in a row. (34)

Elsewhere Linda considers the synesthesia she experiences from complaining about her mother's cooking—"Not again*pancakenosyrup*"—as "restitution for past meals suffered [and] future meals to be endured" (75). For readers first experiencing these passages, knowing that Linda had recently been adopted and that she was an immigrant, likely raised on an entirely different set of staples and flavors, might soften readerly responses to her critiques. But due to the text's strategic paralipses, that knowledge has not yet been shared, and therefore in this case paralipsis regarding non-normative status may actually lead to a harsher response to Linda's critiques. Readers may be more inclined to be generous with narrators who are generous, or at least narrators whose judgments seem warranted by the set of events, sentiments, and relationships that have been shared with us. Withheld information, in other words, can be a double-edged sword.

DeAnne is not the only target of Linda's pointed criticisms; in one passage she describes her "best friend" and perennial pen pal Kelly as "very optimistic for a fat girl" (66). In another passage, Linda dismisses Kelly's suggestion that she might "supplant and overwhelm the phantom tastes with the 'real' flavors on a very full plate" as a "reasonable hypothesis, especially coming from a fat girl" (155). These barbs, which are often included without the appropriate con-text that may have helped readers understand Linda's vitriolic sentiments—it is later suggested that Linda "knew about" Kelly's sexual involvement with Linda's long-standing crush, Wade Harris—may cause readers to question Linda's judgment or even to consider her mean-spirited. Even Linda realizes, toward the end of the narrative, that her judgments could be caustic: "Curios-ity has never been a strong suit of DeAnne's, I thought, and then decided not to say it aloud. Because making fun of DeAnne's cooking was one thing, but making fun of her intellect seemed to me suddenly cruel" (240). This moment is characterized as a realization of Linda's character, as revealed by the retrospective Linda-narrator, but many readers may have already drawn the same conclusion. Strategic paralipsis proves to be a complicated business, and even the latest social science research on this subject has yet to grasp its intricacy.

I would argue that *Bitter in the Mouth* is far more effective at eliciting readers' imaginative identification with Baby Harper than with Linda, perhaps because as an autodiegetic narrator, Linda seems more selfless while promoting Harper's cause than she does while promoting her own. The text also offers more clues about Harper's gay identity early in the narrative than it does about Linda's Asian American / adopted identity, so the fact that he is a gay man comes as more of an anticipated disclosure than Linda's abrupt revelation about her adoption and racial identification. To put it another way, Harper doesn't "keep his secrets" from us as long as Linda does, and even those secrets are mediated by Linda's account, so the fact that they emerge only gradually is not directly attributable to Harper himself. As a result, his identity becomes legible to readers before Linda's does, and once we learn who he "really" is, it is more difficult to fault him (or her) for not disclosing this significant information sooner.

(Great) Uncle Harper is introduced from the outset as the most sympathetic, entertaining, and engaging member of the Hammerick family. He is the relative who teaches Linda to dance, who shares family secrets with her, and who takes her out for barbecue—but only at Bridges Barbecue Lodge, never at Slo Smoking Steakhouse & Bar-B-Que, which he regards with contempt: "Fools" (39–40). Over the course of the novel, Harper grows and changes, becoming the focus of the narrative for extended stretches. Early on, Linda hints heavily at his secret: "My great-uncle was a sixty-two-year-old, never-married male librarian with a velvet divan. . . . These weren't clues; they were flashing signs" (44). We learn that Harper had never "care[d] for his niece" DeAnne, but that he "fell in love with [her] the day she married Thomas" (47, 49). When Linda is finally able (at age eighteen) to tell someone that she was raped as an eleven-year-old, that person is Harper, and he shares her pain and outrage, partly because (as she puts it) "he lived through my body in many ways." Harper's advice to Linda is that "hurt [is] bad enough . . . [we] should never add loneliness to it" (121). Throughout her narrative, he remains a constant presence as a sympathetic listener and a wise voice of experience. And, like the rest of the Hammerick family, he has secrets that resist being spoken, or named.

Readers may also be more inclined to identify with Linda's fondness for Harper than with her anger toward DeAnne because fellow-feeling may be easier to transmit via narrative than irritation. As Adam Smith observed over two centuries ago, while sympathy can "denote our fellow-feeling with any passion whatever," the "furious behavior of an angry man" is more likely to provoke sympathy for "his enemies" if we do not understand the angry man's "provocation" (15). He continues: "Nature, it seems, teaches us to be more averse to enter into this passion . . . till informed of its cause" (16). For much of its narrative, *Bitter in the Mouth* conceals from readers the cause, or "provocation," of Linda's anger with DeAnne. Linda repeatedly suggests that DeAnne is responsible for the fact that she was raped as a child, but the logic behind this claim—that DeAnne "flirted" with the teenage rapist before she left the house, by "smil[ing] and flipp[ing] her hair"—seems tenuous at best (118). And the novel's final revelation of the circumstances by which Linda became part of the Hammerick family seems to bear out the notion that Linda has never fully comprehended DeAnne's subject position. DeAnne's flaws, as Linda deems them, come to seem either inherent in DeAnne's personality (she had not wanted children) or beyond her control (her husband was infatuated with another woman, and he insisted that they adopt her orphaned daughter after he helped bring about that woman's death at the hands of her jealous husband).

Conversely, Linda provides a thorough characterization of Harper and his loveable quirks, and he remains a reassuring presence throughout the novel, even in death. Early on we learn of his "candidgraphs"—candid photos of the Hammerick family, which he collects in albums labeled "H. E. B. One," "H. E. B. Two," and so on, all bearing the initials of the photographer, Harper Evan Burch (40–41). These photographs, Linda explains, allowed Harper to "document us" without being documented himself. "In this clever way, my great-uncle hid from the official history of our family" (41). His photographs demonstrate to Linda that "history always had a point of view" and, therefore, necessarily obscures the "missing details" (52–53). Later in life, Harper takes up a quiet but open sexual relationship with a funeral director named Cecil T. Brandon, and Linda recalls, "When I was growing up, I knew that Baby Harper liked men. That was never a mystery to me. . . . I registered his desire for male members of the species at the same time that I registered my own desire for them" (152). This characterization converts Harper's non-normative orientation (same-sex desire) into shared behavior (Linda and Harper's desire for attractive men). From this first overt statement that Harper is gay, the novel transitions into a frank disclosure about Linda's sexual activity at Yale: "I was in my room in Pierson getting drunk with a boy whom I wanted to touch. We did" (154). Then she narrates Harper's visit to New Haven for her graduation, because he desires "a glimpse of me in my academic regalia" (155). This narrative progression mimics Linda's characterization of Harper's desire for men as being fundamentally similar to hers, and the revelation is framed by descriptions of Harper acting like a loving, supportive family member. In this passage, like many others, the apparent strangeness of Harper's sexual orientation is demystified and contextualized by a narrator who clearly loves and admires him.

Jennifer Ann Ho has argued that one ideological purpose of Asian American literature is "to combat the racist assumptions and portraits of Asians in America in order to ensure that Asian American subjectivity will be defended and upheld" (*Consumption* 19). Truong's novel achieves this goal in various ways: by challenging conventional assumptions that "unmarked" or unidentified narrators or characters must be white, male, and heterosexual; by depicting an Asian American narrator/protagonist who does not emphasize her ethnic identity; and by refusing to foreground the racial and ethnic identity of that character. For much of the novel, Linda's identity seems more clearly defined by Southernness, synesthesia, and animosity for her "mother" than by the fact that she is an adopted Vietnamese immigrant. By offering detailed characterizations of Linda, Baby Harper, and others before revealing their racial, ethnic, or sexual identities, *Bitter in the Mouth* invites us to identify with its characters before considering those identity categories: to know Linda through her word flavors and witticisms, rather than knowing her as "a Vietnamese girl" or as "an Asian girl in a small Southern town." Likewise, we come to know Harper as a photographer, a nurturing uncle, and an opinionated connoisseur of Carolina barbeque before we know him as "a gay man." The novel, therefore, implicitly argues that such identity categories are less important than the individual experiences and self-representations that shape us as human beings and as characters in the stories we tell about our lives. *Bitter in the Mouth* illustrates how powerfully certain withholdings, assumptions, and cultural silences can inflect the ways our stories are lived, remembered, shared, and received.

CHAPTER 9

Rhetorical Narrative Theory and Native American Literature

The Antimimetic in Thomas King's
Green Grass, Running Water

JOSEPH COULOMBE

MANY CONTEMPORARY Native American writers explicitly reference the importance of narrative as a thematic, structural, and theoretic element of their texts. Their treatment of narrative in works of fiction and criticism advances a theory—imbedded organically within the literature—that intersects with two established theoretical trajectories: rhetorical narrative theory (as defined by James Phelan and Peter Rabinowitz) and the antimimetic (as characterized by Brian Richardson). Native authors create texts that function—often quite explicitly—as acts of communication, rather than as objects to be acted upon. This positioning likely emerges, at least in part, from tribal oral traditions, which typically demonstrate a profound respect for the role of narrative/story as a method to understand, define, and teach. Similarly, contemporary written Native texts encourage readers to rethink entrenched Euro-American narratives of discovery and exceptionalism and to consider constructive alternatives.

According to rhetorical narrative theory, this goal corresponds to the "thematic component" of narrative, involving "readers' interests in the ideational function of the characters and in the cultural, ideological, philosophical, or ethical issues being addressed by the narrative" (Phelan and Rabinowitz 7). To engage readers with the thematic, many Native texts—including Thomas King's *Green Grass, Running Water*—utilize antimimetic elements that emphasize flexibility and change. The antimimetic elements confront readers with a dynamic worldview that revises popular Western texts and rejects static notions of identity, culture, tradition, and even narrative itself. Rhetorical narrative theorists define this audience response as synthetic; that is, the focus is largely upon "artificial constructs" (Phelan and Rabinowitz 7), which is closely related to Richardson's treatment of the antimimetic in regard to its effort to instigate change. Richardson writes, "Antimimetic narratives, by contesting conventional or official accounts, invite us to imagine alternative narratives of the world we inhabit" (Herman et al. 178). Whereas the antimimetic is usually understood as a departure from Western conventions, both the antimimetic and the synthetic (as defined within rhetorical narrative theory) highlight aesthetic strategies that encourage readers to formulate ethical responses to cultural and historical narratives.

Native-authored texts like *Green Grass, Running Water* use antimimetic strategies to challenge official narratives and to compel new ways of understanding among readers. Often these strategies draw from tribal traditions and belief systems, and this fact should give non-tribal critics and theorists pause. Richardson writes that antimimetic authors "do not wish to reproduce the world of our experience; they want instead to create original or unprecedented scenes, figures, progressions, and worlds" (22). For many readers, King undoubtedly offers a world that is "original or unprecedented," and this world challenges such readers to reposition themselves in relation to it. Nonetheless, King also communicates, arguably, a set of experiences with precedent for some Native readers, a world familiar to them from their tribal traditions. In short, what may seem radical or transgressive to some readers may seem quite reasonable and commonplace to others. This recognition suggests the importance for narrative theorists (and theory) to learn from Native American writers (and texts), rather than merely apply existing terminology and framing ideas to the text. A Native-centered approach would not only assist the decolonizing imperative advocated by Native scholars, but it also would allow narrative theory to grow by exploring further how the aesthetic and antimimetic shape the historical and thematic.

Many Native writers—including King—characterize narrative as inherently fluid and protean; it shifts and changes in response to evolving circumstances. Narrative is a destabilizing as well as re-centering force that seeks to correct imbalances by encouraging new ways of knowing (that are linked, often, to old ways). As such, many Native texts contain an imbedded theory of narrative that emphasizes the disruption of static concepts—such as the idea of Indianness as an archaic monolith, the presumption of whiteness as a defining norm, even the iconic status of the printed text (a paradox that I will return to)—that have been used to dispossess indigenous peoples. Many

Native American writers utilize what narrative theorists label antimimetic elements to showcase change within the text and compel change outside the text. Readers are invited to witness, and partake in, this change.

Thomas King's *Green Grass, Running Water* provides a strong case in point. It focuses explicitly on the function and power of narrative, and King uses common elements of varied tribal narratives, perceived as antimimetic to many readers, to reimagine and revise Euro-American narratives, thus helping to deconstruct colonial structures of control (or, as the four elders put it, "fix up the world" [133]). *Green Grass* targets a variety of narratives that assert Euro-American hegemony: nationalistic histories, canonical literary texts, religious origin stories, popular culture (such as "westerns"), and pernicious ethnic/racial/gender stereotypes. King's text, however, does not simply offer a counter-narrative; it usurps these hegemonic narratives to redefine and revise popular ways of thinking about history, culture, and identity as well as their effects upon the present and future. Via blended retellings, King advocates and advances a theory of narrative predicated upon change.

Many Native writers have theorized narrative in a similar fashion. It is worth noting, however, that Native writers/theorists sometimes refer to narrative as "story," a usage that includes both syuzhet (presentation/organization/text) and fabula (plot/chronology/story), rather than fabula only. For instance, LeAnne Howe describes the characters in her novel *Shell-Shaker*: "They link the *stories* they've heard about their ancestors with the stories they are living. This linking of the *narratives* breathes meaning into their world (as well as breathing life onto the pages of written stories)" (331, emphasis added). Howe emphasizes the connection of one set of stories (i.e., narratives) to another and how this commingling prompts new ways of understanding. This blending of ancestral and modern narrative infuses vitality into the written text, lessening its static quality and emphasizing its communicative and educational potential. According to Howe, Native stories—that is, Native narratives, both oral and written—embody a theory of living narrative that highlights change and growth both within the text and without. She asserts matter-of-factly: "Stories are Theories" (330). Her character Embarrassed Grief states, "I've been thinking about our old stories. They possess a strong willingness to make new inquiries among themselves to reflect upon and refine their own interpretations of myth and ritual, and to extrapolate deeper interpretations based on further consideration and new evidence" (332). Native narratives are dynamic and responsive, accommodating (and advocating for) new realities and methodologies.

King asserts a similar conception of story-as-narrative, one defined by change. In his 2003 collection of lectures, tellingly titled *The Truth about*

Stories: A Native Narrative, he begins each chapter with a nearly identical statement:

> There is a story I know. It's about the earth and how it floats in space on the back of a turtle. I've heard this story many times, and each time someone tells the story, it changes. Sometimes the change is simply in the voice of the storyteller. Sometimes the change is in the details. Sometimes in the order of events. Other times it's the dialogue or the response of the audience. (1, 31, 61, 91, and 121)

This statement emerges as a foundational touchstone for the collection (and for King's oeuvre), a recurrent assertion of the vitality of narrative that emphasizes the fluidity of tradition. Change is an integral part of how King theorizes Native cultures and narrative, despite the fact that hegemony refuses to acknowledge change as a positive value in Native tradition. When emerging internally, rather than from external coercion and violence, change is equated with self-expression, growth, and survival (both individual and communal) in Native narratives.

Nevertheless, misconceptions abound regarding the supposedly static role of tribal cultures and traditions. To theorize ethically about narrative in Native texts necessitates linking the synthetic/aesthetic and thematic elements within those texts to reductive Euro-American narrative practices in the past and present. In *Narrative Beginnings,* Richardson asserts, "Most institutions and every nation have an official narrative with a decisive point of origin, and where that beginning is established and what it includes will have a considerable effect on the history that follows" (8). The United States and Canada (the locations for *Green Grass, Running Water*) were established in large part using a nationalist origin story of discovery and racial/religious superiority. Most Americans are familiar with the "official narrative," and many have likely internalized the ethics of defining Euro-Americans as intrepid pioneers bringing civilization to a godless wilderness. Richardson, however, asserts that most modern and postmodern texts react against absolutist notions, a position that Stephen Spencer builds upon using Bakhtin's theory of heteroglossia in his essay in this volume on Leslie Marmon Silko's *Ceremony.*

Native authors and scholars often undermine monolithic narratives and instead advocate constructive combinations and transformations. In particular, they reject a static Native identity that depends upon reductive notions of history. Daniel Heath Justice writes that indigenous nationhood and survival "isn't predicated on essentialist notions of unchangeability; indeed, such notions are rooted in primitivist Eurowestern discourses that locate indigenous peoples outside the flow and influence of time" (151). Like Justice, many Native writers combat the concept of a pure past that must somehow be regained, an impossible expectation for any society. For instance, in *Ceremony* Silko explicitly refutes the belief that traditions never change. The medicine man Betonie tells Tayo: "But long ago when the people were given these ceremonies, the changing began, if only in the aging of the yellow gourd rattle. . . . You see, in many ways, the ceremonies have always been changing" (126). Silko characterizes tribal traditions as experiencing healthy, natural growth. Native scholars like Justice have felt compelled to reassert this fundamental component of tribal cultures because, too often, "official narratives" have highlighted images of the vanishing Indian. Justice describes such narratives as "the forces of erasure" (149). Manifest destiny, for example, treats Natives as obstructions to God's will (and U.S. conquest), incapable of accommodating "civilization," thus sanctioning their eradication. The image of the vanishing American ever receding into the past is integral to popular Euro-American narratives of exceptionalism and progress, and it appears in works ranging from James Fenimore Cooper's *Last of the Mohicans* to *The Lone Ranger,* both of which are, not incidentally, integrated and revised into *Green Grass.* King critiques "the blind spots of master narratives" (211 in this volume)—to use Blake Wilder's description of James Baldwin—particularly those that foster reductive images of Natives in the modern world.

Native texts help readers see the blind spots and thus progress toward a more complete understanding of American history and culture. According to James Phelan, "narrativity encourages two main activities: observing and judging" ("Narrative" 323). More specifically, "from the rhetorical perspective, narrativity involves the interaction of two kinds of change: that experienced by the characters and that experienced by the audience in its developing responses to the characters' changes" ("Narrative" 323). These two features of narrativity identified by Phelan are evident within *Green Grass, Running Water.* Not only does King create characters who adapt and grow via narrativity, but the text also encourages readers to observe and judge, taking part in a revisionary process with the potential to complicate and expand their definitions of Indians (and non-Indians).

King begins this process by showing characters struggling with monolithic narratives of Indian identity. Characters such as Eli, a published scholar and professor emeritus, are accused by others of failing to be a "real" Indians, as if there is only one way to be an Indian. For instance, Clifford Sifton, the Canadian architect of the dam on Blackfeet land, tells Eli: "You guys aren't real Indians anyway. I mean, you drive cars, watch television, go to hockey games" (155). Sifton upholds the damaging narrative of Native peoples as objects that have been frozen in time. Supposedly "real Indians" exist in a static world imagined by people like Sifton, who is named, not coincidentally, after the nineteenth-century Canadian promoter of western expansion. Sifton attacks "that barrel load of crap about Native rights" (150), distorting the legally binding "treaty rights" into special privileges predicated upon a narrowly conceived Indian identity. As Craig Womack writes, "To talk about treaties is to discuss living nations; it is more palatable to an Indian-hating public to present Indians as historical artifacts" ("Theorizing" 369). George Morningstar, Latisha's white ex-husband, also has rigid images of Native identity, and he is "pleased that [Latisha] was, as he said, a real Indian" (145) because she was born on a reservation. Such limiting definitions of authenticity deny Native peoples change and choice. Even Norma, an advocate for traditions like the Sun Dance, buys into narrow definitions of Indianness, and she berates Lionel and Eli repeatedly for "want[ing] to be a white man" (36), as if living in a city, going to a university-trained doctor, or marrying a non-Native somehow negates their ethnic identities. Ultimately, Norma wants them both to reengage more fully with the tribe—undoubtedly a positive direction within the novel—but her accusations also echo reductive colonial narratives that restrict individuals to an impossibly small range of options.

Native scholars react against these simplifications, and they recognize the potential for narrative and narrative theory to institute change. In *Reasoning Together: The Native Critics Collective,* Womack identifies "a recurring problem," which he situates within Native studies and which Norma exemplifies in *Green Grass, Running Water,*

> where certain experiences—namely, those associated with attending ceremonies, telling or hearing oral stories, and being present in cultural milieus—are privileged over other kinds of experiences such as reading, interpreting, or authoring books; articulating theoretical notions; teaching university courses; engaging in various intellectual practices; and so on. ("Theorizing" 358)

If Womack's construction is applied to *Green Grass,* then Eli should still be considered fully Indian while living in Toronto and teaching at a university, and Lionel is still Indian even though he sells televisions. Attending the Sun Dance ultimately brings them both closer to their community, a constructive change for each of them, but to calculate their relative "Indianness" based upon a narrow essentialism is to privilege a rigid narrative that serves colonial control.

Native narrative theory strives to disabuse readers of this notion by emphasizing complexity, fluidity, and change. Justice writes, "Simplification is essential to the survival of imperialism, as complication breeds uncertainty in the infallibility of authoritative truth claims" (155). King and other Native writers embrace the complications and issue their own challenges—often via the antimimetic—to readers. As Womack writes, "Stories provide key opportunities for community members to present images of themselves on their own terms, another powerful form of sovereignty" ("Theorizing" 362). Emphasizing dynamic, blended narratives is central to self-definition and sovereignty.

Many Native-authored publications utilize an aesthetic emphasizing improvisation and revision not only to decenter Western perspectives dependent upon hierarchy and conquest but also to prompt readers to reimagine a more harmonious world. That is, Native narrative involves a call to ethical action, and narrative theorists should be at the forefront of the response in their criticism and teaching. Phelan links aesthetics to ethical reader responses:

> Individual narratives explicitly or more often implicitly establish their own ethical standards in order to guide their audiences to particular ethical judgments. Consequently, within rhetorical ethics, narrative judgments proceed from the inside out rather than the outside in. It is for this reason that they are closely tied to aesthetic judgments. ("Narrative Judgements" 325)

The text leads readers to conclusions about historical events, current circumstances, and future possibilities using thematic and synthetic components to prompt revaluation.

In *Green Grass,* an emphasis upon change is imbedded within the narrative form itself. King signals an improvisational quality from the outset, thus preparing readers for more explicitly antimimetic strategies. *Green Grass* begins with the one-word paragraph "So," suggesting a narrator who is gathering his or her thoughts before embarking upon a complex task involving memory/recitation as well as choice/performance. It implies that the narrator must select significant elements out of a vast amount of material. In this way, King acknowledges the arbitrariness of narrative beginnings, much as Sterling Bland argues in his analysis of Ralph Ellison's *Invisible Man*: "narrative expression is the only way to provide shape and meaning to a real world that is essentially without coherence and form" (141 in this volume). Likewise, in *Analyzing World Fiction,* Richardson argues that postcolonial narrative theory "contest[s] the possibility of any absolute beginning and affirm[s] instead that all narratives, fictional and nonfictional, are always already *in medias res*" ("U.S. Ethnic" 6); as such, postcolonial—and decolonial—narratives resist "traditional forms of closure" ("U.S. Ethnic" 7). Certainly, *Green Grass* resists closure as well as clear-cut beginnings. In the novel's final line, the narrative

"I" responds to Coyote's complaint about the ubiquitous water, stating: "And here's how it happened" (469), which repeats verbatim the line introducing section 1. Readers are given the impression that the story will be retold again and again, not identically, but instead with the myriad interruptions and revisions that characterize the existing text. No closure can occur until the world is fixed, which is unlikely to happen, as such an event would imply perfection and stasis—perhaps even death. Thus, readers are drawn into its cyclical structure and compelled to recognize the necessity of ongoing correction, balance, and revision. The aesthetic form of *Green Grass*—which enlists a synthetic response—privileges continuity and flexibility over rigidity and control.

The narrative "I" and Coyote administer and represent these revisionary processes; they both facilitate and embody strategies that narrative theory terms the antimimetic. Both have supernatural powers and exert their individual influence over characters and events. Both move fluidly through the various time-stages of the novel—existing outside of linear time entirely—and serve as explanatory guides and trickster interlopers. Both mediate between readers and recurrent revisions of canonical/mythic Western narratives. When Coyote's "silly dream" is told that it is a dog, for example, it (that is, the dream/dog) reverses the spelling and claims god status. This antimimetic act, which occurs in the opening pages of the novel, simultaneously reframes and redefines a Judeo-Christian narrative within a Native worldview, while alerting readers to the specifically textual nature of King's narrative: the word "dog" can only be inverted into "god" in written English, and it can only be capitalized (i.e., God) on the printed page. The willingness to revise and adapt is directly at odds with colonial structures presented within the text. The recurrent "Christian rules," in particular, are characterized as overbearing and inflexible.

Green Grass humorously revises and repurposes Euro-American narratives. Structurally, King's novel mimics the four Christian gospels—with each of the four sections told "according to" one of the four elders. In addition, each elder is not only identified with a mythic being from a tribal tradition (First Woman, Changing Woman, Thought Woman, Old Woman) but also with a character from the Western literary canon (Lone Ranger, Ishmael, Robinson Crusoe, and Hawkeye) that is defined, at least in part, by a hierarchical cross-racial relationship. The four elders enter and modify the ongoing narratives—religious, historical, literary, pop-cultural, and textual—to revise and correct misinformation as well as to disrupt and subvert colonial power. Amongst other examples, they insert themselves into a John Wayne movie in order to help enable an Indian victory over the U.S. cavalry, thus reversing the original ending. They are actually forced to alter the Hollywood version a second time, thus underscoring Wilder's contention about the difficulty of counter-storytelling. In all their efforts, the elders acknowledge and negotiate the difficulties, undermining the static quality of the text as they transform well-known narratives. This adaptability furthers the impression of a narrative under construction, all of which helps promote a narrative theory privileging change and integration in the service of advocacy (not merely entertainment). Readers must adjust to ongoing textual adjustments, thus augmenting their own intellectual flexibility.

Each of the four sections blends and revises a variety of different narratives to challenge the status quo. They make liberal use of antimimetic elements to challenge white male dominance within the Judeo-Christian Bible as well as satirize the gender and racial politics of Herman Melville's *Moby-Dick* and Daniel Defoe's *Robinson Crusoe*. The four elders enter and modify these popularized literary and religious narratives, disrupting rigid worldviews and showcasing an independent, protean outlook. For example, First Woman leaves the "garden of Eden" on her own behest (rather than being forced out), revising the story of Eve's transgression, before masking herself as the Lone Ranger to escape capture; Changing Woman escapes Noah's lechery and then rejects Ahab in favor of Moby-Jane, the great black whale; Thought Woman dismisses Gabriel's overture to assume the role of "Virgin Mary" as well as refuses the subservient position of "Friday" to Robinson Crusoe; Old Woman tries to help Young Man Walking on Water (read: Jesus), who will not accept assistance from a woman, before she narrowly escapes Nasty Bumppo, who is fatally shot (probably) by Chingachgook. Their adaptations and improvisations revise existing narratives, blending Western and tribal elements to negate the very idea of postcolonialism, a term that King and many Native scholars reject as self-evidently false. *Green Grass* resituates colonial texts within protean indigenous narratives that highlight tribal nationalisms and cosmologies, rejecting the linear trajectory of Western "progress" and civilization in favor of cyclical patterns of Native resistance and autonomy. The antimimetic elements point to the possible.

Within this expanded context, characters enact self-definition at a personal level. Three characters, in particular, seek to reassert control over their own narratives and identities: Lionel is stuck in a dead-end job at age forty after being mislabeled in his youth as an AIM activist with heart trouble; Alberta wants a child without a husband, but the medical establishment treats her choice as immoral; and Eli is fighting an illegal dam on reservation land. Each struggles with intolerant colonial narratives of race and gender. Lionel, for instance, harbors a lifelong desire to be John Wayne, a self-defeating inclination that springs from Euro-American constructions of masculinity, which, in turn, drive nationalistic narratives of discovery and conquest, all at the expense of Native agency. Alberta is boxed in by moralistic gender codes and "Christian rules" in her desire to have a child, even as she attempts to educate a new generation of college students about tribal (and white) histories. Eli struggles with his own life choices as he confronts Euro-American hubris in the form of the dam—a concrete image of colonial rigidity. Sifton tells him, "Government's got no sense of humor" (85), a statement signaling the intolerance that King's narrative combats with humor and flexibility.

The four elders attempt to help these characters—by correcting systemic problems involving narrative—with narrative. Ostensibly, they set out to explain the origins of the water, a recurrent image that reinforces the narrative aesthetic of fluidity and change, but their goal is much more ambitious: they seek to "fix up the world" (133) nearly destroyed by rigid narratives. To this end, the elders perform the very stories that they tell, highlighting the antimimetic to help others recognize (and act within) alternative narratives. For instance, they escape a locked institution to position Lionel to accept the importance of the Sun Dance, and he ultimately chooses to intervene on behalf of tribal privacy and sovereignty. The elders appear suddenly to certain characters, including Charlie and Eli, as well as Lionel, and then disappear in the next moment, unnoticed by other characters who are in the same place. They are affiliated with major natural and cultural events over an impossible expanse of time: Mt. Saint Helens in 1980, Krakatau in 1883, the Alcatraz occupation in 1969–71, the stock market crash of 1929, and the Wounded Knee standoff in 1973. They also converse on familiar terms with Coyote, the inveterate trickster whom others cannot always see, unless they note him at a distance as a particularly unusual dog.

For his part, Coyote enacts several radical revisions. A mischievous, disruptive, and comic character, at odds with almost anything resembling stability or rigidity, Coyote targets the dam that represents yet another colonial trespass upon Native sovereignty. The dam prevents the water from flooding the cottonwood trees with nutrients, thus imperiling the Sun Dance, which depends upon the cottonwoods. Revamping the popular history of the "pilgrims'" arrival upon the *Niña*, *Pinta*, and *Santa Maria*, Coyote sends three automobiles—a Nissan, Pinto, and Karmann-Ghia—through the dam, thus freeing the water and, significantly, reasserting the treaty rights that are figuratively dependent upon the (titular) narrative of green grass and running water. Movement equals life: in nature, narrative, ceremony, and Native lives. Moreover, Coyote impregnates Alberta, thus appropriating an antimimetic element of Christian narrative—that is, the immaculate conception—to help counteract stories used to subjugate Native rights and beliefs.

Green Grass—with its talking dogs, lesbian whales, and death-defying elders—clearly embraces what narrative theory terms the antimimetic. Kings' novel avoids verisimilitude and flaunts a willingness to break Western rules, or, perhaps more accurately, it asserts its own autonomy. By highlighting the constructedness of narrative, *Green Grass* calls attention to multiple possible truths, rather than a single absolute truth. It uses the antimimetic to reaffirm the power of narrative to decenter, reframe, and teach—both within the text (for characters like Lionel and Eli) and outside it (for attentive readers). Toward the end of the fourth section, the narrative "I" tells Coyote, "I wasn't talking to you," and Coyote responds, "Who else is there?" (432), signaling both a comically inflated self-regard and, more importantly, the participatory role of the audience. Readers (much like the characters) are invited to shift and adapt their relation to multiple narratives that intersect, loop, and grow. The antimimetic elements unsettle readers, encouraging them to resist absolutes, embrace change, and consider new versions of old stories.

King uses narrative not to reject, but to transform, and *Green Grass* does much to destabilize colonial constructions and reshape them into powerful and inclusive narratives. *Green Grass* contains multiple narrative perspectives that, while distinct, run together and merge with that of the narrative "I." It eschews a single authoritative narrative in much the same way that it challenges the notion of one wise, all-knowing Judeo-Christian god. As the narrative "I" tells Coyote, "'There are no truths, Coyote,' I says. 'Only stories'" (432). Far from erasing the incontrovertible facts (and atrocities) of history, the narrative "I"'s assertion points to the myriad perspectives and narratives that shape individual and collective opinions. Historically, many Native experiences have been silenced, and King and other Native American writers are asserting their own narratives even as they call for additional voices. Dean Rader emphasizes this feature of Native literature: "Indian communities have distinguished themselves by making polyvocality, multiplicity, and interactivity part of their ontology" (4).

In *Pushing the Bear* (1996), Diane Glancy also advocates for polyvocal narrative. Her text, which recounts Cherokee removal to Indian Territory (now Oklahoma) in the 1830s, commonly known as the Trail of Tears, involves many different narrators who relate their individual experiences and opinions in the present tense. Its immediacy and diversity reinforce the sense that there is no One Truth, only versions of the truth conveyed via individual narrative. Thus, the power of narrative is connected to its complexity, variety, and creativity. The Basket Maker, for instance, compares stories (defined, again, as narrative involving both syuzhet and fabula) to baskets, asserting that both "hold meaning" (153); when another Cherokee objects, the following dialogue ensues:

"You're making that up."

"What's wrong with that?"

"I don't like it."

"We need new ways."

"You can't make stories on your own."

"Why not? The trail needs stories."

Stories are created to understand and shape; they are responsive as well as generative, not static. Another character in *Pushing the Bear* states that stories "gave us a place to order our disorder, a direction for our directionlessness" (158). Narratives provide clarity and definition, particularly for oppressed peoples. Similarly, Sterling Bland argues in this volume that Ralph Ellison's narrator in *Invisible Man* creates "a narration that somehow helps him make sense of his experiences" (139 in this volume). In Native texts, stories assert continuity and autonomy; they are a vital component of kinship and survival. For example, the story of Selu in *Pushing the Bear* links Cherokee people to their tribal land, and stories such as Kinchow's comically successful hunter provide hope and humor during a time of despair. Narratives—new and old—provide strength and cohesiveness to the listeners under genocidal assault.

Pushing the Bear also invokes the performative power of narrative. That is, words and their expression can effect a material shift; they have creative power. Glancy writes, "The wind had a moan to it. It was like the stories of the old ones. The voice carried power. What was spoken came into being" (95). Native narrative not only advocates for change; it often enacts change. Likewise, in Silko's *Ceremony,* readers are informed that Thought-Woman uses language to create: "Thought-Woman, the spider, / named things and / as she named them / they appeared. // She is sitting in her room / thinking of a story now / I'm telling *you* the story / she is thinking" (1, emphasis added). Silko uses the performative power of language to harness the involvement of readers (i.e., "you"), thus multiplying its effect. By taking part in the narrative, readers become part of the solution, and the performative power of the narrative is extended exponentially.

In Louise Erdrich's *Tracks,* the emphasis upon individualized perspectives again underscores the importance of varied versions. The two narrators, Nanapush and Pauline, represent nearly opposite reactions to colonial subjugation; no single story captures the entire truth. Nanapush treats narration as a pragmatic method of survival: "I talked both languages in streams that ran alongside each other, over every rock, around every obstacle. The sounds of my own voice convinced me I was alive" (7). Language shifts and bends, like water, around obstructions both physical and narrative. He says, "I got well by talking. Death could not get a word in edgewise, grew discouraged, and traveled on" (46). While orality is privileged in *Tracks,* the printed word is associated with treaties and laws that dispossess the Anishinaabe. Margaret Kashpaw avoids even the touch of printed language: "She didn't want the tracks rubbing off on her skin" (47). Written words are presented as irrevocable and dangerous. White intruders quote them for their own ends, treating written words as bounden law, whereas they simply constitute another narrative, one that is particularly intrusive, rigid, and destructive.

Native writers undoubtedly write for many different reasons, but most seem intent upon exposing the inadequacy of colonial narratives, filling in the gaps of American history, and reeducating the reading public. Many Native texts involve readers in an experiential fictional world that requires their engagement and imagination. Kimberly Roppolo asserts that Natives have "colonized English as much as it has colonized us" (303). Her assertion of Native narrative authority, existing in a reciprocal relationship with the English language, suggests likewise that Native writing "colonizes" its readers, compelling them to change. The inclusiveness of Roppolo's articulation, however, is the opposite of polemic or dogma. Roppolo values "communally made meaning, as Native cultures have since time-immemorial" (310). Native texts serve as a creative intervention into colonial thought by blending disparate narratives, asserting intertextual connectedness, and linking text, culture, and history. They guide readers toward an ethical response that values inclusion and growth.

Narrative theory, broadly conceived, will benefit from further engaging the historical and cultural realities as presented with Native texts, particularly by recognizing how the antimimetic elements advocate fluidity, change, and growth. Native narratives, and the theories advocated within them, create and foster new alliances while undermining static institutionalized perceptions and theories. Justice writes, "Indigenous intellectual traditions have survived not because they've conceded to fragmenting Eurowestern priorities, but because they've challenged those priorities" (150). This challenge involves an inclusive understanding of peoples and cultures, and it promises to create new systems of flexible, shared thought. Robyn Warhol argues that emerging narratives—what she labels neo-narratives—arise within a complex matrix of receptive readers and forward-thinking writers seeking to correct omissions: "Indeed, shifts in the category of the unnarratable are, I would say, significant indicators of generic change itself, and they both reflect and constitute their audiences' developing senses of such matters as politics, ethics, and values" ("Neonarrative" 221). This shift in what is narrated simultaneously responds to an audience's desire for more complex and ethical truths while it also actively promotes these truths. Native texts embody a new theory of narrative that uses the antimimetic to engage readers in their own ongoing philosophical and ethical development.

Central to this trend, *Green Grass, Running Water* attempts to fix the world one person at a time, much like the four elders. King's playful intermingling of revised narratives invites readers to adapt and shift their respective worldviews and theories while joining a larger global process that aims to offset the damage of colonization. The stakes are high, and King helps build communities that will continue cycles of ethical reimagining and retelling . . . until we get it right.

CHAPTER 10

Narration on the Lower Frequencies in Ralph Ellison's *Invisible Man*

STERLING LECATER BLAND JR.

> But it is worth remembering that one of the implicitly creative functions of art in the U. S. A. (and certainly of narrative art) is the defining and correlating of diverse American experiences by bringing previously unknown patterns, details and emotions into view along with those that are generally recognized.
>
> —Ralph Ellison, "The Little Man at Chehaw Station"

RALPH ELLISON'S invisible protagonist begins his narrative with the sentence "I am an invisible man." But what the reader quickly realizes is that this is not the beginning of the story at all. This is the end. The story itself has begun many years earlier, as the narrator, about to graduate from high school, witnesses the death of his grandfather. The story precedes the narrator's telling of it (or, at least, it seems to) though, at the same time, the narrator's presentation of the narrative seems to generate the story itself (Culler, "Story and Discourse"; Abbott). The narrator, unreliable as he is, creates a narrative that produces as many gaps as it provides definitive explanations. The reader is forced into the position of reconciling what the narrator tells with what he fails to tell. Like the narrator himself, the reader is at the mercy of often conflicting narrative accounts and personal and political agendas.

From the very opening of the novel, Ellison's unnamed narrator finds himself placed in a position in which he must explain the reality and consequences of racialized invisibility and how he understands his identity. That explanation takes the form of an extended narrative of race and alienation. The novel's theme and plot are inseparable from its narration. Perhaps more importantly, the narrative provides an important corrective commentary on the influence of segregated, pre–*Brown v. the Board of Education,* pre–civil rights America. It also provides commentary on the ways a narrative concerned with race is both produced and consumed. By using the inextricable relationship between race and identity as a point of departure, my goal in this chapter is to examine the ways the narrator's ever-evolving sense of racialized identity in *Invisible Man* provides insight into the ways the very form of his narrative should be understood. Put differently, my point is that the narrator's production of race and identity is the most valuable lens through which to understand the workings of the narrative. *Invisible Man* is grounded in the stark disparity between the possibilities contained in America's democratic ideal and the realities of blackness in segregated, pre–*Brown v. the Board of Education* America. The tension between narrative attempts to create order in a disruptively chaotic social environment—for which Blake Wilder argues in this volume in his examination of "Going to Meet the Man"—echoes the very dynamics with which Ellison's narrator contends.[1]

The shifting narrative presence in *Invisible Man,* ambiguous and often unreliable, reframes the ways in which the design and purpose of this kind of narrative text may be understood. While this kind of examination rests on the imprecise boundary where literary analysis meets narratological study, the point is that in order for narrative theory to serve as a useful tool for examining black writing in the age of Jim Crow, it must necessarily be attentive to the fact that black narrative authority is profoundly constrained by its historical context. As Blake Wilder observes in "Black World / White World," there is a two-way dialogue at work between racialized segregation and narrative potential.

The racialized paradox that Ellison presents is the ambiguous, ever-shifting border between invisibility and hypervisibility that is so central to the novel's intentions. The racialized experiences that are shared between the narrator and the narratee make it clear that not only is the narrator preoccupied with the consolidation of characteristics that define racialized subjects like himself, but the very form of the novel's emphasis on storytelling reinforces the novel's racialized implicit meaning. By linking critical race theory with the defined

---

1. For discussions of the use of rhetorical models to try to understand both the meaning and the purpose of storytelling, see also Alber and Fludernik, *Postclassical Narratology* 1–15; Herman, *Narratologies* 2–3; Lanser, *Fictions of Authority* 3–24, 120–38 and "Sexing the Narrative" 85–94; Warhol, *Gendered Interventions* 25–44, 192–206; Alcoff 97–119; Awkward 70–91; Harding 120–36; Phelan, "Rhetoric/ethics" 210 and *Reading the American Novel 1920–2010* 149–69.

Palmer 28–52 and Zunshine 16–22 each propose strategies that see narratives as fluid and understood by context (readerly and intuitional), rather than as modes that are inherently fixed and essential. Both argue for approaches in which the reader understands the narrative by understanding the mind of the narrator, which is precisely the rhetorical access that Ellison presents to the reader in *Invisible Man.*

parameter of Jim Crow's influence on narrative and with some of the concerns (if not the actual design) of rhetorical narratology, the novel reenvisions the ways in which historical context ultimately constrains the very possibilities of narrative authority that the novel implicitly seeks to foreground and expand.

The prologue to *Invisible Man* opens with what Melba Cuddy-Keane in *Narrative Beginnings* refers to as "beginning's ragged edge." The beginning of the central action does not begin until the first chapter. The prologue contains references to earlier events that the narrative itself never fully explains. The reader sees right away that the world to which the narrator so fervently aspires is narrow and constricting at best and at worst, dangerous and even life-threatening. The instability the narrative presents throughout its progression promises to resolve (or at least explain) the profound precariousness of the narrator's understanding of his identity (that is, his growing awareness of his own invisibility) and its relation to the society in which he lives. This is a narrative of the past that concludes in the present and looks toward the future. Its issues of race and identity provide an important place of intersection that encourages an examination of the workings of its narrative form.

The invisible narrator's quest is for some understanding of his own identity in a world that does not allow him to establish and maintain a singular, cohesive identity. What the narrator fails to realize until he nears his decision to go underground and accept his invisibility is the performative, fluid nature of identity and the relationship of identity to the various social roles in which that identity performs. What he does not know is that identity is not a static, monolithic entity. It is plural and entirely a function of contextual suitability. More precisely, these identities are an aggregation of performative identities. They function, along with memory, in ways that create some semblance of connection between their performance roles and their contextual frames of reference (Fludernik 260–61). The narrator's experiences through much of the novel refute Jacques Lacan's belief that people see themselves as others see them (Fludernik 260–61; Homer 17–31).[2] For the narrator, either people do not see him at all or they see him only as playing a particular role in a particular context. Since identity is neither singular nor stable, it is continuously reassembled in ways that connect the immediacy of lived experience to the constant pull of memory and the past.

Though the narrator does not entirely understand it, his narrative does not uncover some intrinsic core self or even a set of core, unchanging truths about himself. What the narrator is left with is a narration that somehow helps him make sense of his experiences. While his successes all disintegrate into chaos,

---

2. See Lacan 1–7 for a discussion of his ideas on the mirror stage.

his narrative leaves him with something approximating hope (though there is a considerable amount of ambiguity about the actual nature of his hope) (Fludernik 262–63). The constructive process of identity formation that the narrator experiences reveals that there is no truth and there is no reality. By the conclusion of the novel, which is its beginning, the time of the narrator's story has merged with the time of his narrative in such a way that the reader has been brought to some understanding of the events that led to the narrator's current condition. As Catherine Romagnolo observes in "Narrative Disidentification," the narrative's disruption of beginning and ending ultimately forces the reader to reconsider the elements connecting the two.

Although *Invisible Man* is most often read as a narration of the protagonist's unsatisfied pursuit for coherence and identity, it is important to note that the novel takes place between the First and Second World Wars, when all facets of life in the United States were defined by legalized racial segregation. In many ways, the narrator's thwarted attempts to come to terms with his identity are reflective of the nation's larger attempts to reconcile the often-conflicting nature of its own identity. In the essay "Twentieth-Century Fiction and the Black Mask of Humanity," which he wrote shortly after World War II but did not publish until 1953, Ralph Ellison notes,

> Either like Hemingway and Steinbeck (in whose joint works I recall not more than five American Negroes), [America's best authors] tend to ignore them, or like the early Faulkner, who distorted Negro humanity to fit his personal versions of Southern myth, they seldom conceive Negro characters possessing the full, complex ambiguity of the human. . . . Naturally, the attitude of Negroes toward this writing is one of great reservation. Which indeed bears out Richard Wright's remark that there is in progress between black and white Americans a struggle *over the nature of reality*. ("Twentieth-Century Fiction" 82, emphasis added)

The protagonist's narrative concerns itself with this struggle.

For Ellison, America's struggle with illusion and "the nature of reality" was more than simply a narratological distinction. It was the responsibility of the writer to make distinct the real from the unreal and, perhaps more importantly, to drive the direction of national conversation. What Ellison's narrator grapples with is a rendering of the reality of what the democratic ideal, as understood by Emerson, Thoreau, Whitman, and others, means to blacks living in America.[3]

---

3. For expanded discussion of Emerson and the influence of Emerson's ideas on the invisible narrator's attempts to narrate and interpret his experiences, see especially Hanlon 74–98

The novel is composed in an underground apartment on the border of Harlem. The narrator lives rent-free in a section of the basement "that was shut off and forgotten during the nineteenth century" in a building rented exclusively to white residents (Ellison, *Invisible Man* 6). Those in the building do not know of his existence in much the same way that they do not know of the existence of the unilluminated portions of the nation's past that have been relegated to underground storage places, boarded up, and forgotten. The novel's implication is that there can be no true ability to do as one wants in a country defined by segregation. This is subverted by the fact that the narrator, to some extent, eventually realizes how much the narrative recitation of his experiences bestows much of the freedom denied to him in his daily existence.[4]

Ellison has devised a protean narrative pattern that shifts and evolves as the narrator's understanding of himself and his position in society progresses. Catherine Romagnolo's persuasive assertions about the importance of narrative beginning in "Narrative Disidentification" suggests the ways the narrative's circular configuration reflects both the disintegration of boundary between story and discourse and the narrator's attempts to take control of his own experiences through writing and speech. In the essay "On Initiation Rites and Power," Ralph Ellison notes that "although *Invisible Man* is my novel, it is really his memoir" (537). Ellison's observation reveals the fundamental tensions in the novel related to written composition and narrative reconstruction. His narratological self-creation functions on the apparently paradoxical assertion that the invisible narrator's form is inseparable from his invisibility: "I myself, after existing some twenty years, did not become alive until I discovered my invisibility" (*Invisible Man* 7). The narrator's ultimate awareness is that external reality often arrives without either form or substance and that narrative expression is the only way to provide shape and meaning to a real world that is essentially without coherence and form:

> I am invisible, understand, simply because people refuse to see me. Like the bodiless heads you see sometimes in circus sideshows, it is as though I have been surrounded by mirrors of hard, distorting glass. When they approach me they see only my surroundings, themselves figments of their imaginations—indeed, everything and anything except me. (3)

By embracing his own invisibility and insubstantiality, the only thing the invisible narrator is left with is the perception of reality that he radiates to

---

and K. J. Lee 331–44.

4. For a fuller discussion of the relationship between race and democratic individuality, see J. Turner 655–82.

the reader. Because of his extraordinarily limited perspective, the only thing he can reliably convey to the reader is his eventual awareness of the chaotically absurd nature of his experience. In a narrative that functions around the ambiguity of what is real and what is illusion, the only real things available to the reader are the words composing the narrative itself (Schaub 130–31).

Ellison's comment in the introduction to *Shadow and Act* that "the act of writing requires a constant plunging back into the shadow of the past where time hovers ghostlike" is certainly reflected in the ways his narrator's story unfolds (56). Ellison's invisible narrator's primary concern is to explain to his reader the circumstances that have led him to the point where he is capable of relating his story. There is a profound difference between the individual in the present (most fully realized in the prologue and epilogue to the novel, each of which is written in a voice defined by literary, cultural, and musical references that is very distinct from the voice contained within the novel) and the individual whose past experiences form the body of the novel. His narrative impulse is not simply animated by a desire to transcribe experience; it is driven by a desire to immerse the reader in a process of recovering experience and its meaning. It is his grandfather's deathbed warning to "live with your head in the lion's mouth . . . overcome 'em with yeses, undermine 'em with grins, agree 'em to death and destruction, let 'em swoller you till they vomit or bust wide open" that most effectively pushes the narrator simultaneously back into the past and forward into the future (16). As Ellison notes in his essay "Change the Joke and Slip the Yoke," the grandfather's

> mask of meekness conceals the wisdom of one who has learned the secret of saying the "yes" which accomplishes the expressive "no." . . . More important to the novel is the fact that he represents the ambiguity of the past for the hero, for whom his sphinxlike deathbed advice poses a riddle which points the plot in the dual direction which the hero will follow throughout the novel. (Ellison 111)[5]

The narrator's freedom—such as it is—from the ambiguity of his grandfather's deathbed riddle into an awareness of his own invisibility should more precisely be seen as the narrator's eventual ability to usurp from others the right to navigate and interpret the meaning and significance of his own experience. While each of his experiences of confronting the limits of self-reliance is representative of the inability of the nation's African Americans to fully par-

---

5. For a discussion of the ways the narrator constructs a social reality that is inseparable from the historical context enabling that process, see Steele 486–87.

ticipate in Emerson's ideas of self-reliance, each reflects the narrator's improving ability to give voice to his thoughts.

The development of the narrator's voice, which is represented in the novel by his increasing proficiency at giving speeches, runs parallel to his narrative: as he gains insight into the most effective qualities of speech making, his narrative gains insight into the realities of his social status. The first speech contained in the narrative is a rereading of the narrator's valedictory address that he has been asked to deliver to the most powerful men in his Southern hometown. It is both a satire of Booker T. Washington's 1895 Atlanta Exposition Address (widely seen as advocating a profoundly accommodationist agenda that traded black social equality for the possibility of economic advancement) and a poorly delivered, poorly received speech. The narrator has been humiliated by being blindfolded and forced to fight other blindfolded black boys before he is allowed to give his speech to an audience that was not listening: "I spoke automatically and with such fervor that I did not realize that the men were still talking and laughing until my dry mouth, filling with blood from the cut, almost strangled me" (30). At one point, the narrator mistakenly uses the phrase "social equality" in place of "social responsibility." His mistake immediately brings him hostile displeasure from the audience. This mistake also suggests the narrator's larger implication that Ellison's notion of equality is something much closer to an acknowledgment of the profound differences woven into the fabric of American society than an attempt to enforce adherence to an indistinct gathering of rights. The narrator's production of his story does not exhibit a blanket call for egalitarianism so much as it demonstrates the differences inherent in equality (Steele 486–88).

One important turning point in the novel is the events leading to the narrator's move to New York after being told during his third year to leave the state college for black students, to which he had been awarded a scholarship. The narrator's expulsion comes after he is asked to serve as a chauffeur to Mr. Norton, a white philanthropist from Boston, who is a college trustee and whose donations support the college. In his confusion while chauffeuring, the narrator inadvertently drives past the former slave cabin on the outskirts of the campus occupied by Jim Trueblood, a sharecropper notorious to the local community for impregnating his own daughter. The narrator's confusion is caused, in part, by Mr. Norton's rambling conversation in answer to the narrator's question to him about how he became interested in the school. Mr. Norton's response reveals a convoluted explanation about how African Americans were somehow interwoven with his fate: "I felt even as a young man that your people were somehow closely connected to my destiny" (41). Perhaps more tellingly, Mr. Norton sees the school as a monument to the memory of his daughter, for whom he seems to have an incestuous attraction.

Jim Trueblood is the exact kind of African American that the narrator and those at the college hope to render invisible by keeping him on the out-skirts of the campus. He is a poor, uneducated sharecropper who is directly connected to the nation's slave past. But Jim Trueblood is also the blackened mirror image of Mr. Norton's repressed incestuous desires. Unlike Mr. Norton, who conceals his guilt, Jim Trueblood ultimately decided not to camouflage the extent of his guilt. After a period of exile, he simply returned home and accepted himself for who he is: "All I know is that I ends up singin' the blues. I sings me some blues that night ain't never been sang before, and while I'm singin' them blues I makes up my mind that I ain't nobody but myself and ain't nothin' I can do but let whatever is gonna happen, happen" (66). Ironi-cally, although he is marginalized by the black community at the college, he is sought out by members of the white community.

As the invisible narrator will eventually do himself, Jim Trueblood takes control of his story. In fact, Jim Trueblood actually profits from the story he tells. White visitors ask him to recite his story, particularly the details con-cerning the impregnation of his daughter, and financially reward him. Jim Trueblood concludes by saying, "But what I don't understand is how I done the worse thing a man can do in his own family and 'stead of things gitin' bad, they got better" (68). Trueblood takes control of his own story as a way of giving his life and experiences meaning. He was not destroyed by the chaos his actions created. Instead, he thrives because his narrative creates a kind of order and meaning within the chaos.

Jim Trueblood, to his own disbelief, is able to use his story to create some kind of transcendent rhetorical chronicle of experience and meaning. Jim Trueblood has indeed returned home without guilt after a period of exile. But that does not eliminate the guilty reality that he has gained his finan-cial success and apparent insight at the expense of his daughter Matty Lou's rape. In the midst of sexually violating his daughter, Trueblood realizes the conundrum of the situation that in some way provides him with his own justification:

> But once a man gits hisself in a tight spot like that there ain't much he can do. It ain't up to him no longer. There I was, tryin' to git away with all my might, yet having to move without movin'. I flew in but I had to walk out. I had to move without movin'. (68)

Mr. Norton is moved to the brink of hysteria and death. The narrator is moved to shame and embarrassment for what Jim Trueblood and his story represent. Jim Trueblood alone remains unmoved. The power Jim Trueblood derives from taking control of the meaning and interpretation of his story is the power he took from his wife and daughter, neither of whom is given the rhetorical opportunity to control her own story (68).

After this episode, the narrator arrives in New York City clinging to the only identity that he has ever known. When he sees an old couple being evicted from their Harlem apartment, the narrator is moved to words: "And beneath it all there boiled up all the shock-absorbing phrases that I had heard all my life. I seemed to totter on the edge of a great dark hole" (275). It is here that the narrator most convincingly begins the process that links him to the importance of controlling language as a way of defining reality. This awareness of the "great dark hole" he faces will eventually lead the narrator underground to the recognition and acknowledgment of the invisibility that frames the novel. As he also does in his essay "Harlem Is Nowhere," Ellison remarks on the very nature of the world the narrator attempts—in his speeches and in the narrative itself—to describe:

> There is an argument in progress between black men and white men as to the true nature of American reality. . . . Following their own interests, whites impose interpretations upon Negro experience that are not only false but, in effect, a denial of Negro humanity. . . . Too weak to shout down these interpretations, Negroes live nevertheless as they have to live, and the concrete conditions of their lives are more real than white men's arguments. (Ellison 326)[6]

Ironically, the narrator is actually profoundly visible through the majority of the experiences he narrates. The white men force him to fight the other black boys in the battle royal before he gives his first speech precisely because he is black, his grandfather's deathbed warning was given with the awareness that blacks living in a nation segregated by race must at times wear a minstrel mask in order to survive, and he is identified as Mr. Norton's destiny and later recruited by a leftist organization in Harlem called the Brotherhood precisely because of his race. The piece of his experience that remains truly invisible is the writing process. We read the narration of his experience, but we do not see him actually composing the narration. The act of writing is completely absent in the body of the novel. We see the invisible narrator preparing for speeches, delivering speeches, and reacting to the consequences of his speeches, but the reader does not see him writing.[7] To some extent, this is one of the qualities that differentiate the prologue and the epilogue so profoundly from the body

---

6. For an examination of the world the narrator inhabits and its implications on the narrator's attempts to control and make sense of his reality, see Schaub 132–33.

7. See Rice 11–12 and 25–56.

of the narrative itself. The voice in the narrative body has come to realize that it is by taking rhetorical control of his own story that he develops an awareness of his invisibility. Memoir, in the form of the narrative he constructs, transforms that awareness into something greater than the narrator. This is no longer a fragmented personality whose experiences can only be narrated solely through the incoherent, stereotyped perceptions of those he encounters. This is now a unified consciousness perhaps capable—"Who knows but that, on the lower frequencies, I speak for you?" (581)—of articulating the meaning of his own experiences as a way of producing a single egalitarian experience, containing all of the inconsistencies and opportunities of life in the United States.

For the narrator, narrative construction is a conscious act that is precariously balanced between a desire to speak and a desire to write. His experiences have been given to him, beyond his control. But his narrative is a form of active construction. He recovers from his experiences by reconstructing them. The reader does not watch the narrator construct his story any more than the reader witnesses the narrator construct his identity. And this, perhaps, is the very lesson of the double consciousness to which his grandfather's defiantly ambiguous deathbed words have been leading since the opening chapter, where the narrator began his attempt to put words to his experiences. The narrative reveals no breakthrough and certainly no moment of sudden awareness. Instead, his story is an incremental series of experiences that lead him to the subterranean hole where he sees what goes on around him with none of the obligations that are part of being noticed. One of Ellison's beliefs was that the work of the writer was to shape the direction of the public conversation about race and national consciousness.[8] But as the narrator has come to realize, it is virtually impossible for people who have been written out of the public sphere to influence the direction of its conversation about self-determination and individual agency. The control the narrator takes from the production of his story has less to do with rendering his experiences and much more to do with stripping away the layers of cultural illusion that shaped his experiences in the first place. By acknowledging his own invisibility, the narrator is actually able to realize the unstable nature of identity and the world identity occupies. He constructs the roles he inhabits to suit his purposes, rather than trying to fit his needs to the roles assigned to him by a society that cannot see him. By writing his story, the chaos he repeatedly experienced is replaced by the evaporation of boundary and by his increasing awareness of possibility.

---

8. See Ellison, "The World and the Jug," especially 158 and 178.

This should not minimize the fact that the epilogue is profoundly problematic. Ellison fragments the narrator's personality by making a distinction between the narrative voice that experiences the action of the novel and the narrative presence that composes, explains, and evaluates those experiences. The novel's prologue and epilogue form an encircling presence that is united by a narrative voice of experience that emanates from the underground apartment to which the narrator fled to escape Ras during the riot that engulfs Harlem at the conclusion of the novel. But in the epilogue, the universalizing position the narrative voice strikes relative to the body of the novel itself seems almost contradictory to the indictment the novel has earlier leveled on all ideological systems that minimize the roles of the individual in favor of ideologies that emphasize a collective approach.

The epilogue also profoundly reduces the distance the novel has often imposed between the narrator and the narratee by reorienting itself around a bifurcated assessment.[9] The narrator's invisibility for much of the novel's progress has functioned as a tool of exclusion. But when the reader reaches the epilogue, invisibility begins to function as a tool of critique (Cheng 133). Invisibility becomes transformed by the narrator's voice of experience into a tool of representational expression. Ultimately, the narrator can only find the identity and coherence for which he has spent the novel searching by withdrawing to a place of isolation. This is the narrative sleight of hand that allows Ellison to renegotiate the boundaries of political and social intervention away from the racialized subject and toward a collaboratively universal, multiracial entity. With this clash of narrative agendas coalescing in the narrator's final remarks, it is no revelation that the meaning of the novel's resolution is ambiguous and opaque.

What the narrator discovers in hibernation is that in a segregated nation, individual identity for a black subject can be as ineffectual as the group ideology he has relied upon during so many of his experiences in the chapters leading to the epilogue. Particularly in the epilogue, Ellison has fractured the

---

9. See Foley 325–49; "Prologue," Box 147, the Ralph Ellison Papers; "Fragments and Partial Drafts," F1 Box 150; "Notes 1942–50," F. 9 Box 152, the Ralph Ellison Papers; "Original Typescript," F.6, Box 147, the Ralph Ellison Papers; "Fragments and Partial Drafts," F. 3, Box 151, the Ralph Ellison Papers. Foley argues that Ellison's notes and drafts indicate that the novel's conclusion was problematic for him in a number of ways. His notes, for example, do not indicate that he had even originally planned to include an epilogue. In its final version, the epilogue thematically expanded invisibility from the racial context described in much of the novel into a universal, multiracial condition that substantially softened the racial indictment contained in most of the novel. He replaced the novel's critique with a conclusion much more palatable to the mainstream, white readership that eventually embraced the novel and established it in the nation's consciousness. See also Phelan, *Reading* 165–68.

implied reader as completely as he has separated the narrative voice. The epilogue does not definitively see the implied reader as either an adversary or a partner. The narrator's concluding remarks seem only partially intended to recruit his reader to his way of thinking. Since he never fully achieves his goal of finding his identity, his recitation of experience actually sounds like an ominous caution against following his course of action. The narrator's affirmation is countered by his denial and presented to implied readers who may be read as either supportive or potentially antagonistic.

In a larger narrative sense, what is important about the novel is that it is only through the imperfect frame surrounding the narrative—its prologue and ambiguously universalized epilogue—that many of the questions raised by the narrator's recitation of experience can be addressed. The narrative structure itself is the primary lens through which the relationship between race, history, social structure, writing, and speech can be understood. In the final passages of the novel, the writer rhetorically asks, "So why do I write, torturing myself to put it down? . . . Why should I be dedicated and set aside—yes, if not to at least tell a few people about it?" (579).

The narrator, unnamed but not unraced, has expended his narrative capital trying to reconcile two points of orientation that define his experiences: his race and the nation itself. The nation's black citizens are imbued with the social and psychological significances of America's ideals and its focus on the endless possibilities available to all of those who participate in and pursue its aspirations. America itself is indelibly marked by the imprint of African Americans who contributed tirelessly (though invisibly) to all aspects of the nation's social and cultural presence. Though the narrator considers his imminent reemergence from his underground apartment to be a sign of hope, perhaps the only true sign of hope is that the narrator has come to understand that the relentless contradiction of race and nation is the most essential reality for African Americans in the world they inhabited and helped to create in the years between Reconstruction and *Brown v. the Board of Education*.[10]

---

10. See Adell 18–19.

CHAPTER 11

Race as Interpretive Lens

Focalization and Critique of Globalization in Jhumpa Lahiri's "Sexy"

SHAUN MORGAN

AS THE ESSAYS in this collection suggest, there have been numerous recent attempts to take the tools of the narratological tool kit and reformulate them for understanding the representation of race and ethnicity in narrative. Of particular interest has been attention to the ways narrative functions associated with narration can enable critics concerned with issues of race to explain how narratives represent aspects of race. Patrick Horn's essay in this collection, for example, explores the way in which a "strategic parelepsis"—in this case, the way in which the narrator of Monique Truong's novel *Bitter in the Mouth* delays the revelation that she is Vietnamese American and other markers of race in the novel—can significantly alter the way a narrative is received by readers in terms of its claims about race. By confronting readers with the assumption of the narrator's whiteness, the novel illustrates how the normativity of whiteness informs narratives that do not directly identify characters and narrators as nonwhite. In a related vein, Christian Schmidt in his essay on Percival Everett's novel, *I Am Not Sidney Poitier*, explores the concept of the implied author to explain how Everett creates the narrative distance necessary to establishing a "postblack" aesthetic that resists the identification of a raced author with raced characters and subject matter. By refusing to be read as a mimetic character narrator, Everett's narrator further refuses to be identified autobiographically with the author of the novel, and thereby the novel resists being read as a mimetically "black" text.

Taken together, the essays by Schmidt and Horn demonstrate the importance of attending to matters of race when dealing with character narrators who are raced and of understanding how the work of raced authors may impact the reception of narratives told by such narrators. Other critics have sought to explore the relationship between race and the functions of narration by focusing on focalization. For example, in his essay "Focalization, Ethics, and Cosmopolitanism in James Welch's *Fools Crow*," James J. Donahue explains that Welch's novel employs what he calls a "culturally-focalized narrator" that exists on a "plane between" focalized narrators and nonfocalized narrators and that filters the narrative discourse through the perceptions of the culture of the Blackfeet and Anglo American peoples presented in the novel (57). This observation builds on the work of theorists of focalization like Gerard Genette and Mieke Bal. As Donahue notes, the "controlling metaphor" of Genette's conception of focalization (in which focalization refers to "who sees" in a narrative) limits the concept to an embodied and therefore singular subject. Donahue's conception of a "culturally-focalized narrator" expands the concept of focalization in order to allow for a collective, cultural form of focalization that is not embodied in a single perceiving subject. Further, Donahue turns to Bal's notion of "levels of focalization" to distinguish between the functions of character focalizers (which exist at the level of story) and external focalizers (which, because they have access to information not available to character focalizers, exist at a "higher" level of focalization). It is this distinction, based on Bal's relational conception of focalization, that enables Donahue to move beyond the metaphor of focalization-as-vision to consider the question of ideology's relationship to focalization (Bal 149).[1] As Donahue puts it, "What I am concerned with here is not the act of sight, but rather how ideology binds the narrating agent, providing a limit not to what the narrat-

---

1. I describe Bal's notion of focalization as relational because, according to Bal, "focalization is the relationship between the 'vision,' the agent that sees, and that which is seen" (Bal 149). Unlike Genette, Bal posits a theory of focalization that emphasizes the relationship between the perceiving subject and the perceived object. For the purposes of identifying and explaining how ideologies such as race focus the perception of a narrating subject, Bal's theory of focalization provides a mechanism for describing the ideological character of perception. While Genette's notion of focalization disaggregates the "speaking" subject of a narrative (voice) from the "seeing" subject of a narrative, it effectively treats focalization as the representation of a direct perception of an object (*Narrative Discourse* 186). Bal's theory of focalization, however, allows for "levels" of focalization embedded within a narrative, and this indicates the possibility of multiple levels of perception and interpretation in a narrative. As such, it is better equipped to explain the ways in which different levels of focalization can present different perceptual experiences and therefore can also make readers aware of the ideologies that constrain those different perceptions.

ing agent can 'see,' but rather what it can know, which in turn colors how that focalized object is seen" (60).

What Donahue's reformulated notion of focalization allows him to describe is the way in which focalization serves to convey the impact of ideology, in the form of culture and race, on the perceiving faculty of individual subjects. This is a valuable development for a critical race narratology because it illustrates the ways narration can convey the psychological and social significance of race as an identity and the ways the control of information made possible by narration can affect the interpretation of raced narratives. In this essay, I build on the work of Horn, Schmidt, and Donahue by examining how race is represented in Jhumpa Lahiri's short story "Sexy." "Sexy" takes up a central space in *Interpreter of Maladies*, Lahiri's 1999 collection of stories focused on the experiences of people living in the South Asian diaspora. However, "Sexy" stands apart from other stories in the collection because it concentrates on the experience of a twenty-two-year-old white woman from Michigan whose relationship to the social world of the South Asian diaspora is a vicarious one, achieved through her relationships with a coworker, Laxmi, and Dev, a Bengali man with whom she has an affair. Following on Donahue's suggestion that analysis of focalization can help to explain how certain narratives represent modes of perception that have been conditioned by racialized identities and experiences, I examine the levels of focalization employed in Lahiri's story to reveal racial differences between the characters, differences that are never spoken as dialogue because the characters are unable to address their racial differences openly or even consciously. By alternating between the position of an externally focalized narrator and an internal character focalizer, Lahiri represents race as an ideological component of character perception, a filter through which material evidence of the social world passes and is then marshaled to explain elements of the social world of the narrative in terms of race. By passing the material of story through multiple levels of focalization, Lahiri is able to demonstrate how race both motivates and constrains the interracial communication symbolized by interracial relationships in a globalized, diasporic social context.[2]

---

2. The relationship between race, globalization, and cosmopolitanism in Lahiri's work has been the subject of much criticism, and I am not the first to note that "Sexy" represents a significant intervention by Lahiri on these subjects. Elizabeth Jackson, for instance, suggests that "Sexy" complicates elitist and colonialist notions of cosmopolitanism by contrasting Miranda, "a rustic native from Michigan," with Dev, an Indian man who "is figured as a sophisticated cosmopolitan" (114). In a different vein, Susan Koshy uses the short stories collected in *Interpreter of Maladies* (though, interestingly, she does not address "Sexy") to illustrate what she calls a "minority cosmopolitanism," a term she coins "to refer to translocal affiliations that are grounded in the experience of minority subjects and are marked by a critical awareness of the

"Sexy" explores an interracial extramarital affair between Dev and Miranda, but the story begins by relaying the circumstances of a parallel extramarital affair between a South Asian man and "an English girl, half his age" (83). This affair is presented in the opening paragraph in a way that serves to establish the global, diasporic social setting of the narrative and to establish the levels of focalization that filter the story into narrative discourse:

> It was a wife's worst nightmare. After nine years of marriage, Laxmi told Miranda, her cousin's husband had fallen in love with another woman. He sat next to her on a plane, on a flight from Delhi to Montreal, and instead of flying home to his wife and son, he got off with the woman at Heathrow. He called his wife, and told her he'd had a conversation that had changed his life, and that he needed time to figure things out. Laxmi's cousin had taken to her bed. (83)

This paragraph locates the story in a world of globalization and diaspora with its references to the international network of cities of South Asian diasporic migration—between Delhi, Montreal, and London (in the offhand reference simply to "Heathrow")—made possible by the air transportation and telecommunications technology so central to globalization. Further, it establishes the relationship of the reader to this social setting through a subtle use of indirect discourse. Narrated by an externally focalized narrator who takes a position outside of the storyworld of the characters, the passage is presented as the reported speech of a character Laxmi, whose name and relationship to the characters in the story she narrates suggest her intimate familiarity with this

constraints of primary attachments such as family, religion, race, and nation and by an ethical or imaginative receptivity, orientation or aspiration to an interconnected or shared world" (594). As such, Koshy highlights the ways that Lahiri's stories present cosmopolitan subjects who are nevertheless aware of the constraints placed on cosmopolitan existence by diasporic, minority status. Readings such as these helpfully suggest that Lahiri's fiction imagines a cosmopolitan subjectivity emerging out of the experience of diaspora, a subjectivity that is cognizant of the inhibiting factors of race and nationality. They could go farther, however, in explaining and exploring Lahiri's interrogation of the limits of race as it is treated in the United States in the late twentieth century.

A critic who examines such limits quite closely is Stephanie Li, who, in an insightful chapter of her book *Signifying without Specifying: Racial Discourse in the Age of Obama*, argues that while it might seem "incidental" in Lahiri's fiction about interracial relationships, race "becomes paramount as [Lahiri's] characters construct one another through sexual fantasies dependent on racial constructions" (104). In "Sexy," Li notes that "silence" about the differences in race "fosters [Miranda's] fanciful projections and prevents her from understanding South Asian culture as anything more than a series of polarizing sexual images" (110). Thematically, my reading of "Sexy" is very close to Li's, but by emphasizing the significance of Lahiri's method of focalization, I extend Li's analysis to explain how, as a matter of form, the narrative presents and confronts the racial silences Li identifies.

social context. Through reported speech, the narrator gives voice to Laxmi in this paragraph (she is the speaker here), but Laxmi's voice and embedded narrative are presented through the internally focalized position of a character, Miranda, who is receiving the story of Laxmi's cousin's husband's affair because, unlike Laxmi, she is not a member of Laxmi's family (thus, the necessity of identifying familial relationships) and also because she is not familiar with the globalized, diasporic social context Laxmi so easily presents.

This structure of focalization permits the reader to engage the story of the narrative from the position of Miranda, but it also allows the external narrator to delay revealing information about the extent and nature of Miranda's distance from Laxmi's world until the scene introduced by the opening paragraph is completed. As Miranda continues listening to Laxmi lament her cousin's situation, Miranda's responses to Laxmi are indicated via subtle instances of indirect and free indirect discourse that serve to qualify Miranda's relationship to the globalized world of the South Asian diaspora. For example, as Laxmi continues relaying her cousin's situation, she eats from the bag of Hot Mix she keeps in her desk, "which" the narrator tells us, "looked to Miranda like dusty orange cereal" (83). Miranda's unfamiliarity with South Asian culture is indicated by her unfamiliarity with a typical South Asian food and her attempt to translate that food into a culinary language that she understands. This revelation is made possible by the externally focalized narrator's use of indirect discourse, giving the reader access to Miranda's perception of Laxmi but maintaining a narrative position outside of Miranda and the story of the narrative.

This seems to be the case, as well, a bit later in the scene, when Miranda overhears Laxmi talking to her cousin on the phone in the next cubicle over, in the public radio station office where they work: "She [Miranda] could hear Laxmi clearly, her sentences peppered every now and then with an Indian word, through the laminated wall between their desks" (84). The sentence presents itself as another instance of the narrator's use of indirect discourse, by which the narrator remains an external focalizer reporting *about* Miranda's perceptions of Laxmi and thus maintaining a distinction between the levels of focalization—external narrator and internal character. However, the description of Laxmi's conversation with her cousin is presented wholly from within Miranda's character. It is Miranda's ignorance of South Asian languages that makes possible the claim that Laxmi is occasionally using "Indian" words in her conversation, and it is Miranda's stereotypical understanding of South Asian food and culture that motivates the description of this as "pepper[ing]." The narrative structure in this passage produces a kind of double focalization that establishes distance between narrator and character and thus primarily functions as an external report of the character's actions, while also presenting the passage through the filter of Miranda as character focalizer. As such, Lahiri not only positions Miranda as the primary focalizer of the story but also demonstrates the cultural and racial ideologies informing Miranda's understanding of South Asian cultures that make her unreliable as an observer of the South Asian diasporic experience.

This structure of focalization serves to characterize Miranda as an uninformed and inexperienced observer of South Asian diasporic culture, and this characterization is complicated by the plot of the narrative, which centers on Miranda's extramarital affair with a Bengali man named Dev. It is this relationship that makes clear that Miranda's ignorance of South Asian culture is a product of racial ideology. On first meeting Dev in the cosmetics section of a Boston department store, Miranda finds him mysterious and attractive precisely because he does not fit easily into the narratives of race and masculinity with which she is familiar. As she struggles to place Dev in terms of his race ("She thought he might be Spanish, or Lebanese," and "she detected only the hint of an accent"), the external narrator makes it clear, once again through internal focalization, that Miranda's interest in this exotic stranger is at least partly motivated by anxieties about her own racial status (87). While Dev looks on, the saleswoman at the cosmetics counter applies blush to Miranda's face, remarking that it "gives you some color," and Miranda notices her appearance in the mirror. This is reported in the narrative through her language:

> She had silver eyes and skin as pale as paper, and the contrast with her hair, as dark and glossy as an espresso bean, caused people to describe her as striking, if not pretty. She had a narrow, egg-shaped head that rose to a prominent point. Her features, too, were narrow, with nostrils so slim that they appeared to have been pinched with a clothespin. Now her face glowed, rosy at the cheeks, smoky below the brown bone. Her lips glistened. (87)

This is a verbal self-portrait of a makeover transformation that achieves its effect because it addresses Miranda's anxieties about lacking "color," particularly as her self-conception as a white American woman (with "skin as pale as paper" and "narrow" features) contrasts with the exotic, colored appearance of Dev, whom she notes is "tanned, with black hair that was visible on his knuckles" and dressed in comparatively flamboyant colors, a "flamingo pink shirt, a navy blue suit, a camel overcoat with gleaming leather buttons" (86).

The structure of focalization that makes these perceptions available to the reader achieves its effect because the descriptions of Miranda and Dev presented in these passages seem as if they are external reports of primarily visual observations. However, because these descriptions are focalized through

Miranda, the significance of the physical markers associated with racial identification (the visual markers of color and the verbal markers of accents) are not presented as explicitly racialized, and as a result, the reader is not prepared to fully understand the motivation behind Miranda's attraction to Dev. That is, the two levels of focalization present in the story make the reader aware of information about Miranda's racial anxieties, but that is information that Miranda has but which she cannot consciously acknowledge or speak in the story. Further, this illustrates the significance of moving beyond, as Donahue suggests, the "controlling metaphor" of focalization as vision. If the focalization of the narrative makes it possible for the reader to "see" race in the color perceptions of Miranda, it also makes it possible for the reader to "hear" and "taste" race in her concerns about South Asian food or her assumptions about South Asian accents. In short, Lahiri's method of focalization brings to bear the full perceiving faculty of the character Miranda in order to illuminate the ways in which race makes the physical data she receives legible to her as evidence of racial identity and difference.

As the narrative turns from the initial encounter between Dev and Miranda to their relationship, Miranda's ignorance of South Asian culture and her assumptions about Dev's racial identity are developed only to be discounted as insignificant to the relationship. Dev, an older and well-traveled man, serves as a kind of tour guide for Miranda, explaining to her some aspects of South Asian culture and introducing her to the cosmopolitan city of Boston. During this initial period of their relationship, which occurs while Dev's wife is visiting family in India, Miranda submits to Dev's knowledge of the world as he points out Bengal on a map in an issue of *The Economist*. Their relationship seems to be developing in intimacy as they discuss their experiences of loneliness and enjoy the varieties of cultural products made available in the globalized city of Boston:

> They ate pulled pork and cornbread in Davis Square, a paper napkin tucked like a cravat into the collar of Dev's shirt. They sipped sangria at the bar of a Spanish restaurant, a grinning pig's head presiding over their conversation. They went to the MFA and picked out a poster of water lilies for her bedroom. (90)

Against the backdrop of this multicultural, global experience of Boston, Dev and Miranda's interracial relationship seems the most natural thing in the world. Matters of race, culture, and geography seem insignificant when cultures from all over the planet are easily accessed thanks to international trade and technologies of communication and travel.

The unifying power of globalization, which promises to bring people from different cultures, nations, and races across the world into a harmonious relationship in which differences of culture, race, and nation cease to matter, is most fully symbolized at the moment when Dev takes Miranda to his "favorite place in the city," the Mapparium at the Christian Science center. There, while standing on opposite sides of the transparent bridge inside a stained-glass replica of the globe, figuratively on opposite sides of the world, Dev takes advantage of the unique acoustics of the Mapparium to whisper to Miranda, "You're sexy" (91). Miranda's response to this moment suggests the degree to which she has assimilated the "color-blind" race ideology of globalization: "She watched his lips forming the words; at the same time she heard them so clearly that she felt them under her skin, under her winter coat, so near and full of warmth that she felt herself go hot" (91). Just as globalized trade has brought nations from across the globe into economic relationships that had not before seemed possible, Miranda and Dev have been brought together from opposite sides of the world by the same economic and political forces that have structured the movements of the South Asian diaspora.

The internal focalization through Miranda in this passage serves to indicate more than the intensity of the feelings Miranda experiences; it also further indicates Miranda's interpellation into the racial ideologies of globalization, ideologies that encourage her to see the social significance of race as reduced or eliminated. The image of the world that the Mapparium presents is a static one, frozen in time at the point of its construction in 1935. While the couple stands at the center of the bridge "so that they felt they were standing in the center of the world," Dev points out to Miranda "that many of the countries no longer existed in the same way; the names had changed by now" (90). For Miranda, Dev's observation is further evidence of his cosmopolitan knowledge of the world beyond the United States, but she fails to consider that it is also evidence of a history of European colonization. She sees the world, and herself, through the lens of an ideology of globalization that elides the histories and conflicts between cultures that have existed prior to the late twentieth century, when globalization promises to make cross-cultural connection so easily accessible that a relationship between a white woman from Michigan and a Bengali man can seem to transcend their racial differences.

This moment of connection in the Mapparium is the high-water mark of Miranda and Dev's relationship, and it allows Miranda to imagine herself fulfilling the role of a mistress. Nevertheless, it is built on the racial logic of globalization that presents cultural differences as exotic products for consumption with no material, political significance. As such, Miranda and Dev have ignored, perhaps willfully, the ways in which their racial differences have affected their understandings of each other. For example, when Dev expresses affinity with Miranda's experience of moving to Boston, a city "where she knew no one," from her home in Michigan, Miranda interprets this as an appreciation for the pleasures she takes in her solitude in the busy city: "Miranda felt he understood her—understood how she felt some nights on the T, after seeing a movie on her own, or going to a bookstore to read magazines, or having drinks with Laxmi, who always had to meet her husband at Alewife station in an hour or two" (89). Interpreting Dev's comment in this way, Miranda misses the fact that Dev's understanding of loneliness is based on his experience of displacement after having been sent to a college in New York "during something called the Emergency" (94). Further, Miranda fails to recognize that Dev may find her exotic and, therefore, attractive for the same reason she found herself attracted to him: her exoticness as a racial other. When, after making love, Dev observes that Miranda's legs are longer than her torso, he notes that this was the first time he had a sexual partner like her: "'You're the first,' he told her, admiring her from the bed. 'The first woman I've known with legs this long'" (89). The hesitation between the initial statement ("You're the first") and the second ("The first woman I've known with legs this long") is not credited to Dev. Instead, it is the product of Lahiri's use of the external narrator as focalizer to maintain distance from the characters even as the scene is primarily focalized through Miranda's subjectivity. As such, it does not reveal the likely subtext of Dev's comment, that Miranda is the first white woman with whom he has had sex. Like Miranda, then, the reader is prevented from a full appreciation of the ways in which race and, in particular, the racial ideologies of a supposedly color-blind globalization have structured their relationship. These ideologies have made the relationship possible, on the one hand, by making the two lovers available to each other as objects of exotic sexual desire while, on the other hand, making it unlikely that they will achieve true intimacy because of their inability to express and confront the racial ideologies that underlie their entire relationship.[3]

Following the scene in the Mapparium, Dev's wife returns from India, and instead of romantic dates on the town, Miranda settles for a weekly rendezvous made possible when Dev claims to be running in the city. With their relationship confined to these brief afternoons, Miranda begins to look for other avenues of connection to Dev and his experiences as a South Asian.

---

3. In this way, Lahiri's narrative can be seen as advancing the notion of "color-blind racism" as it has been developed by Eduardo Bonilla-Silva. In particular, the narrative suggests that a triumphalist attitude toward globalization, which might be associated with celebrations of cross-cultural connections made possible by developments in technology, relies upon an ignorance (willed or passive) of differences between races and cultures.

First, Miranda attempts to place her understanding of Dev's racialized existence in the context of her memory of the Dixit family, the only South Asian family in her neighborhood as a child. The Dixits, she recalls, were generally excluded from the social life of the neighborhood. The Dixit children were the targets of racist epithets from the other children in the neighborhood, Mrs. Dixit was not invited to swimming parties, and Mr. Dixit's unorthodox habit of jogging in his "everyday shirt and trousers" and failure to comply with his neighbors' expectations for lawn care marked him as an outsider. The strangeness of the Dixits and South Asian culture is most poignant for Miranda in her recollection of a birthday party for one of the Dixit girls. While in the Dixit home, Miranda encountered a painting of the Hindu goddess Kali. As a child, Miranda found the strangeness she had associated with the Dixits figured in the image of Kali:

> It was a painting of a naked woman with a red face shaped like a knight's shield. She had enormous white eyes that tilted toward her temples, and mere dots for pupils. Two circles, with the same dots at their centers, indicated her breasts. In one hand she brandished a dagger. With one foot she crushed a struggling man on the ground. Around her body was a necklace composed of bleeding heads, strung together like a popcorn chain. She stuck her tongue out at Miranda. (96)

This passage of ekphrasis is filtered through Miranda-as-child, and it is her perception, influenced by anxieties about the Dixits' racial difference, that makes it possible to see the image of Kali as sticking her tongue out *at* Miranda. Thus, when Mrs. Dixit attempts to explain the image to Miranda, she is too frightened to listen or to eat cake at the party. This experience positions Miranda as an utterly uncosmopolitan figure, someone who has had little experience with South Asian culture and whose ideas about it are parochial and based on ignorance. For readers, many of whom would have similarly limited experience with South Asian cultures, the focalization of this passage through Miranda exposes the critical function of racial ideologies in structuring the cognitive experience of encountering racial otherness. Miranda's discomfort is shown to be a product of her ignorance about Hindu religion, which extends that ignorance by discouraging her from interrogating that discomfort. The affective response of being repulsed by difference exacerbates her inability to understand that difference.

This experience of fear at the threat of South Asian racial otherness is a source of shame in the adult Miranda, who has relationships with two different South Asians, but rather than confront the ignorance of South Asians that motivated her fear, Miranda-as-adult displaces her racial fear with an exoticized image of her Indian lover: "Now, when she and Dev made love, Miranda closed her eyes and saw deserts and elephants, and marble pavilions floating on lakes beneath a full moon" (96). This romanticized view of Dev's South Asian identity motivates her to try to intensify her connection with him via the same kinds of cultural consumption that she and Dev practiced early in their relationship. She goes to an Indian restaurant, where she eats tandoori chicken and tries to memorize the phrases printed in the menu; she visits the foreign-language section of a bookstore to study the Bengali alphabet in hopes of learning to transcribe "Mira," which, according to Dev, is the Indian part of her name; and finally, she visits an Indian grocery. It is there that she is faced with the fact that Dev's wife is beautiful (he had told her that his wife resembled the Indian actress Madhuri Dixit) and that therefore, his attraction to Miranda is based on something other than simple physical attractiveness. Finally, her distance from Dev and South Asian culture is announced when the clerk in the grocery cautions her that the Hot Mix she has seen Laxmi eating at her desk is "too spicy for you" (99).

Miranda's awareness of this alienation from Dev and his culture is only implicitly presented through Miranda's multiple failures to fully acquire, through consumption, the accoutrements of South Asian culture and her apparent discomfort in the Indian grocery. These issues are not addressed in dialogue between characters or through narratorial description. Instead, by maintaining a dual structure of focalization—Miranda as an internal character focalizer and the narrator as an external focalizer—Lahiri suggests both Miranda's anxieties about her relationship to Dev and her inability to fully express those anxieties to herself or other characters. It is only when Rohin, the son of Laxmi's cousin who is in Boston while his mother visits Laxmi, comes to Miranda's apartment that any character in the story speaks frankly about the challenges of racial difference to interracial communication and relationships. Rohin is presented as a diminutive double of Dev: he is a young South Asian man who is more traveled than Miranda and who declares his cosmopolitan sophistication through his knowledge of national capitals around the world. Further, Rohin's experience of witnessing his mother's reactions to his father's affair has given him a surprising, if still naïve, appreciation for the intricacies of such relationships. He rightly interprets, for example, that his mother does not have a cold but instead has been crying over her husband's indiscretions.

This positions Rohin to be a strikingly accurate interpreter of Miranda and Dev's relationship, even if he has little information about it. When he persuades Miranda to model the dress she had bought to wear on the dates with

Dev that never occurred after the return of his wife, Rohin echoes Dev's line in the Mapparium when he tells Miranda, "You're sexy" (107). Caught off guard by the young boy's attempt to sound like an adult and by the unexpected repetition of the sentence that had signaled intense connection and intimacy between her and Dev, Miranda realizes that she may have misinterpreted Dev's meaning in the Mapparium. Thus, she pushes Rohin to explain what he meant by the sentence. She holds him down until he confesses his understanding of what it means to say someone is "sexy": "'It means,'" he answers, "'loving someone you don't know'" (107). Having listened to the reports of his father's affair with a woman he didn't know, Rohin had come to understand sexiness and love as the product of relationships without connection: "[Rohin's father] sat next to someone he didn't know, someone sexy, and now he loves her instead of my mother" (108).

Miranda hears Rohin's definition of sexiness with the same degree of intensity that she felt when Dev uttered the words "You're sexy." As before, she feels the words "under her skin" (107). However, instead of "going hot" with the feelings of attraction usually associated with sexiness, Miranda now goes "numb" with the same feeling of alienation she experienced while at the Indian grocery. In short, she has come to the realization that she had misinterpreted her relationship to Dev. What she thought was a relationship built on mutual understandings that transcended the cultural differences between them was actually a relationship built on a mutual exoticism: the only aspect of their relationship that was mutual was that they both found themselves attracted to each other because of their stereotypical notions of each other as representatives of racial otherness. These suspicions are confirmed, later, when Miranda questions Dev about that moment at the Mapparium, and Dev misremembers what he said as "Let's go back to your place" (109). Following Rohin's declaration, Miranda and Dev's relationship dissolves as Miranda apparently disengages from the exotic fantasies that had initially motivated their relationship.

Through Dev and Miranda's ultimately failed relationship, Lahiri thematically critiques the racial ideology of globalization for celebrating the differences between races and cultures inasmuch as they can be made into commodities of exotic consumption while ignoring (or being ignorant of) the histories of the cultures represented by those commodities. This critique is mirrored in the structure of focalization employed in the narrative, which, through an internal character focalizer, gives us access to Miranda's interior experience and, through an externally focalized narrator, maintains a level of perception separate from the character. This structure of focalization allows Lahiri to present the racial anxieties and fantasies that motivate Miranda's behavior even when the character is not fully able or willing to articulate them. Just as the racial ideology of globalization presents a world of harmony among racial and cultural differences while at the same time burying the material political differences that must be ignored in order to maintain the illusion of such harmony, the structure of focalization in "Sexy" makes available to the reader the experience of inhabiting the racial ideology of globalization as well as the information necessary to perceive it *as ideology*, as a fantasy that overrides the material realities associated with racial difference.

The abstract, formal vocabulary of narrative theory may seem to be thoroughly separate from the political concerns of a critical race literary studies, but attention to the ways narratives like "Sexy" engage the politics of race demonstrates that race is a concern at the levels of theme *and* form. Focalization can provide critical race narratology the beginnings of a formal terminology that can explain how narratives concerned with race as an ideology represent the lived experience of such an ideology as well as the structural, social conditions that perpetuate it. Lahiri allows readers to perceive Miranda's racial confusion at the same time that she makes readers aware of the material conditions that produce such confusion. It is this awareness, made possible by Lahiri's manipulation of levels of focalization and which is not available to Miranda through most of the narrative, that makes Lahiri's critique of the racial ideology of globalization legible at the level of theme. This is the promise of a critical race narratology, a method of criticism that utilizes and adds to the tool kit of formal narrative analysis to show how narratives address issues of race and to consider how issues of race shape the formal functions of narrative.

CHAPTER 12

Race, Cosmopolitanism, and the Complexities of Belonging in the *Open City*

Teju Cole's Transcontinental Aesthetics

CLAUDIA BREGER

IN RESPONSE TO Sue J. Kim's recent provocation, according to which "narrative theory" too often still functions as the "langue," and "minority texts merely the parole" even in contextual narratologies, my reading of Teju Cole's *Open City* contributes to a project of *reconstituting* this langue through the paroles of transcontinental worldmaking. Probing Susan Lanser's groundbreaking contributions to feminist and queer narratology for the (different) context of narratological critical race studies, I begin by exploring the narratological significance of the un/marking of identity—or, in explicitly nonessentialist terms, positionality—categories, in order to approach the interrelations of positionality, narrative voice, and authority ("Toward a Feminist Narratology"; "Sexing the Narrative"). Intertwining models of rhetorical narratology with African diaspora aesthetics, I specifically challenge the implications of individual control and sovereignty haunting notions of unreliability. Instead, I conceptualize *Open City's* experientially dialogic, call-and-response informed character voice as *nonsovereign*.

The transcontinental or critically cosmopolitan aesthetics of *Open City* described in these terms enables a complex engagement with questions of race in twenty-first-century society. While engaging contemporary desires for moving beyond race after the end of "the century of the color line" (Gilroy *Against Race* 1), *Open City's* poetics of nonsovereign narration simultaneously complicates these calls by pursuing the enduring affective legacies of racism.

Integrating the outlined paradigms of narrative voice also with contemporary affect studies, this essay contours Cole's transcontinental narration as an experiential process of configuring attachments, associations, experiences, disaffections, gestures, and memories with and into words.

Open City (2011) was released into a literary market driven by a demand for so-called world literature with canonical and still dominantly European, even if "multicultural" ancestry. Invited by the publisher to compare Cole's debut to the oeuvres of Joseph O'Neill and Zadie Smith, J. M. Coetzee and W. G. Sebald, reviewers overwhelmingly responded by affirming Sebald, in particular, as a major influence.[1] While some of their observations, for example about *Open City*'s "meandering structure" and "solitary, scholarly narrator" on a quest of revealing "unknown histories" in cityscapes (Lewek para. 7), are quite apt, these placement strategies curiously correspond—or fall prey?—to a particular element of the character narrator's initial self-presentation. In the novel's opening pages, he foregrounds his high-cultural European affiliations, for example by reporting on his habit of listening to classical music programs on Canadian, German, and Dutch Internet stations (Cole 4).

In the absence of other information on the narrator's background (except for the casual introduction of his first name, "Julius") (12), this introductory emphasis on classical music almost seems designed to test reader assumptions about narrator positionality. Reminiscent of Lanser's questions about gender and sexuality, might (specific groups of) readers default to assuming an unmarked narrator's majority European/Western background and/or whiteness rather than positional proximity between narrator and author? Or, what normative connections between race, cultural background, and taste do "we" still make? While the author's belonging to the African diaspora is marked by a photograph of Cole on my edition's back cover, and a closer look at its descriptive paratext may have informed the reader that the narrator is "a young Nigerian doctor," the novel itself complicates such simple accounts of positionality. Delaying the disclosure of respective information, the text eventually relates the narrator's background through the report on two different racist incidents. As variations on Frantz Fanon's classical scene of negative interpellation (see 109–40), they activate two different vectors of identification. First, a film on *The Last King of Scotland*—referring to Idi Amin Dada, dictator of Uganda in the 1970s—triggers a memory of a dinner scene during Julius's studies, where the Indian host had expressed his anger at having been expelled by Idi Amin as an anger at "Africans" in general (Cole 30). As the narrator reports, he "couldn't help feeling" that the anger "was partly directed

---

1. See Wood; Messud; Kakutani; E. Turner; and Foden.

at me, the only other African in the room," regardless of the fact "that I was Nigerian" (30–31).With its layers of mediatization—movies and memories—and the (nonwhite) racist's own history of displacement, this scene of (in the novel, initial) racial identification dramatizes the complexity of positionality, while indicating the impact of rac*ism* on identity. As unsupervised kids from out of town then hail Julius as a "gangster" on his way home from the movie theater, he has a "feeling that my oma (as I am accustomed to calling my maternal grandmother) should see me again" (32). The German term foregrounded here indicates the narrator's part-European background, in which he will, for those of the novel's readers desiring respective stability, on the following pages anchor his initially foregrounded cultural affiliations.

Insistently alerting the reader to her variously sub/conscious expectations and assumptions, the novel's intricate process of positional marking through implicit coding, ellipsis, and gradual disclosure in competing scenes of interpellation thus initiates a multilayered analysis of the significance of race and ethnicity in the contemporary world. Translating this complexity to the level of aesthetics, I want to suggest a more intricate account also of the novel's aesthetic lineage. If the Sebald association makes sense, it might be pertinent to begin with a general reminder that European post/modernisms have been significantly co-constituted by cultural flows across the "Black Atlantic."[2] A closer look at Cole's novel itself can start from the observation that the mentioned introductory report on the narrator's radio habits is developed into a poetological affirmation of orality. While listening, Julius explains, he would variously read Roland Barthes, the Viennese modernist Peter Altenberg, and Tahar Ben Jelloun and, as he sometimes spoke "the words in the book out loud to myself," notice "the odd way my voice mingled with the murmur of the French, German, or Dutch radio announcers" (5). Associating St. Augustine's astonishment at the technique of reading silently, Julius proposes that "a book suggests conversation . . . and audible sound is, or should be, natural to that exchange" (5).

Despite its ostensibly mostly European intertextuality, this scene certainly resonates also with major concerns of African diaspora aesthetics. Importantly, I am not suggesting to simply reclassify the novel, which might get me accused of ignoring textual surface (Best and Marcus), or worse, of adhering to essentialist notions of African diaspora aesthetics as a privileged, presumably authentic locus of orality aesthetics. As indicated above, I am, rather, interested in the novel's transcontinental affiliations as the background of what I describe as its critically cosmopolitan worldmaking, whereby "critically" marks the attempt to free cosmopolitanism from its Eurocentric baggage. In

---

2. See, for example, pointedly Mercer 146.

other words, I argue that the novel's intricate narrative form, which enables its complex thematic negotiations of cultural belonging in the contemporary world of uneven globalization, can be conceptualized in terms of multidirectional, layered cultural flows across the Atlantic as well as the Mediterranean.

Elsewhere, I have detailed some of these flows for the context of transnational German literature in terms of *An Aesthetics of Narrative Performance*. With this notion, I designate multifaceted configurations of performative narration techniques that have shaped twentieth- and twenty-first-century European (as well as American) literature at large.[3] However, these techniques have often been excluded from the domain of narrative "proper," not least through racialized associations with "premodern" and "non-European" literature, and in positive terms, they have found much of their early conceptualization in scholarship on African diaspora aesthetics. Foregrounding the aesthetics of narrative performance thus allows me to trace post/modernist European literature's contingent foundations in the transcontinental traffic of colonialism and migration, translation, adaptation, and appropriation. With respect to Cole's novel, which highlights such travels also thematically, a close-up on its African diaspora resonances, supplementing its initial marketing and reception primarily on European ground, seems warranted for balance. More generally, my reading demonstrates the productivity of such a close-up for the conceptual intertwining of narrative theory and critical race studies that composes this collection's goal.

Specifically, most critics missed the significance of the novel's aesthetics of storytelling, or its—decidedly literary, nonclassical—form of call-and-response performance. Based on *Open City*'s ostensibly European intertextuality, reviewers variously characterized the voice of the main character narrator on a scale from Sebaldian erudite commentary (implying highly overt narration) to "meandering stream-of-consciousness narrative" (that is, narrator invisibility?) or, puzzlingly, foregrounded both the text's diary-style immediacy and the narrator's "slightly god-like distance" (Kakutani; Rockwell). Then, they wondered how Julius's evidently authoritative account is undone through the disclosure of his apparent unreliability at the end of the novel, when his life story is shattered by a charge of rape. While the disclosure of that charge is doubtlessly crucial for the reader's experience, I argue that these diverging categorizations of the novel's narration can be displaced through a positive account of its multivoicedness.[4] This multivoicedness characterizes

---

3. With a focus specifically on (secondary) orality in contemporary literature, see Kacandes.

4. In European literary theory, Mikhail Bakhtin, of course, provides another conceptual reference point.

both the narrator's own telling and the interplay between his voice and that of a range of diegetic respondents, as well as the reader, whose active involvement in the sense-making process is not invited through direct address in Cole's emphatically literary development of narrative call-and-response performance, but through the narrator's implicit poetological commentary. In the spirit of Julius's programmatic description of a book as a "conversation," the novel's interplay of voices favors an ongoing process of sense-making over any achievement of closure, be it by virtue of narrator authority or via his deauthorization through an unreliability diagnosis (Callahan 15).[5] In and beyond Lanser's categories, the model of conversation allows me to reconceptualize narrative authority beyond the diagnosis of its absence on the one hand, and its reassertion on the other hand, whereby absence has been theorized alternatively through a history of racist deauthorization or the post/modernist critique of narrative authority as such, and reassertion alternatively understood as liberating or problematic (*Fictions of Authority* 198). Instead, the model of conversation describes a relational process of nonsovereign agency in contouring "the first-person narrator as a locus of empowerment, contest, and collaboration" (Jablon 124). Importantly, Cole's twenty-first-century form of call-and-response does not postulate any community as given, but rather investigates the conditions of community in and for contemporary society.[6]

Most conspicuously, the (virtual) opening of the narrator's individual consciousness into intersubjective experience is dramatized in Julius's encounter with a Haitian shoe shiner "in the underground catacombs of Penn Station" (70). Over several pages, the shoe shiner's first-person direct narrative of having fled Boukmann and his army and later having purchased his freedom alternates with Julius's account, without demarcating quotation marks. Afterwards, Julius normalizes the initially disorienting sequence for the reader by commenting on the "afternoon, during which I had flitted in and out of myself, when time became elastic and voices cut out of the past into the present" (74). Nonetheless, it stands out—as, possibly, another poetological signpost—in an otherwise largely realist process of narration. In less conspicuous ways, however, the voices of other characters momentarily also assert themselves—ranging from Julius's former literature professor and a troubled Turkish patient to a Belgian airplane acquaintance, Dr. Maillotte (13–14, 55–56, 88–93). Compared to Sebald's—principally equally multivoiced—narrative signature, Cole's narrative performance is less ostensibly mediated, and in effect less distancing. In

---

5. On conversation, see also Kacandes xiii; on the "radical" democracy inherent in call-and-response, see Wideman in Baker.

6. On storytelling as a "call . . . for community" in African American literature, see Kacandes 39.

Sebald, extensive citations of other texts, the obsessively repeated markers of layered telling (e.g., the characteristic "Austerlitz said" following virtually every first-person pronoun or feeling report) and the foregrounding of the narrator as witness more than experiential focus in his own right insistently separate the reader from the related experiences and thematize memory as the evocation of what is irrevocably past (*Austerlitz*; see also *Die Ausgewanderten*). Importantly, there is no immediacy conceit in Cole, either: the main narrative voice overall remains visible and does not pretend to a situation of oral communication with the reader. However, Cole's less rigorously artificialized process of telling allows his readers to get closer to the narrator's present experiences, including their penetration by the past. In this way, the novel enables us to participate in the narrator's ongoing processes of orientation and nonsovereign worldmaking.

The fact that Cole's narrator, in contrast to Sebald's characteristic voices, refrains from providing extensive summaries of the books he reads does not make intertextual references any less significant. It does, however, make them more open-ended—material for conversation rather than occasion for authoritative elaboration. Exemplarily, this can be shown for the book that perhaps resonates already in the novel's title, *Open City*. While its literal reference is to the World War II status of Brussels, where Julius travels roughly at the center of the (otherwise New York–based) novel (97), the title's metaphorical play simultaneously initiates the novel's discussion of cosmopolitanism. In Brussels, Julius hopes to reconnect with his German grandmother but, failing to locate her, instead meets the Moroccan immigrant, philosopher, and Internet café attendant Farouq. In a tense discussion in a smoky bar, Farouq and his Marxist friend Khalil provoke Julius's New York sensibilities by not fully distancing themselves from Islamist radicalisms. Upon his return home, Julius responds by sending Farouq a copy of Kwame Anthony Appiah's 2006 *Cosmopolitanism*. Although the explicit reference to this title thus comes late in the novel, and remains brief, I argue that the dialogue with Appiah shapes the novel throughout and that the gesture of sending the book indexes Cole's novelistic intervention—perhaps if not least in "displacing" its philosophical content. Thus, *Open City* critically reconfigures cosmopolitanism not through rigorously formalized scholarly discourse but through conversation, that is, contextualized, embodied, intersubjective worldmaking. Intriguingly, Appiah himself similarly programmatically highlights the notion of "conversation" also in its older meaning, "of living together" (xix)—and we can thus suspect a first hint at Appiah already in *Open City*'s introductory poetological reference to the model of conversation.

Appiah's book is the only scholarly work on the topic explicitly quoted in the novel, but not Cole's only possible theoretical reference point: concepts of cosmopolitanism have gained new prominence since the millennium. This twenty-first-century return to the ancient notion, redeveloped for modernity by Immanuel Kant, can be contextualized as part of broader trends toward more positive articulations of collective identity, belonging, and, in Gilroy's words, "conviviality" (*Postcolonial Melancholy* 8). While these trends have gained traction in response to September 11 and the following wars, they started to emerge already at the end of the twentieth century, arguably from longer-standing discontents with "postmodern," and specifically postcolonial, insistences on the socio-symbolic regimes of difference and violence. In scholarship as well as the larger public sphere, this "affirmative" turn has taken the form of rearticulations, on the one hand, of universalism, and of belonging and tradition on smaller scales of collectivity, on the other.[7] Appiah's *Cosmopolitanism,* in fact, combines both of these moves: tempering his plea for "universal concern" with the "respect for legitimate difference," he argues for a "partial cosmopolitanism" (Appiah xv, xvii). Explicitly positioning his intervention against the War on Terror backdrop, Appiah sets out to make it "harder to think of the world as divided between the West and the Rest" through an ethics of conversation about values, without "a promise of final agreement" (xxi, 44). In more poetic terms (adapted from the nineteenth-century traveler Sir Richard Francis Burton), Appiah characterizes the cosmopolitan attitude through the metaphor of "the shattered mirror—each shard of which reflects one part of a complex truth" (8). Rather than holding on to our shard in relativistic resignation, however (as postmodern skeptics might do), Appiah asks us to sort through the pieces in an ongoing assessment of situational truth.

Cole's novel explores the productive potential of Appiah's intervention—and the described contemporary reorientations more generally—but simultaneously insists on the continued weight of the "negativities" threatened to be left unattended by these twenty-first-century turns: namely, the historical legacies of racism, slavery, colonialism, and the Holocaust, all of which figure prominently in *Open City*. In some respects, *Open City*'s complex configuration of cultural encounters virtually unfolds the philosophy of Appiah, who, in turn, compares conversation to "the sort of imaginative engagement you get when you read a novel" and underscores that "evaluating stories together" is "one of the central human ways of learning to align our responses to the world" (85, 29). In this spirit, Cole's reader may be engaged in a conversation with Julius, as he evaluates the stories he encounters in navigating the complex

---

7. For more detail, see my "Configuring Affect."

worlds of his Manhattan home, the Nigerian childhood of his memory, and post-9/11 Brussels.

In many passages of the novel, Julius himself acts as an exemplary cosmopolitan, in Appiah's sense, by ceding ground to other voices but also making his own heard in an explicitly evaluative, but cautious and sometimes self-corrective, rather than definite, fashion. For example, Julius repeatedly readjusts his take on Farouq: he balances initial admiration ("Farouq spoke without the faintest air of agitation") with more distanced evaluation ("He, too, was in the grip of rage and rhetoric) (104, 107), but he also situates his own gestures of distancing with contextualizing self-analysis. Thus, Julius calls Farouq's friend Khalil an "extremist" when Khalil qualifies his condemnation of the September 11 attacks with expressed understanding for "why they did it," but adds—in his narrator function—that he was playing "the outraged American" because "anger" was "easier to handle than sorrow" (120). While Julius diegetically performs the confrontational dynamics of (majority U.S.) public discourse here but notices his discrepant affective response, he later censors his own emotional alignment with collective political discourse. When Farouq develops his anti-Zionist stance on Palestine through slippage into anti-Semitic tropes about Jewish business skills, Julius suppresses his urge to tell Farouq "that, in the States, we were particularly wary of strong criticism of Israel because it could become anti-Semitic," suspecting that "my own fear of anti-Semitism, like my fear of racism, had through long practice become prerational" (124).

This latter moment of affective self-censorship, however, also marks the anti-conversational turn that the exchange with Farouq now takes: instead of responding at all, Julius decides to "save" his "breath" (124). When he later sends Farouq the copy of Appiah's book, he indirectly continues the conversation—but does the gift confirm a successful, if at moments uncomfortably agonistic, cosmopolitan exchange? Or does Julius—for whom Farouq's face, in the midst of their discussion, "resolved itself" into that of "the young Vito Corleone" in *The Godfather II* (121–29)—indirectly communicate that he ultimately read his interlocutor as one of Appiah's Islamist *counter*-cosmopolitans, whose universalism violates the cosmopolitan commitments to pluralism and fallibilism? ("Their mirror is not shattered, it is whole" [Appiah 145].) Julius does not answer this question for us; although explicitly given, his rationale for the gift remains underdetermined: "The memory of my conversations with him had convinced me to send him . . . Appiah's *Cosmopolitanism*" (186).

As perhaps suggested by the diverging critical assessments of Julius's narration discussed above, this evaluative restraint is as indicative of his overall voice as his active engagement in the sense-making process. Another indirect poetological comment at the outset of the novel may point to the significance of this aspect of Julius's narration. On his relationship with his retired literature professor, Julius says: "I learned the art of listening from him, and the ability to trace out a story from what was omitted" (9). Drawing on James Phelan's investigations into "the complexities of the indirect art of character narration," the "proper" narratologist inside myself grasps for taxonomical precision: I want to detail that Cole's novel has elements of "restricted narration" (that is, recording without evaluation), if not "suppressed narration" (where even the implied author would fail to deliver evaluation), and decide where exactly Julius underevaluates, underreads (that is, lacks the knowledge needed for a full evaluation), or even underreports (*Living to Tell* 1, 29, 138, 51). Or should the unreliability diagnosis inherent in the latter descriptions be challenged by instead categorizing some of Julius's actions as "reliable *elliptical narration*"—that is, postulating that he himself wants us to fill the gaps he leaves? (52).

Julius indirectly adds to such explorations when he diagnoses small instances, "not of unreliability, but of a certain imperfection in Farouq's" narrative performance (114).[8] But perhaps, the dialogue between rhetorical narratology and African diaspora aesthetics suggested here can reorient these various taxonomical energies. Like Julius's own contribution to the narratological endeavor, Phelan's rhetorical model demonstrates ethical sensibility about the limits of human agency, and it prepares the ground also for my own suggestion by insisting that un/reliability is not a binary opposition, but unfolds on a wide spectrum (*Living to Tell,* 53). Nonetheless, Phelan's model remains tied to standards of (authorial, and indirectly also narrational) "control," individual sovereignty, and ethical certainty, against which the various forms of unreliability fall morally short (*Living to Tell* 71, 151).[9] Instead, the notion of a dialogic call-and-response process underlines the quintessentially nonsovereign nature of both subjectivity and narration, as produced in the social flows of circulating affects, words, and positions (see Ahmed, *Cultural*

---

8. With yet another twist and on a different level, Cole himself, on the occasion of a visit to my home university, responded to an open-ended question about his relationship to Julius with the assertion that while there is distance (not least in political terms), Julius was not "unreliable" but rather "not that different from us" in his efforts at sense-making (Cole, in colloquium discussion, Indiana University, Bloomington, 2 April 2015). While the flesh-and-blood author does not have to have the last word in the interpretative conversation, either, his wording seems consonant with my reading.

9. In the case of Cole's novel, the formal diagnosis of Julius's unreliability is, in particular, closely (and, in the reader's experience, perhaps appropriately) linked to our moral judgment of him for the apparent sexual assault (see below for a more detailed discussion). On the interplay between interpretative, ethical, and aesthetic judgments in the process of reading, see Phelan, *Experiencing Fiction.*

Politics). In the ongoing processes of telling, listening, challenging or filling in, the exchange with a narrator who will not, or cannot, do all the work for us but does not, therefore, categorically fail, produces nonfinal accounts inviting ongoing (re)evaluations.

In part, this account of Julius's narration still resonates with Appiah's philosophy (itself inflected by African diaspora aesthetics): rather than providing any pretense to an unshattered mirror, Julius's narrative demands engaged puzzle activity with some ill-fitting shards from us. However, I argue that Julius's nonsovereign narration also becomes a vehicle for evaluating Appiah's theoretical narrative, which fails to adequately account for important dimensions of human nonsovereignty. This critique aligns the novel, in part, with more skeptical perspectives on cosmopolitanism's claims, cautioning us about the concept's implication into the histories of colonialism and its association with "elite Western subjects" formed by "European bourgeois culture" along its gendered ideals of sovereignty (Ong, *Flexible Citizenship* 14; ca. *Neoliberalism as Exception* 17–18). Alternatively, the novel unfolds a "critical cosmopolitanism," which accounts for the "inescapabilities and particularities of places, characters, historical trajectories" (Rabinow qtd. in Ong, *Flexible Citizenship* 14). Specifically, Appiah undertheorizes the crucial legacies of power and violence in the formation (and disruption) of cultural belonging: he foregrounds neither histories of trauma nor (with Ann Cvetkovich) "public feelings," that is, the "affective legacy of the racialized histories of genocide, slavery, colonization, and migration" not generally at the center of trauma theory (175). In Appiah's (more or less Wittgensteinian) narrative, in contrast, affects and attachments primarily figure as the "deep *habits*" by which cultural affiliations acquire their relative stability (Appiah 84).[10] When Appiah presents Muslim notions of gender as his example for these habits, and identifies them as one of the "roots" of Islamism, he remains trapped in a moderate version of the very "culture clash" concepts he set out to overcome (82).

Julius and Farouq do not discuss gender, but the staging of their encounter theorizes cultural orientation—including Farouq's oppositional belief in cultural "difference" (114)—as a result of power and violence rather than tradition or habit. In engaging Appiah, the novel thus confronts his commitment to building a shared world through the "exercise of reason" with the weight of trauma and public feelings in (what Appiah himself calls) the "intimate texture of our everyday lives" (Appiah 170, 83). When Julius first arrives in Brussels, he hesitates to evaluate the racial tensions he observes, perhaps because he wants to believe the claim to the city's "color-blind[ness]" articulated by

---

10. For the Wittgensteinian bent, see more generally chapter 2.

his majority-Belgian plane acquaintance, Dr. Maillotte, whose age and gender associate her with the grandmother Julius came to locate (89; ca. 98–99). But immediately after his first conversation with Farouq, Julius corrects himself in imagining the impact of the stares Farouq gets on the trams (106). When their conversation later reaches its ideological impasse, Julius instead asks about Farouq's life, and Farouq tells him how his European "dream," including his academic ambition of becoming "the next Edward Said," was crushed: right after September 11, his MA thesis in critical theory at the University of Brussels was rejected on (unspecified) grounds of plagiarism, making him suspect that "they were punishing me for world events in which I had played no role" (122, 128). After several paragraphs that feature Farouq's voice uninterruptedly, Julius picks up his narration by commenting: "The wound ran deep. How many would-be radicals, just like him, had been formed on just such a slight?" (129).

Despite the judgment inherent in Julius's response, the textual interplay of voices thus reinforces the centrality of (in Sara Ahmed's words) "histories that hurt" ("Happy Objects" 50). While Julius finds himself unable to fully relate, he now confronts Dr. Maillotte about her color-blindness claim by citing Farouq's experience and insists against her racist generalizations about "such people" that Farouq's "hurt is genuine" (143). No less importantly, Julius's nonsovereign narration also enables the reader to trace how his own wounds inflect his distancing gestures. The first of these (on Farouq being "in the grip of rage and rhetoric") had followed Julius's realization that he "was in a situation not so radically different from Farouq's," in that his "presentation" as "the dark, unsmiling, solitary stranger" made him a target for racist projections (106–7). With a wording foreshadowing the disclosure at the end of the novel, he adds: "I could, in the wrong place, be taken for a rapist" (106). In the face of their shared experience of racism, however, Farouq and Julius have taken opposite routes. While Farouq politicizes cultural difference—if in a way ironically aligning him more with Appiah than with the fundamentalism Julius suspects[11]—Julius resists all uncomplicated claims to collective identity. Repeatedly, he is angered by cabdrivers, museum guards, or—at the occasion of mailing Appiah's book—the postal clerk insisting on their shared African-ness (40, 53, 186–87).

For one reviewer, Julius's response in these situations indicates "a posture of a superior mind" and "refusal to engage the world" that he identifies with the "cosmopolitanism" of both Cole and Appiah (Falk para. 13). To be sure, advocates of cosmopolitanism have defended the notion against this "popular" mistaking of it as "an elite form of rootlessness and a state of detachment,"

---

11. Farouq emphasizes individuality, historicity, and the textuality of the Qu'ran (see 126–27) but simultaneously the relative autonomy of culture (e.g., 112).

insisting that the cosmopolitan is "nowhere a stranger" but imagines "a universal circle of belonging" (Cheah 487). The novel complicates both of these assertions. While Julius in some respects does remain a stranger in his various environments, the reviewer's charge is unfair to him insofar as he engages with dissenting positions—for example, by accompanying his own distancing from Farouq with the question whether "having no causes" was "not an ethical lapse graver than rage itself" (107). But the reviewer's charge also fails to account for how Julius's dialogic, nonsovereign narration calls on *us* to reflect on *his* stance, investigating his reluctance to identify. Julius himself diagnoses his negative feelings toward the cabdriver insisting on their shared Africanness as "the anger of a shattered repose" (141). In part guided by him, in part beyond his insights, the novel's sustained conversation enables us to position his political detachment as a defense mechanism—and legacy of disaffection—rather than an ideal.

Against the backdrop also of Julius's professional research on "affective disorders in the elderly," the novel pursues the genealogies of his hurt, and disturbances of his sense of belonging, back to his Nigerian childhood shaped by "a sense of being different" by virtue of his name, passport, and (lighter) skin color (7, 78), as well as by his mother's emotional withdrawals and their subsequent estrangement, which fuels Julius's present longing for his mother's own estranged mother in Brussels, but simultaneously his inability to actually connect with her. Although unable to spell out the "inchoate" reasons for these broken connections, Julius relates them back to his mother's postwar German childhood, suspecting that he himself is "in some odd way, . . . the unaware continuation of" her "experiences, sensations, desires" (34, 80). His mother's childhood story is a majority German "story of suffering," of rubble and possible rape by Red Army soldiers, a life overshadowed by the "rule" to "refrain from speaking" about the "horrors" of war and the Holocaust (79–80). Julius's own life story, then, unfolds at the intersection of dramatically heterogeneous histories of trauma and public feelings—legacies that confound dichotomies between victims and perpetrators. To the novel's advantage, Julius's inability to fully spell out the connections prevents any grand-scale gestures of parallelization or historical allegory. More cautiously, his tentative, nonsovereign narration links the German context to "touching tales" of violence in postcolonial Nigeria,[12] where the adolescent tried to find "some sense of belonging" at the military academy with its reputation for discipline—and a teacher nicknamed "Hitler" (81–82).

At the end of the novel, Julius's layered positional implication into these transnational histories of violence is dramatized by—although not short-cir-

---

12. On the concept of "touching tales," see Adelson 21.

cuited into—the above-mentioned charge of rape: upon meeting him in New York, Moji, the sister of a childhood friend, accuses Julius of having "forced" himself on her at a party as a drunk fourteen-year-old (244). Without diminishing the significance of all of the other (individual and collective) hi/stories of violence that may have, directly and indirectly, contributed to his affective withdrawals, the disclosure of this piece of information about the narrator's past adds an emotionally dramatic, formally intricate layer to the novel's complex investigations, inviting us to foreground our ongoing reflections also on the affectivity of Julius's narration. His belated disclosure of Moji's charge indicates his struggle with its impact on "the story of my life": "we are," as he words it apologetically, "not the villains of our own stories" (243). While thoroughly nonsovereign, however, Julius does himself ethically engage with the situation: cautiously, he authorizes Moji's charge by asserting that, in contrast to all the "bad stories" he hears from his patients, she had told it "as if, with all her being, she were certain of its accuracy" (243–44). In fact, the reader may conclude that Julius himself is the patient here, on whose narrative the psychiatrist depends (according to Julius's professional reflections a few pages earlier), but whose "lens" itself may be "symptomatic" (238). Julius's pessimistic conclusion that most psychiatrist work "was a blind spot so broad that it had taken over most of the eye" then seems to present an indirect indication of his own unreliability, as diagnosed by himself (239). But our interpretative conversation does not have to stop at this juncture of heightened self-reflexivity and looming paradox. In fact, the performance of Julius's narration does offer an alternative to the dilemma of expert discourse. Although he is, at the time of narration, unable to fully integrate Moji's story with his own account, his dialogic discourse makes room for it: in eventually reporting on what she said, he slips into free indirect discourse and then cedes narrative authority to her direct speech for a couple of paragraphs. Moji's concluding question to Julius, "Will you say something?" (245), to be sure, remains unanswered. The reader never learns what, if anything, Julius himself remembers of the event. While the dramatic impact of Moji's charge on him indicates a sense of guilt, it is up to us to spell out ethical judgment in the absence of positive evidence, and against the background of the then-adolescent's complex life story.

The question of personal agency vis-à-vis a legacy of public feelings is dramatized in a different context, when in an earlier conversation Moji expresses empathy for Julius's African American friend by declaring that the "racist structure of this country is crazy-making," and the friend's girlfriend provokes shared laughter with her spontaneous response, "Oh man . . . don't give him excuses" (203). Drawing our attention to both connections and gaps between political structure, personal history, and agency, the novel's nonsovereign, polyvocal worldmaking does not suspend judgment, but perhaps invites us to keep it "provisional, hesitant, and as kind as possible," in line with Julius's respective description of "what psychiatry really ought to be about" (208). Julius then associates Sigmund Freud here, whom he claims to only read for "literary truths," but whose "writings on grief and loss, I found, remained useful" (208). In the twenty-first century, Freud's confident practice of "symptomatic reading" has lost its cultural authority, perhaps not least via modernity's racist developments of the "theory of Signs," or hermeneutic tradition, that Julius also associates with the diagnostic enterprise (237). However, Cole's intricate poetics of hints, associations, and gaps also refuses to settle for the "surface reading" developed as a programmatic alternative to symptomatic reading in contemporary literary studies (Best and Marcus). Instead, the novel invites a provisional practice of sense-making faithful to the psychoanalytic ethos of attending to the psychic remnants of the past: with Freud, Julius underscores the importance of "mourning" vis-à-vis melancholic "incorporation," which he suspects is responsible for the "neatness of the line we had drawn around the catastrophic events of 2001" (208–9).

Time and again muddling the neatness of historical lines, Julius's meandering narration connects the trauma of September 2001 with the earlier "erasure[s]" on the site of the World Trade Center buildings, which "was a palimpsest, as was all the city," recalling histories of immigration as well as the "echo across centuries, of slavery" (58–59, 221). Hoping "to find the line that connected me to my own part in these stories," Julius keeps refusing easy answers, but in a "less impatient" mood retracts his resistance against collective identifications, in acknowledging the significance of shared historical experience and its representation: "Ellis Island was a symbol mostly for European refugees. Blacks, 'we blacks,' had known rougher ports of entry: this, I could admit to myself now . . . was what the cabdriver had meant" (59, 55). Later, the novel concludes with the narrator's reflections on the "fatally disoriented birds" that had found their death at the Statue of Liberty during its service as a lighthouse, which, in the novel's intricate web of resonances, reconnects to Julius's opening thoughts on "bird migrations" as "the miracle of natural immigration" (258, 1–2). For the reader attentive to these connections, the bleak closing scene (indicative also of Julius's unresolved personal crisis) · opens onto the ongoing task of attending to the histories indexed by the city's rougher ports of entry.

The difficulty of closure is played through at the occasion of Julius attending a Berlin Philharmonic Orchestra performance of Mahler's *Ninth Symphony*—the last completed symphony of this "master of the ends of symphonies"—in Carnegie Hall preceding Julius's concluding trip to the Statue of Liberty (250). His concert experience is framed by both his thoughts on the presence of anti-Semitism in Mahler's life and his own discomfort with the almost exclusively white audience, to which he responds with "a quick complex series of negotiations: chiding myself for even seeing it, lamenting the reminders of how divided our life still remains, being annoyed" at the inescapability of these thoughts (251). If "Mahler's music" itself is, as Julius insists in response to the looks he gets in the bathroom line, "not white, or black," this emphatic cosmopolitan affirmation attains its concrete contours in his subsequent comparison of "the first movement" to a "great ship slipping out of port"—onto the (not just) black-and-white Atlantic (252). The multidirectional process of cultural appropriation and exchange, through which my reading has characterized the novel's aesthetics, finds its diegetic echo in the ways in which Julius, listening with "both" his "mind and" his "body," discovers "new . . . points of emphasis and articulation" in Simon Rattle's performance of Mahler's score (252). Rattle "was also communicating—at least to me, as a longtime partisan of that music—with other performers, . . . mostly European men, many of them now dead" but each "connected to a specific mood and inflection . . . on the symphony's vast score" (252–53). As Julius's nonsovereign, polyvocal narrative performance unfolds the novel's open-ended process of affective-cognitive worldmaking, it traces the complexities of dis/connection and non/belonging in the contemporary world, in which the legacies of modern regimes of racialized violence no longer easily translate into collective identities, but—as "histories that hurt" (Ahmed, "Happy Objects" 50)—nonetheless form crucial building blocks of the narrator's, and his interlocutors', worldmaking. While this challenge does not undo the promise of a cosmopolitan ethics, it underlines the importance of anchoring this ethics in sustained attention to the legacies of division and violence that continue to haunt its dreams.

CHAPTER 13

Caribbean Book Nerds

Recentering to Possible Worlds in Judith Cofer and Junot Díaz

DEBORAH NOEL

> The barrier between worlds is not airtight.[1]
> —Kendall Walton

IN HIS "plea for narrative" in the *Michigan Law Review* in 1989, Richard Delgado observes: "Oppressed groups have known instinctively that stories are an essential tool to their own survival and liberation" ("Storytelling" 2436). When we combine elements from stories and our "current reality," he argues, "we may construct a new world richer than our own" (2415). Stories enable us not only to *examine* our world but also to *imagine* it. David Herman transforms "story" into a verb in *Storytelling and the Sciences of the Mind* (2013). "Storying the world" involves using narrative "to make sense of what is going on" (Herman 228). As we study the role of narrative in human survival, liberation and sense-making, we should consider how the activities of reading and writing themselves have been depicted. *The Latin Deli* by Judith Cofer and *The Brief Wondrous Life of Oscar Wao* by Junot Díaz present fiction, myth, and fantasy as *sources* and not simply *reflections* of cultural identities. *The Latin Deli* offers multiple female perspectives on the Puerto Rican American experience in the mid-twentieth century through poems, fiction, creative nonfiction, and essays largely drawing on Judith Cofer's own experiences, and several narratives in the collection feature young girls learning to cope with life as Latina teens in Paterson, New Jersey. Throughout the collection, these girls confront the trials of puberty and cultural rifts within the family and community; they also consistently identify as bookish outsiders who turn to fantasy for comfort and inspiration. *The Brief Wondrous Life of Oscar Wao* explores multi-

---

1. Walton, "How Remote Are Fictional Worlds from the Real World?" 22.

ple generations of the Cabral family, but Oscar holds center stage while the narrators work through Oscar's family biography, blending history, folklore, family legend, personal experience, and myth. The primary narrator and fictional author, Yunior, recognizes Oscar as a book nerd early on and identifies this nerdiness as both a fatal flaw and, paradoxically, a great strength. While Cofer's and Díaz's narratives are formally and structurally different, their similarities are striking: these narratives feature central characters who defy racial and gender stereotypes and align themselves with intellectual cultures construed as antithetical to sexual and social power. They also share some significant cultural markers in their views from the diaspora in twentieth-century immigrant Caribbean communities of New Jersey. Both are situated historically and both involve autobiographical elements; Díaz and Cofer use their texts' generic hybridity and the voices of their narrators to position their main characters among a network of influences that shape their lives, including, especially, their beloved books. As they navigate life in the United States from young childhood to adulthood, these protagonists experience radical shifts away from the ideological orientations of their parents and social groups and forge unique identities in the fires of discovery, conflict, isolation, and purpose. Díaz's and Cofer's "book nerds" cope and sometimes thrive through their reliance on fantasy and science fiction narratives that are major sources of their personal values even as their immersion in books causes social and familial isolation.

Some concepts from possible worlds[2] theories provide useful ways to explore character-readers and writers. According to Marie-Laure Ryan, while writing, the author "relocates to what is for us a mere possible world, and makes it the center of an alternative system of reality" (*Possible Worlds* 22). When a reader becomes totally immersed in a novel, it is the result of a "recentering" to the possible worlds established in that narrative, which temporarily cuts that reader off from the "actual world." "For the duration of our immersion in a work of fiction," Ryan writes, "the realm of possibilities is thus recentered around the sphere which the narrator presents as the actual world. This recentering pushes the reader into a new system of actuality and possibility. As a traveler to this system, the reader of fiction discovers not only a new actual world, but a variety of [alternative possible worlds] revolving around it" (22). Furthermore, when characters think, dream, and read, they become travelers themselves and access points to yet more systems:

---

2. Marie-Laure Ryan describes the origins and applications of these theories to narrative studies in the "Possible Worlds" in *the living handbook of narratology* <http://www.lhn.uni -hamburg.de/article/possible-worlds>.

Just as we manipulate possible worlds through mental operations, so do the inhabitants of fictional universes: their actual world is reflected in their knowledge and beliefs, corrected in their wishes, replaced by a new reality in their dreams and hallucinations. Through counterfactual thinking they reflect on how things might have been, through plans and projections they contemplate things that still have a chance to be, and through the act of making up fictional stories they recenter their universe into what is for them a second-order, and for us a third-order, system of reality. (22)

The complicated recursions described here seem to open up endless possible worlds. Ryan elevates fantasy worlds formed by "dreams, hallucinations, fantasies and fictional stories" to the status of separate universes because they are modal systems themselves (Ryan, *Possible Worlds* 119). Readers who recenter to these universes "have at their disposal the entire array of world-creating activities: the characters in a dream may dream, the heroes of fictional fictions may write fictions. This type of recursive embedding . . . does not propose ever new points of view on the same system, but transports the experiencer to ever new realities" (119).

Possibilities that may be limited by a test of plausibility in realistic narratives are readily available in speculative fiction. But, just as the possibilities proliferate, so does the text require a more radical recentering. During his discussion of possible worlds theory in *Basic Elements of Narrative*, David Herman observes: "The world evoked by the text may be more or less accessible to the world(s) in which that narrative is produced and interpreted" (114). When interpreters identify a narrative as fantastic or otherworldly, they "engage in strategies for worldmaking that are not fully continuous with those used to make sense of their everyday experience." (114). Such strategies may be honed through continuous encounters with fantasy universes, which could explain why avid fans of speculative fiction can more easily slip into such narratives and become fully immersed. Like seasoned travelers, they know what to pack and how to reorient themselves in that new place. They may be what Robyn Warhol calls "susceptible readers," or readers who are more than willing "to engage in the set of emotional exercises set out in a narrative" (*Narrative Theory* 148). In the case of speculative fiction readers, susceptibility may be their most remarkable and notorious characteristic, having produced whole subcultures of avid fans willing to dress as and even speak in the fictional languages of their favorite characters, as Díaz's Oscar does. Readers lacking in the necessary strategies or affinities may not be susceptible, and they may find it much more difficult to recenter to a fantasy universe, much less navigate its worlds with pleasure. Still other readers may be drawn to fantasy precisely *because* it requires a significant departure, as with Cofer's and Díaz's book nerds, whose familial and social worlds are often hostile and alienating. Reading speculative fiction, for some, is not only an engaging pastime but also an essential exit, the opening of crucial alternatives.

As characters navigate their private and text-actual-worlds,[3] they invariably make decisions and engage in behaviors that reflect the sensibilities, goals, and values of their private worlds. Those behaviors that are "indispensable" to the plot may be labeled *moves*. Building on Thomas Pavel's use of the term,[4] Ryan describes moves as actions "with a high priority goal and a high risk of failure" (*Possible Worlds* 130). The goal of character moves is the alignment of their private worlds with the text-actual-world, and misalignment is a major source of conflict. When a character's private possible worlds differ substantially from the text-actual-world, the challenge of alignment is amplified. This accounting of reading transforms a potentially and stereotypically passive "move," what I'll call the "move to reading," into a meaningful imaginative and performative activity closely related to what Herman calls "storying the world," or deploying narrative as a "resource for sense-making" (*Storytelling* 23). The bibliophile characters featured in *The Latin Deli* and *Oscar Wao* identify with literary subcultures as a means of resistance against cultural hegemony and tradition. They become immersed in alternative possible worlds, and in the process, they imagine possible selves in order to cope with their existence in hostile text-actual-worlds. In her work on "Storyworld Possible Selves," M. Angeles Martínez expands theories of narrative immersion via cognitive narrative theory and blending theory.[5] One type of storyworld possible self, according to Martínez, is the "desired possible self," those selves that "have not been confirmed by social experience," such as "the successful self, the loved self, the adventurer self, or the hero self" (Martínez 123). Readers may be drawn to narratives that introduce or reaffirm an aspirational possible self, and such narratives often have escapist qualities. Sterling Bland explores how identity, which is "plural and entirely a function of contextual suitability," must be "continuously reassembled" through the sense-making process of narration in Ellison's *The Invisible Man* (139 in this volume). As Cofer's and Díaz's book nerds compare and contrast the cultural identities prescribed by dominant social forces with the possibilities they find in fiction, they learn to

---

3. Ryan uses the phrase "text-actual-world" to reference the primary world in any narrative.

4. See Pavel's 1980 "Narrative Domains."

5. As a source for blending theory, Martínez cites Giles Fauconnier and Mark Turner, *The Way We Think: Conceptual Blending and the Mind's Hidden Complexities* (New York: Basic Books, 2002).

cope with difference and to reconfigure their values. Their move to reading is both a defensive *choice* and a productive alternative, and as these characters "reassemble" themselves and their worlds, they establish alternative "rules"[6] by which actual readers may judge subsequent moves.

In *The Latin Deli*, the stories about girlhood may be labeled fiction (as in "American History," "Not for Sale"), creative nonfiction ("Advanced Biology"), and essay-memoir ("The Paterson Public Library," "The Story of My Body"), yet particular features of these narratives make generic distinctions especially complicated; they feature extradiegetic-homodiegetic narrators with nearly identical characteristics as intellectual Puerto Rican women looking back on their bookish adolescence during the middle of the twentieth century in Paterson, New Jersey. In effect, Cofer sets up a generic continuum in this collection, presenting some narratives as closer to the facts of her own history than others but none very remote from her life. Treating these particular works from *The Latin Deli* collectively as narratives enables scholars to bypass some of the problems introduced by Cofer's memoir-fiction continuum through focusing on features of narrative and setting aside, if temporarily, problems introduced by generic labels. The differences among the narrators are barely perceptible. By bringing together this group of narratives in *The Latin Deli*, Cofer invites readers to treat them as a story cycle that explores the tension arising when the private worlds of a certain character type are frequently misaligned with the text-actual-world.

In the book nerd narratives of *The Latin Deli*, particular conflicts arise as the private worlds of the narrators clash with those of the teen establishment at the public school and the conservative Catholic Puerto Rican parents. As a student at the local school, the narrator feels alienated from the dominant group due to her body type and skin color, her ethnicity, her personal lifestyle, and ultimately, her values. Her physical body and her sexuality not only defy cultural stereotypes, offering a counterexample to what Cofer has called "the myth of the Latin woman" (Cofer 150), but also limit her power within a social group that prizes size, strength, and conventional, sexualized, and white "good looks." In "American History," she is called "Skinny Bones" (8); in "The Paterson Public Library," she is "the skinny Puerto Rican girl" (131); in "The Story of My Body," she is "Skinny Bones and the Shrimp" (135), "4f" during playground sports at school, "skinny, short, bespectacled" (139). Moreover, the young girl is an academic, a bespectacled bookworm. She lingers in libraries and studies for fun. In "Advanced Biology," she is "considered odd because [she] is one of the few Puerto Ricans on the honor roll" (123). In "American History," she is a

---

6. In "Narrative Domains," Pavel describes "rules" of action and action evaluation.

"straight A student" who is nevertheless excluded from honors classes because English is not her first language (9).

The narrator's already difficult interactions with schoolmates are often complicated by parental prohibitions against certain kinds of socializing, especially as she gets older and wants to date. Her attempts to find allies among the few book nerd peers she encounters are thwarted due to cultural differences. In "American History," for instance, the narrator has "only one source of beauty and light" at her school, and that is her book nerd neighbor, Eugene. From her own private book nook, her fire escape perch on an upper floor of "El Building," she enjoys an alluring view of the only single-family house with a yard in her neighborhood, and therein, she notices, Eugene sits at his kitchen table and "read[s] books for hours" (9). The narrator watches him surreptitiously, and this parallel reading goes on for weeks without Eugene's knowledge, though, to the narrator, this feels like "company" (9). After they meet and bond at school, that "secret sharing" (10) intensifies because they choose the same books from the library. But just as the relationship seems poised to become legitimately social, outside of school, Eugene's mother squelches their study session and library date and effectively ends their relationship, rejecting and othering the narrator with a simple observation. Gesturing toward the narrator's largely immigrant, run-down apartment building, she says, "You live there? . . . I don't know how you people do it. . . . Eugene doesn't want to study with you. . . . I am truly sorry if he told you you could come over" (14–15).

Young book nerd love is thwarted again in "Advanced Biology," and in this case, the stakes are even higher. This is one of several stories in which Cofer charts the book nerd's gradual move away from her parents' deep Catholicism. Cofer frames this clearly autobiographical narrative with a familiar yet enduring question: how can believers "reconcile" "God's Mysterious Ways" with enormous human tragedies, such as the Holocaust? Learning about the persecution and murder of Jews during the Holocaust leads to her "first serious clash" over religious doctrine with her mother. She has this theological dilemma in mind as she embarks on an exciting new relationship with her Jewish "prodigy" of a biology tutor, Ira. This story explores the power of narrative possible worlds to shape human behavior and social institutions on a much grander scale. Cofer ironically reinforces the crucial role of storytelling in meaning-making throughout human history by dramatizing the moment in her life when the narrator first begins to question the veracity of Bible stories. The narrator's passionate tutoring sessions with Ira "becom[e] more exciting with every chapter in his biology book" (125). She and Ira debate a key plot element in human history—how humans reproduce—during the steamy, overdetermined scenes of their library dates. There, giggling uncomfortably, Ira sets the stage for the narrator's dual fall into sexual awareness and skepticism. Due both to her bookish, honor-student profile and the sexual attraction she feels, the narrator finds the coursework in biology and the biology textbook sexy; even a photograph of a fetal pig's "blurry sexual parts" causes her to blush. Using his phallic "number two pencil" and his mastery of the subject matter, Ira usurps the authority of the narrator's mother, and even God's authority, as he delivers his declarations on human reproduction in "the seductive language of the scientific laboratory" (124–25). When the narrator reminds Ira that the Immaculate Conception was an exception to these basic biological rules, she is "totally unprepared for the explosion of laughter" (124). Ira confidently denounces the story of the virgin birth and God, too; the narrator is "both offended and excited by Ira's blasphemy" (124).

Through her relationship with Ira and her education, the narrator becomes sensitized to the salient ontologies of her now much more complicated world. While she begins to view the story of the Virgin Mary's Immaculate Conception as a fiction, her mother's feet remain firmly planted in a world that affirms the reality of that story. For the narrator, the tale is suddenly parallel with other myths and legends, and her mother is revealed as a deep believer in a world made possible only through story. This significant paradigm shift coincides with another social and sexual prohibition from her mother: Ira is both sexually and ideologically dangerous, so her mother forbids relationships with "people who do not have God" (126). In retaliation, the narrator lashes out, ultimately calling her mother a "Nazi," which she views as "the harshest thing [she] could have said to anyone" (127). In a way, this narrative can be read as a cautionary tale about the dangers of dogmatic belief, a reversal of the Garden of Eden story. The narrator's fall into skepticism makes it possible for her to question some foundational stories and certain cultural divisions fundamental to her mother's identity and opens up possibilities that exist beyond her nuclear family's belief system. The framing narrator in this autobiographical story finally reconciles the secular and the sacred worlds by imagining them spatially. Preparing for a trip to visit her mother in Puerto Rico, she decides,

Why not allow Evolution and Eve, Biology and the Virgin Birth? Why not take a vacation from logic, I will not let myself be tempted to remain in the sealed garden of blind faith; I'll stay just long enough to rest myself from the exhausting enterprise of leading the examined life. (129)

In "Not for Sale," the most extreme example of the sexual-social prohibitions in the collection, the narrator is kept indoors by her traditional parents, who tell her that "teenage girls in Puerto Rico did not go out without chaperones . . . they stayed home and helped their mothers and obeyed their fathers" (20). Despite her declarations of independence ("We are in the United States. I am an American Citizen. I speak English better than Spanish and I am older than you were when you got married!"), she remains confined, "an exile in the foreign country of [her] parents' house" (20). As with the other book nerd protagonists, this narrator escapes through stories. "They allowed me to imagine my circumstances as romantic," she explains, "some days I was an Indian princess living in a *zenana*, a house of women, keeping myself pure, being trained for a brilliant future. Other days I was a prisoner: Papillon, preparing myself for my great flight to freedom" (16–17). Her susceptibility to fantasy stories exposes a weakness, though, when the outside world invades their apartment in the form of "the storytelling salesman" (16). Using one of his products, a Scheherazade bedspread, as an excuse to linger with the lonely girl and tell some tales, "El Árabe" ingratiates himself, but he has more to sell than linens and jewelry. He needs an American bride for his son. The narrator, utterly immersed in El Árabe's tales, feels that "the subject" of his son "seem[s] to arise naturally out of the last tale" (18). "Under the spell of his words as he describe[s] a heroic vision of a handsome man," the narrator does not pick up on El Árabe's motive until her father arrives home only to be propositioned: sell me your daughter "for a fair price" (20). It takes an enormous effort for the mortified father to "break through the expert haggler's multilingual stream of offers and descriptions of family wealth," but he manages "an anguished scream of *Not for Sale! Not for Sale!*" (21). As the "dangers" of the outside world, of growing up and facing the challenges of a sexual/marital economy, invade the apartment, it seems as if there is no protecting this young girl from the inevitable future beyond her threshold. Consequently, her father eases his restrictions on her and "learn[s] the word 'yes' in English" (21). But this story occasions a powerful observation made possible by the narrator's narrative competence. Her fascination with "El Árabe's" stories may have made her vulnerable momentarily, but she is not fooled by the implausible endings of fairy tales. She observes, "'Happily ever after' was a loose knot tied on a valuable package" (18). In the end, she makes the stories her own: "On my bed Scheherazade kept telling her stories, which I came to understand would never end—as I had once feared—since it was in my voice that she spoke to me, placing my dreams among hers, weaving them in" (21). By suspending "El Árabe's" intended ending and investing storytelling with a radically different purpose, the narrator foils the marriage plot and substitutes a kinship with the most famous practitioner of survival by storytelling, Scheherazade herself.

When Cofer's book nerd narratives are considered together, it becomes clear that as the narrators recenter to fiction and fantasy, as they "story" the world, they are not only liberated but ultimately empowered. In "Not for Sale," the narrator's stories keep her "from going mad" (16). When she is last at school-yard pick during gym class yet again in "The Story of My Body," she relates, "No wonder I read Wonder Woman comics and had Legion of Super Heroes daydreams. . . . I fantasized about scooping my enemies up by their hair from the playing fields and dumping them on a barren asteroid" (140–41). Although the narrator's initial move to books may be interpreted as a reaction and a retreat, as evidence of her *failure* to align herself with the dominant forces in her actual world, it is equally possible to view the narrator's misalignment as a fortuitous opportunity to discover another constellation of private worlds, one that is ultimately aligned with a subculture strong enough to sustain her through the trials and major transitions of her adolescent life and on into adulthood.

In each of these narratives, the narrator's own private worlds are often woefully misaligned with those of the most influential forces in her life. Her body and her intellect predetermine the sanctioned "moves" within the domain of her public schools, and her parents' insistence that she behave according to traditional Catholic and Puerto Rican rules further curtails her ability to adapt to the youth culture around her. The narrators thereby find themselves within a domain of the excluded in the general world of adolescence depicted in these narratives because they cannot make the available moves that might give them place, power, and value within the dominant social groups. Finding little solace in their text-actual-worlds, each of these narrators turns to the private world that affords the greatest escape, that of fantasy and fiction: "I read to escape and also to connect: you can come back to a book as you cannot always to a person or place you miss. I read and reread favorite books until the characters seemed like relatives or friends I could see when I wanted or needed to see them" (133). Her reading is not merely a default time-passer; rather, it is elevated to a "move" in the Pavel/Ryan sense when it becomes clear that through reading, the narrator makes a conscious turn away from the hostilities of her text-actual-world to engage more fully with the possible worlds inhabiting her books, worlds that offer sustenance for her mind and an escape from her body, which she has learned to undervalue in her social/sexual economy. Furthermore, the move to reading perpetuates central plot elements and conflicts in these narratives. Sometimes this move is enacted defensively; at other points, it is clear that reading has become a way of aligning herself with like-minded characters and differentiating herself from others. And Cofer's book nerd is willing to take enormous risks to protect her access to stories. In "The Paterson Public Library," her desire for books is "strong enough to propel [her] down the dreary streets" to the library despite the fact that a bully, herself humiliated by her comparative failures at school, has assured her that she will be beaten mercilessly if she makes the trip (131). She perseveres because the library is "a Greek temple in the ruins of an American city" (130). It is her "sanctuary," and books represent her "spiritual life" (134). Ultimately, though, the bully carries out her threat, and the narrator is beaten in front of her classmates, who do not intervene. She explains: "To this crowd, it was one of many such violent scenes taking place among the adults and children of people fighting over a rapidly shrinking territory. It happens in the jungle and it happens in the city" (134). This blunt analogy amplifies the importance of "a mental life" and internal spaces, such as those the book nerd finds in stories. And the escape into those internal spaces ultimately serves both a spiritual and a practical purpose as the book nerds in Cofer's narratives (and Cofer herself) turn reading *and* writing into a vocation. Importantly, Cofer acknowledges that this move may not be obvious:

> It requires something like obsessiveness for a young person growing up in an environment where physical labor and physical endurance are the marks of a survivor—as is the case with minority peoples living in large cities. But many of us do manage to discover books. In my case, it may have been what anthropologists call a cultural adaptation. Being physically small, non-English speaking, and always the new kid on the block, I was forced to look for an alternative mode to survival in Paterson. Reading books empowered me. (134)

All of Cofer's book nerd narratives in *The Latin Deli* feature narrators who are, implicitly or explicitly, the writers of their tales, suggesting a direct progression from avid reader to writer and confirming the productive role early reading plays in survival and cultural adaptation. Storying the world as a writer confers even more power: "it was the way I absorbed fantasy in those days that gave me the sense of inner freedom, a feeling of power and the ability to fly that is the main reward of the writer. . . . As I read those stories, I became not only the characters but their creator" (132–33).

While *The Brief Wondrous Life of Oscar Wao* addresses these themes, too, the complicated structure and scope of the novel offer a deeper glimpse into the activity of storying the world. Díaz's narrative exhibits several affinities with *The Latin Deli,* not the least of which is that significant move to reading fiction and fantasy made by a central book nerd character whose physical features and intellectual bent render him "other." But the novel further explores the role of recentering in survival, liberation, and value formation with the added layer of a dramatized narrator book nerd who is also the fictional author. Yunior is a closeted book nerd who outwardly follows what David Herman calls "the dominant social script" (*Basic Elements*). He describes himself as a muscle-bound, macho, womanizing stereotype—a self-described typical Dominican male. Yet his interests in science fiction, fantasy, and writing, as well as his own deep ambivalence about his playboy habits, perfectly position him to offer an insider/outsider view of the main character and ultimate book nerd, Oscar. Since Oscar is only accessed through the filtering lens of the first-person narrators (Yunior and, to a lesser degree, his sister Lola), to fully comprehend the nature of Oscar's recentering to speculative fiction, it is crucial that at least one of these narrators is both fluent in "nerdery" and sympathetic to Oscar's habits and vocation. By virtue of his own frequent allusions to popular and esoteric science fiction and fantasy worlds, Yunior models the kind of nerd who dabbles widely in speculative fiction but suppresses that interest in his everyday life. In his writing, however, Yunior seems open to slippage between the fantasy worlds he and Oscar admire and the text-actual-worlds of New Jersey and the Dominican Republic, which Yunior describes. In fact, as an "author," Yunior makes clear narrative choices that finally reveal his true admiration for Oscar and his ultimate subversion of cultural values and gender stereotypes. Storying Oscar, Yunior learns that the very things that made Oscar outcast also gave Oscar strength.

Looking back on Oscar's life, Yunior identifies him as "a social introvert who trembled with fear during gym class," a guy who "used a lot of huge-sounding words like *indefatigable* and *ubiquitous* when talking to niggers who would barely graduate from high school" (22). He writes that Oscar is "one of those nerds who was always hiding out in the library. . . . His adolescent nerdliness vaporizing any iota of a chance he had for young love" (23). According to Yunior, Oscar believed his central conflict, his inability to find love and lose his virginity, was precipitated by a fateful early "move": ironically, it was Oscar's first and last attempt at being a player, like Yunior. As a child, Oscar was a "Casanova. . . . Because in those days he was (still) a 'normal' Dominican boy raised in a 'typical' Dominican family, his nascent pimp-liness was encouraged by blood and friends alike" (11). When the seven-year-old, charismatic Oscar finds himself in the middle of a love triangle and callously dumps the less attractive girl, "Shazam!—his life start[s] going down the tubes" (16). In the ensuing years, Oscar becomes obese and covered in acne, "too dorky," "too shy," and "too *weird*" (17). The physical manifestation of Oscar's otherness, in the form of his extreme obesity, seems to fulfill the narrative's prophecy: when he botched his first breakup, Oscar triggered his fall from masculine sexual potency into a passive, feminized impotency that would last. As Yunior's plot unfolds, Oscar's significant "moves" are cyclical. He finds "love" and attempts to advance the relationship only to learn that his "girlfriends" regard him as a "girl friend." With each failure to consummate a relationship, he retreats deep into his books, movies, comics, and games— his fantasy worlds. To Yunior, acting as the voice of sexual and social norms, Oscar's obesity and his allegiance to "nerdom" are both cause and evidence of his failure to realize the Latino male potency that should be his birthright; as he moves on to high school and college, friends and family no longer recognize him as male or Dominican.

As a narrator and "author" of Oscar's biography, Yunior himself seems deeply sympathetic to Oscar's values and unwilling or unable to separate Oscar's life story from fantasy. From his introduction to the very end, Yunior wonders whether Oscar's story fits into a larger mythology with some claim on the truth. Pavel uses the term "salient structures" to describe those narratives wherein a dual ontology obtains (*Fictional Worlds*). Although the gritty realist in Yunior wants to dismiss the notion of the fukú, or the curse originating in the European colonization of the Americas, the persistence of fukú in the popular belief of his family and community prevents its total dismissal. And Yunior draws the reader into this ontological quandary with what David Herman has called the "doubly deictic you"[7] in his discussion of the fukú's believability: "It's perfectly fine if you don't believe in these 'superstitions,'" Yunior writes. "In fact, it's better than fine—it's perfect. Because no matter what you believe, fukú believes in you" (5). Ultimately, Yunior's narrative exhibits a salient ontology and, thus, dual text-actual-worlds. In the primary world, fukú is simply a myth belonging to the private knowledge worlds of the characters who believe in it, and firmly exiled to the fantasy universes of others. In the secondary world, the curse is evidenced in the plot itself and embodied in the figures of the talking Mongoose; the "zafa," or counterspell; and the faceless man, the harbinger of doom. Yunior's narrative choices reveal his own affinity for fantasy but also his suspicion that the text-actual-world and fantasy worlds may, indeed, overlap. This is part of Yunior and Oscar's shared cultural heritage: "In Santo Domingo," Yunior explains, "a story is not a story unless it casts

---

7. In *Story Logic*, Herman points out that "doubly deictic" uses of "you" hail both the fictional and actual audiences. In *Oscar Wao*, Yunior's references to his readers frequently reflect his concern with believability, as if he needs to preempt his readers' inevitable doubts about the fantastic elements in his narrative because he regards "you" as firmly planted in the skeptical, actual world.

a supernatural shadow," something that Oscar and Yunior find very attractive (245–46). And Yunior somewhat hesitantly, but intuitively, turns his story of Oscar's life into a romantic quest for love in defiance of evil forces. Yunior's tentative belief in the curse, the mongoose, and the faceless man, and his suspicion that Trujillo may be the real-life equivalent of J. R. R. Tolkien's Sauron, keep the novel teetering between historical fiction and fantasy, and it is precisely this quality of ontological salience that makes it immersive for Yunior.

In the end, Yunior's Oscar makes the most significant move in the narrative by following romantic-heroic rules. Oscar rejects the identity and values ascribed to him by the dominant social forces in his life and chooses, instead, to realize a desired possible self prefigured in his beloved fantasy narratives: he chooses almost certain death over survival and transforms himself into a heroic martyr for love by standing up to the evil that has oppressed his family for generations. This ending seems purely tragic until viewed, by Yunior, as Oscar's grim but conscious choice. Oscar finally brings his fantasy world into alignment with the text-actual-world, if only temporarily, by losing his virginity to a woman he loves through an act of bravery. This requires a return to the Dominican Republic and a fatal second defiance of the novel's last Trujillo stand-in, Ybón's boyfriend, the brutal capitán. Reflecting on Oscar's final days, Yunior realizes that Oscar was preparing for a dramatic move. "You should have seen him," Yunior writes. "He was so thin, had lost all the weight and was still, still. . . . Something had changed about him. He had gotten some power of his own" (312, 319). When he is predictably recaptured by the capitán's goons, "Grod and Grundy," and dragged back into the cane, Yunior's Oscar delivers a heroic speech about his perfect love, one worthy of high romance and finishing with a curse on the forces of evil. Initially, Yunior utterly deflates the romance by ending Oscar's death scene with a cruel, cheap joke and Oscar's execution. It seems that Oscar's valiant attempt at love has failed, his story becoming yet another pathetic tragedy. But Oscar's final letter reveals that before his death he gleefully consummated his love and achieved a weekend of ecstasy.

Yunior's decision to withhold the good news about Oscar's quest until the end reflects his desire to close Oscar's biography with triumph. By choosing to sacrifice his life for a chance at love, Yunior's Oscar writes himself into a great tragedy worthy of his own high romantic values, and Yunior, who understands Oscar's romantic quest, bears witness to the temporary alignment of Oscar's private worlds and the text-actual-world. This structural decision also reflects the sort of book Yunior wants to write in order to fill the void left by the missing books of Oscar and his maternal grandfather, Abelard. These missing narratives are rumored to have offered answers, and, in part, they represent the missing historical counter-narratives that were repressed or destroyed during Trujillo's regime; they never made it out of the Dominican Republic.

Abelard's famed missing book was "an exposé of the supernatural roots of the Trujillo regime!" (Díaz 245). Yunior explains: "Oscar, as you might imagine, found this version of the Fall very very attractive. Appealed to the deep structures in his nerd brain" (246). Characteristically, Yunior struggles with his repressed inner nerd, as he is unable to entirely reject this famed origin myth even though it is "the kind of shit only a nerd could love" (246). The story of this book's existence and suppression forms a counter-narrative, contrasting the much more "believable" story, "The Girl Trujillo Wanted" (246). This more realistic history links the Cabral family fall with Abelard's refusal to offer his daughter to Trujillo as yet another in his endless line of rape victims; thus, it casts Trujillo's reign as a systematic, violent, violation of an entire people. In this version of the story, Abelard's resistance seems utterly futile. But despite his doubts about the supernatural, Yunior self-consciously explores the possible worlds suggested by the myth of the missing book, reinvigorating Abelard's resistance. In one of his extended historical footnotes, Yunior describes another suggestive missing story, the "blank page, a página en blanco" left in the memoir of Joaquin Balaguer, initially one of Trujillo's "more efficient ringwraiths" and ultimately "the Election Thief" who "unleashed a wave of violence against the Dominican left, death-squading hundreds and driving thousands more out of the country" (90). This blank page represents Balaguer's refusal to tell the truth about the murder of journalist Orlando Martinez, and it was to be "filled in with the truth upon his death" (90). The Dominican history Yunior attempts to tell is riddled with its own blank pages due to the silence imposed by Trujillo and the heirs of his power. The salience of fantasy in Dominican oral histories and the holes in Dominican historiography, figured in Abelard's missing book and the página en blanco, create the conditions and the necessity for Yunior's blend of fiction and reality.

Several scholars have noted that Yunior's counter-narrative questions the segregation of fiction and reality as well as the usefulness of "official" histories through its generic blending. In "Historical Fantasy, Speculative Realism, and Postrace Aesthetics in Contemporary American Fiction," Ramón Saldívar argues, "*Oscar Wao* turns historical fiction inside out in the hope of undoing the aesthetic and social history of the New World" because Díaz understands "the constitutive role of fantasy in the post-postmodern world" (585). Saldívar calls Yunior's narrative "historical fantasy" and "speculative realism," labels he coins "to retain the contradictory impulse suggested by the forcible joining of the gravitas of history with the spectral quality of fantasy" (585). One consequential result of this hybrid form is that "fantasy is no longer simply a private, licentious matter creating a world of pleasure without obligation to what is permissible or possible outside the realm of fantasy. Instead, fantasy now becomes a public progressive energy aiming toward the world it only seems to have left behind" (592). As the text-actual, historical, and possible worlds of Yunior's story begin to overlap, as Yunior quite self-consciously "stories" his world, the resulting narrative gives relevance and value to creative power rather than brute force. Monica Hanna has argued that Yunior offers a "resistance history" that he views as more truthful, "an imaginative reconstruction that can only take place in the literary realm" (500, 504). In the face of the Trujillo master narrative, Yunior "asserts his power to rewrite the story as he sees fit in order to best present the overall reality he seeks to put forth" (Hanna 508). But as Yunior fills in his blank pages, for much of the novel he struggles to resist his own internalized dictator.

Arguably, the most palpable marker of Trujillo's legacy in Yunior's story is his own adherence to the stereotypical Dominican male social script built on Trujillo's model of patriarchal masculine power. A direct consequence of Yunior's callous playboy lifestyle is the loss of Lola, the girl of his dreams. His self-destructive womanizing persists through most of his story, causing him great losses. Blake Wilder (in this volume) suggests that cultural hegemony operates through dominant narratives to influence identity formation, and counter-narratives may not only offer alternatives but also cultivate a sense of loss for those whose dominance is suddenly challenged. Yunior's depiction of Oscar as the powerless, feminized nerd who desperately needs his help establishes a seemingly incontrovertible hierarchy in their relationship: Yunior's masculinity is dominant and Oscar's femininity submissive. As Yunior reexamines his own life in light of Oscar's example, he confronts the corrupting influence of Trujillo-style masculinity on his own values and lifestyle. Just as Yunior finds the possible worlds evoked by myth and fantasy somewhat inaccessible, he struggles to accept the gendered possible world in which Oscar-style maleness is endorsed. Interestingly, his final major move in the novel is catalyzed by his inner Oscar. The ghostly Oscar of Yunior's dreamscapes, his repressed inner nerd, convinces him to change his ways. When he reaches his lowest point, Yunior finally relents: "OK, Wao, OK. You win" (Díaz 325). Though this shift comes much too late to save his relationship with Lola, it is clear that it saves Yunior. He manages to create a decent, Oscar-style life for himself as a teacher and writer: "These days I write a lot. From can't see in the morning to can't see at night. Learned that from Oscar. I'm a new man, you see, a new man" (326). At the end of *Oscar Wao*, Yunior seems to mourn his former confident and dominant self, even though his transformation has saved his life. But in the trajectory of his own story, as well as the structure of Oscar's, Yunior affirms Oscar's type of power, a power drawn from the imagination and from an inner life originating in fiction. The final missing book in *The Brief Wondrous Life of Oscar Wao* was supposed to arrive in Oscar's second package sent from the Dominican Republic after his last trip; it was said to contain everything Oscar had written on his final journey, including "the cure to what ails us. . . . The Cosmo DNA" (Díaz 333). But that package never arrives. Instead, a letter sent to Lola, which arrives after Oscar's death, represents a trace of Oscar's "cure." Referencing his weekend of love in the letter, Oscar exclaims: "So this is what everybody's always talking about! Diablo! If I'd only known. The beauty! The beauty!" (335). This reversal of Conrad's famous line from *Heart of Darkness* confirms the integral role of fiction and counternarrative in sense-making and signals this novel's place in the broader literature of colonization and resistance. Ultimately the novel is the story of Yunior's own resistance and liberation, a "zafa of sorts. [His] very own counterspell" (7).

Distinctions of cultural identity, nationality, race, and gender are constantly challenged in the twenty-first century by instant international communications, increasingly widespread diasporas, multiracial generations, and a heightened awareness of the gender continuum. Narrative remains the most effective mode for communicating the subtleties of racial, ethnic, and gender identities as the easy, often inadequate markers of these differences become blurred; brief strings of descriptors simply cannot convey the elements of our origins and our experience that shape our points of view and values. In *Fictional Worlds*, Pavel considers the age-old and controversial questions surrounding the relationship between the actual world and fiction, and he ultimately rejects the "segregationist" view in favor of an "integrationist" approach that helps explain "why so many of us acquire bits of wisdom" from fiction (27). The possible worlds approach take us some distance further toward understanding why fiction draws us in, how it impacts our lives, and why we often regard it as true. It provides a sophisticated method for examining character behavior and the relationships among the "really real world,"[8] the text-actual-world, and the many private worlds of characters in narratives. In historical and biographical fictions, especially, those relationships are crucial since those genres are framed as particular reflections of our actual world. The possible worlds in Cofer's and Díaz's literary realms constitute sites of ideological resistance and sources of identity formation through the transformational power of the "move to reading."

---

8. Pavel uses this self-consciously simple and charming phrase in *Fictional Worlds*.

CHAPTER 14

Homo-Narrative Capture, Racial Proximity, and the Queer Latino Child

ROY PÉREZ

> The future is only the stuff of some kids. Racialized kids, queer kids, are not
> the sovereign princes of futurity.
> —José Esteban Muñoz, *Cruising Utopia: The Then and There of Queer Futurity*

NARRATOLOGY, POSSIBILITY, PROXIMITY

NARRATION IS a practice of worldmaking, and it follows that narratologists
delve into realms of imaginative representation for which we do not always
have sufficient language, routinely capitalizing instead on terms that signal
uncertainty. Many of the essays in this collection use narrative analysis to
point to formal and social phenomena that are not immediately classifiable,
and it appears that at the intersection of narratology and critical race analysis
there is a prominent and productive concern with the omitted, the delayed,
the not-yet, the possible, and the new. In this vein, Patrick E. Horn uses paralipsis to describe the way in which the protracted withholding (and sudden
disclosing) of an Asian American narrator's race constructively challenges an
implied reader's identification with the novel's point of view. For Horn, the
absence of racial signifiers reveals that color-blind narration paradoxically
triggers leaps of putative racial identification. Similarly, in order to elaborate a
theory about the value of imaginative escape into other "possible worlds" for
marginalized subjects, Deborah Noel must speculate about whether a facet of
a fictional universe will appear well worn and familiar or new and weird to an
implied reader. Unable to account for a given reader's social position or her
affective disposition toward a narrative, these ventures into the indeterminable
dimensions of narrative focus on what new things narrative can make and do,

what Claudia Breger terms "the aesthetics of narrative performance" (165 in this volume). The performative nature of narrative and "how language constructs or affects reality rather than merely describing it" remains a remarkably uncommon proposition within the field of narratology that appears to serve, at least in this volume, as an entry point for a narratology of race and antiracist worldmaking (Sedgwick, *Touching Feeling* 5).

Consistent with this turn to performativity as an important and instructive supplement to the narratology of race, this essay examines how narrative acts, theorized as performances in their worldmaking capacity, can approximate something other than the familiar, rote, and even deadening affects of racial and sexual normativity. For those subjects José Esteban Muñoz calls "racialized kids, queer kids" in the epigraph above, I see in this imaginative escape into possible worlds and the performance of new social possibilities through narrative a way of laying claim to futurity. Narratives offer a fabricated *then* or *elsewhere* within which one can participate in new kinds of affiliation and selfhood (Muñoz, *Cruising Utopia* 95). But making space for an aesthetics of possibility demands a slackening of some of the rubrics of formal and social interpretation. Proximity's light touch, emphasizing figural and material nearness, points to forms of relation that might not register in theories of colonization, acculturation, or formalized structures of interracial kinship that lie at the crux of much postcolonial and critical race analysis. A theory of racial proximity highlights the way queer narrative tactics are practiced as everyday modes of social intervention and survival amid vexed relations to, rather than independent of, the normal. The normal itself can be understood, after Judith Butler, as the repetition unto invisibility of particular narratives about identity, such that a narrow set of practices appear natural (Butler, *Gender Trouble* 31). To approximate rather than fulfill an identity into which a subject is hailed evokes measured imprecision, contingency, unpredictability, and the refusal of repetition and resolution in relation to the normal. Approximation is a strategic falling short of the normal.

In this essay I examine the rhetorical exploitation of the figure of the racialized child in Dan Savage's narrative contribution to the It Gets Better Project. As a riposte to this dynamic, I examine the challenges to racial assimilation embedded in the gender experiments enacted by Justin Suarez on the ABC television series *Ugly Betty*. I focus on two representations of queer Latino childhood—one of homo-narrative secondary possession by a white sojourner and one of figurative, Latino self-possession—in order to show, first, how queer performative possibility becomes trapped within homo-normative discourse, and second, how the racialized queer child's performances of that which seems politically foreclosed by contemporary gay rights discourse not only challenges the familiar and the intelligible but also allows new avenues of queer *latinidad* to emerge.[1] How might narratology theorize the performance of a television actor delivering a narrative? Here I propose that the embodiment of the actor makes elements of narrative unfolding available to interpretation through what Juana María Rodríguez terms "corporeal gestures" that, in their nuanced departures from repetitive gender scripts, are "capable of making gender and sexuality seen" rather than given or natural (*Sexual Futures* 29, 177). The salient question for this collection then becomes how the performativity of the brown body might be read narratologically: what does the actor's play in possession of a role make available for interpretation, and how much of this play registers on the level of narrative?

A set of increasingly mechanized narratives about gay development formally uses and confines the figure of the queer child—a figure that nevertheless, as I elaborate here, manages to squeeze through the strictures of the normal. Through the figure of the child, multiple narratives of queer becoming seem to braid, revealing new intersections of possibility and performing (as in constructing) a politics of queer Latina/o futurity that offers critical alternatives to a white-dominated gay rights movement. This is achieved through the formal incident of narrative and figural proximity, or closeness, between white gay adults and queer brown children. Proximity engenders political possibility through the exchange of narratives. Narratives give flesh to the historical relations on which futures are built, and it is in relation that subjects transmit the "possibility of possibilities" (Delany 17–18). But proximity is both a window of possibility and a site of literal and rhetorical capture.

My view of racial proximity as generative is restricted to its appearance and effects as narrative act, rather than as social reality. In a frequently cited passage from *No Future: Queer Theory and the Death Drive,* Lee Edelman emphatically distances his theory of the reified "image of the Child" from "the lived experiences of any historical children" (17). I am similarly committed to an emphasis on the rhetorical uses of child figures and have benefitted here from Edelman's shrewd deconstruction of the normativity into which gay politics has marched. But at the same time, quarantining "the image of the Child" from any and every historical incarnation of that image forces us to overlook all those ways in which, far from the antithesis of queerness, children might be the original queers. Critics like Kathryn Bond Stockton have developed the child's Freudian "polymorphous perversity" into a growing area of queer studies. In queer Latina/o studies, a productive course appears in

---

1. *Latinidad* serves as connotative way of referring to the presence of Latina/o identity and affect in a text, bracketing national, cultural, and racial particularities whose potency as signifiers can be overdetermining. See Rodríguez, *Queer* Latinidad 22 and Rivera-Servera 22–26.

the child's real "proximity to certain worlds that are defined by national, economic, racial, and sexual modes of behavior," intersections of child discourse
and public health that Rodríguez calls us to examine in her study of the ways
in which queer social spaces have begun to reify children's innocence in the
embrace of normative family politics (*Sexual Futures* 45). Capitalizing on the
child's seeming lack of access to self-narration, political discourses that hinge
on narrow, fabricated ideas of what brown children need and want often work
against the child figure's political and creative vitality. Where child figures
could be voices of possibility, they are instead the recipients of benevolent
constraint. I call this formal effect "homo-narrative capture," and with it I seek
to emphasize the power relation—one at least as old as the capture of Cali-
ban and Ariel by Prospero in Shakespeare's *The Tempest*—that structures the
conjuring and entrapment of the infantilized brown subject in rhetoric and
fiction. Homo-narratives seek sameness, reproducing themselves by educating
and disciplining the infantilized brown figure; they write a queer figure into
being in order to capture her and impose social sameness upon her, though
not always successfully.

HOMO-NARRATIVE CAPTURE

Citing Pierre Macherey's reflections on the methods of the critic and the relation between writing and thought, Rey Chow argues that "'the emergence of
thought institutes a certain distance and separation,' and that distance and
separation is a way to reconceptualize the utterances of narrative fiction" (21).
Distance lets ideas congeal and allows thought to do its work. Alongside this
distanciation, Chow simultaneously credits narrative with the ability to bring
divergent points of view into constructive proximity, perhaps owing to a narrative's function as a kind of third space, engendered by its remove from the
scene of the original dialectical opposition. Through a flowing or entangling
of antithetical narrative codes,

> the literary text itself provides an internal distance from the ideology: rather
> than being a mimetic reproduction or reflection of a preexisting, ideologi-
> cal reality, the literary text is where contradictory social relations confront
> one another, and where ideology is made visible by refraction, as though in
> a broken mirror. (Chow 22)

For Chow, narrative's function is not representational or mimetic, but relational and spatial. Narrativity describes dilations of the space among a series

of dialectically bound ideological oppositions, and their distance and separation can suddenly reverse into confrontation and encounter. Whether or not the contradictory social relations that appear in a literary text constitute separate narratives or just one focally decentered, multivoiced narrative is a valuable question. But rather than quantify the number or strata of narratives that might appear in a text, I am concerned with a dynamic of ideological power that obtains when a rote story about gay well-being and political agency encounters a deviant, queer, racialized subject, and how her competing, contradictory set of desires reveals another possible story. Narrative fluctuates—*is* fluctuation—dividing and combining like biological cells or celestial singularities, altering the proximity of disparate things. Add power to this equation and we can discern narratives dividing into dominant, recognizable fabula and emergent, new fabula. How do social expectations shape narrative, and how do narratives alternately empower or police the figures that populate a story? The proximity of competing social logics in narrative causes refractions and breakages that make the known world feel porous and unbound. These breaches in the ideological fabric of a given narrative offer spaces for performing otherwise.

The paradox of simultaneous distance and proximity is manifest in the dynamic of the trap—snares and cages used to capture animals and the animalized to bring them into close control. Chow finds traps in philosophy and art criticism and uncovers a prevailing discourse of entrapment that lies at the center of Western thought. Might the critic-writer-narrator's "captivation" by an object of study (or subject *cum* object), she asks, reinforce an old colonial dynamic of victor and captor? In the narration of what I call white sojourns into brown space that stage racial proximity, "capture and captivation [arise] as a type of discourse, one that derives from the imposition of power on bodies and the attachment of bodies to power, and that contains the makings of what may be called a heteronomy or heteropoeisis" (Chow 6). Chow's "capture" as a narrative discourse reveals the degree to which any poetics of difference (heteropoeisis) will necessarily entangle the other in a web of biopolitics that assign particular fates to particular bodies in the emergence of something like, for example, gay rights.

Scholars have used the term "homo-narrative" in a somewhat casual way to describe a story's general, thematic concern with same-sex love. It has referred to stories about homosexuality, rather than the doubling, interpellative function of narrative (Allen 82–83; Vincent 383–85). But what might a technical understanding of homo-narrativity as a form of writing and arguing that seeks and produces *sameness* reveal about the sexual and racial politics of a particular genre, like self-help books, travel literature, or a coming-of-age telenovela? Queer children appear at odds with the master narratives that seek to entangle them in proper modes of racial and sexual self-understanding and expression because they anticipate sexual ways of being for which the adults around them do not have a clear language. The tension we find between an adult narrative and a wily child shows that the counterpoint of a homo-narrative is not necessarily heterosexuality, in some binarized way; the homo-narrative's counterpoint is the difference (any difference) it attacks and seeks to assimilate. There can be homo-narratives of heterosexual sameness, and indeed an important charge for the narratology of sexuality and race is to note how neoliberalism has smoothed out the ideological differences between gay and straight, such that any political divergences linked to being gay or straight have dissolved in the name of equality. Homo-narratives attempt to obliterate difference by casting the queer child in a series of pedagogical performances of impossible, racialized sexual normalcy. These performances entangle the child in discourses of moral rectitude that attempt to enforce assimilation, but whose splintered executions ultimately reveal more about the instability of the discourses themselves and the anxieties of the protagonist-teachers than about the presumed pupils. Gay uplift has become synonymous with economic mobility, and gay pride is achieved vis-à-vis middle-class assimilation. Homo-narrativity describes the formal dissemination and social effect of this gay politics of uniformity.

The term "hetero-narrative," on the other hand, has benefitted from sharper technical honing. Judith Roof describes hetero-narrativity as a putative heterosexual's drive against a "risk of sameness" (82). Detectable in a character's speech and actions (what Rodríguez might call a "gesture"), hetero-narrative tension occurs in the rubbing together of what is allowed and what is not allowed to trespass through a character's sexual self-awareness (Roof xvi–xvii). However, developments in the way queer scholarship has come to understand the cultural politics of sexuality reveal a mainstream ideological position emerging that no longer understands sameness as *risk* (homosexual contamination), and a gay politics in which sameness is a commodity, a form of capitalist reproduction, and a technology of white biopower. Gay is like straight, but better. As scholars like Lisa Duggan, José Esteban Muñoz, Jasbir Puar, and Cristina Hanhardt have argued with historical and theoretical breadth, gay politics in the United States has shifted away from its early trajectory as a countercultural civil rights movement and toward a neoliberal economics that now invests sexual sameness with a late capitalist drive for reproduction, wealth accumulation, and the actualization of an individual self—a particular kind of consuming, consumptive, conforming selfness.

A theory of homo-narrativity that indexes the new gay normal interrupts the focus on homophobia that has long occupied LGBT studies, in order to pay mind to the way contemporary gay identity has been folded into popular culture and reshaped into a profitable enterprise by late capitalism. Homo-narrative capture, wherein a nonconforming queer figure is trapped, shrouded, and re-subjected by a mainstreaming gay political imaginary, is one disciplining arm of an increasingly white and politically centrist gay rights movement, the result of what Keith M. Harris has termed the "heterosexualization of homosexuality" (2). The narrative sojourns by white masculine figures into brown spaces I examine here are scenes of proximity where homo-narrative traps attempt to lure queer children into sameness.

SOMEDAY, SOMEHOW, SOMEWHERE? WHITE SOJOURNS INTO THE BROWN FUTURE

Futurity is a narratological concern. To inhabit a future is to be furnished with forward-reaching narratives in which you feature, perhaps thriving, maybe just getting by, but nonetheless present as an agent in an alternative, imaginary social fabric. As Eve Kosofsky Sedgwick argues in "How to Bring Your Kids Up Gay: The War on Effeminate Boys," many of the ways in which adults speak of the well-being of the queer child—through narrative co-optation, conscription, and speculation about potential harms to the child's future well-being—tell us more about the "haunting abject of gay thought itself" (femininity) than about actual children (157). Homo-narratives suck up the child's potential like oxygen into the biosphere of a privileged white gay subject, the favored beneficiary of contemporary gay rights politics. The figure of the child provides futurity, or more precisely, political rhetoricians of different leanings regularly exploit the figure of the child to serve particular futures. The child figure is a rhetorical boon: innocence, promise, a blank slate. This potential is the primary rhetorical resource of child figures. As Stephen Bruhm and Natasha Hurley put it, "utopianism follows the child around like a family pet" (xiii), but whose utopia, and how do we read a utopia for its underlying interests?

In 2010, after a spate of teen suicides linked to homophobic bullying, sex columnist Dan Savage and his now-husband Terry Miller posted a video on YouTube titled "It Gets Better: Dan and Terry." In the video, the two men sit before a mike at a neighborhood bar and discuss their personal and professional success despite the privations of queer childhoods. Thousands of video contributions followed from users around the world, and the It Gets Better Project (IGBP) emerged and quickly transformed into a nonprofit foundation that produces books, websites, and cable TV specials, sharing banner space at gay pride parades nationwide with corporate partners like Wells Fargo and AT&T. Given this trajectory, perhaps it is not surprising that even within its first few weeks on the Web, IGBP was the target of biting criticism from scholars, journalists, and activists for its liberal evangelizing of a bootstrap success narrative (Puar, "In the Wake"; Nyong'o, "School Daze"). While the "more than 50,000 user-created videos" on the foundation's website to date offer a diverse stock of narratives, the IGBP's philosophy of suicide prevention still banks on a promise of a "better" life defined by the entrepreneurs, politicians, and celebrities the videos most prominently showcase (It Gets Better Project, "What Is?"). The appeal of "it gets better" lies not in the desire to redact suffering, but to transform suffering into a rich resource of strength for adulthood.

The capitalist and racist "common sense" that underwrites the "it gets better" narrative has been thoroughly deconstructed in the blogosphere by Jasbir Puar, Tavia Nyong'o, and other critics. Here I would like to focus on a particular moment of racial possession in Savage's video that stages the kind of racial sojourn into brown space that enables the homo-narrative to seize the Latino child. By virtue of a neoliberal equivalence that binds salvation with consumption and geographic mobility, Savage's narrative produces a remainder child figure: an *other* child with limited economic purchase, who is geographically bound, racially marked, beyond saving.[2] This brown child is conjured literally when Savage describes attending a Broadway performance of *West Side Story* as a teenager. "If my adult self could talk to my fourteen-year-old self and tell him anything," says Savage in a tone of storybook wonder, "I would tell him to really believe the lyrics of 'Somewhere' from West Side Story. There really is a 'place for us.' There really is a place for you" (It Gets Better Project, "It Gets Better"). Restoring the context of this song from Steven Sondheim's musical reinvention of *Romeo and Juliet* reveals the narrative hijacking that takes place here. Set among the balkanized working classes of the Upper West Side, the "us" and "you" of these lyrics refer to Maria and Tony, an interracial couple whose relationship ends with Tony's murder. Near the end of the musical, Maria sings these lines through tears as she holds Tony's dead body. The complete phrases from the song give us the time stamp for Maria and Tony's utopic wish: "There's a place for us, somewhere a place for us / There's a

---

2. For Jesse Matz, Savage and Edelman offer complementary ventures in queer narrative temporality (231). However, both Matz's and Edelman's inattention to race with regards to the way the child figure circulates in gay media limits the reach and possibility of their otherwise indispensable critiques of the queer temporality and the brand of gay rights discourse that guides Savage's project.

time for us, / Someday a time for us / Someday, Somehow, Somewhere!" That "someday, somehow, somewhere" projection into a future time and place is politically critical: for all of *West Side Story*'s guilelessness concerning race, the *not yet here* of Maria and Tony's postracial future is one of the musical's most truthful and condemning insights on mid-century race relations.[3] This postracial dream has not yet manifested, despite the mainstream gay movement's persistent homologizing of racial and sexual liberation with such taglines as "gay is the new black."[4] Like the brown-face worn by the white actress Natalie Wood to "Ricanize" her visage in the film adaptation of the musical, Savage's casting of his fourteen-year-old self as the addressee of the song's political message is a rhetorical act of brown becoming, as well as an act of figural brown childing, through which his story extorts the utopic energy of antiracist thought to paint his social and economic mobility as a consequence of liberation movements. The postracial "place for us" imagined by Maria becomes Savage's utopia, a political vision that siphons futurity from antiracist political energy and speculation. But such sojourns by white subjects into brown space can also serve as sites for the brown child's performative conjuring of alternative, antiassimilationist forms of queerness and survival.

THE TELENOVELA AND THE POLICE

Mark Indelicato was eleven years old when he debuted as Betty's queer nephew Justin Suarez on the ABC network television series *Ugly Betty*, making him the youngest queer-presenting character to have appeared on primetime television. An hour-long dramatic comedy that aired from 2006 to 2010, *Ugly Betty* is the U.S. adaptation of a Latin American telenovela and transnational phenomenon that began with the wildly popular *Yo soy Betty, la fea*, which aired on the RCN network in Colombia from 1999 to 2001. The show was adapted for U.S. audiences by Cuban American and openly gay writer and producer Silvio Horta. Mexican American Betty is a college graduate who aspires to write hard journalism but unexpectedly lands a job at a fashion magazine called *MODE*. The main arc of the series, for both Betty and Justin, is a bootstrap first-generation coming-of-age story about class mobility and feminine self-fashioning. In this unfolding, the show often participates in a tradition of social-problem sitcoms, like those of TV guru Norman Lear (*All in the Family, Sanford and Son, The Jeffersons, Good Times, Maude,* and others) that pushed viewers on issues like racial integration and sexual liberation (Villarejo 23,

---

3. See Sandoval Sanchez for a careful and generous analysis of Sondheim's racial politics.
4. See Carbado.

85). *Ugly Betty* enters this tradition with queer and Latino representations TV had rarely handled before. Much of the show entails characters traversing the uneven class topography between lower Manhattan and Queens, often setting the stage for sojourns across racialized space that ultimately prompt Justin's slow and unconventional coming-out story as he encounters different ways to inhabit or do gender.

But to label Justin's narrative a "coming-out" story is misleading. The "coming-out" genre easily falls prey to a set of familiar narrative expectations about homophobic exclusion, tragic violence, and spectacular gay actualization, and these never really play out over the course of *Ugly Betty*'s four seasons. Justin's growth from gender-nonconforming tween to sexually active queer teen is shaped by a queerly matrifocal home life (his mother and aunt are assisted by their widowed grandfather, a smooth-tempered homemaker who cooks and routinely wears an apron around the house), in which his gender expression is nurtured and protected. As early as the pilot episode, we find Justin at home with the family gluing gemstones to a secondhand Polo shirt while watching *Fashion TV* (*Ugly Betty*, "Pilot"). What remained to be seen during that opening season was if and how the show would develop the character's sexuality long-term. Justin's queerness in the pilot episode triggers a proleptic narrative investment in the character—"seeding" sexual difference but offering only enough information to suggest that his sexuality will unfold at a later point in the story. It is perhaps a testament to the centrality of sexuality as a narrative concern that narratologist Gérard Genette uses the deferral of evidence of "homosexuality and its subtle variant, heterosexuality," in Proust to help explain prolepsis as a rhetorical device that requires cultural literacy about the tension that surrounds a particular inference. Genette sees entrapment here, too, in the "snares" a narrative lays out as part of the fort/da of narrative play (*Narrative Discourse* 76–78). In popular culture, a proleptic narrative gesture at sexuality is typically fulfilled through the discursive unfolding of a now-familiar coming-out story that prime-time television had previously reserved for adult characters and usually executed in a condensed manner that flattened gay experience into a universal journey of trauma and self-acceptance. The child figure, as a "cipher into which adult anxieties are poured," is already charged with proleptic narrative value, and a kind of struggle ensues on *Ugly Betty* to capture Justin's proleptic potential and guide him along one of a number of competing narrative trajectories (Bruhm and Hurley xii). Rather than through Justin's coming out—which never happens in word, but only in action, when he starts dating his classmate, Austin—the show uses scenes of white sojourn into the Suarez home space to tease out Justin's sexuality. The implication of such interventions is that no cultural paradigm or precedent exists for this unfolding to occur organically within a Latino family living in a Latino community, without white proximity. Meanwhile, the Jackson Heights/Elmhurst neighborhood in Queens in which the story takes place is home to the annual Queens Pride street party and to a number of established Latina/o-owned and frequented gay bars. In a very material way, Queens has much to offer an emerging queen. The white characters who sojourn from Manhattan into this Latina/o cultural matrix bring with them a homo-narrative of gay actualization. These homo-narratives fail to take over the political landscape of Justin's coming out because Justin rejects them for something more affirming of his racial experience and his feminine gender presentation, ultimately performing a new family politics of queer *latinidad*. Importantly, such a representation might be new to U.S. media and network television, but to this author, it doesn't feel new to Latino family politics at all—it is, rather, a timeworn and transnational tradition of improvisational kinship and child rearing that has perhaps required the exhausted slackening of Latino gender stereotypes for its popular emergence.

A pivotal moment in Justin's gender identity that occurs in the show's second season is prompted by the appearance of a white police officer at the Suarez home. Much of Justin's arc in the first season is dedicated to rekindling a relationship with his estranged father, Santos. Just as Santos begins to reform his initially homophobic attitude toward Justin, he is killed as a bystander in a convenience store robbery. Reeling from his father's murder, Justin begins season two grief stricken and grasping for a way to honor his father by shedding his queerness, donning his father's old leather jacket and assuming a bad-boy attitude with a belligerent swagger. One night, to impress a girl, he takes the family car for a joyride, hits a tree, and is subsequently escorted home by a solemn policewoman, Rita. Rita, who reads as ethnically white and more comfortably butch than Justin, warns Justin's mother, Hilda, of the criminal future she sees shadowing Justin, and advises: "Listen, this one's between us. I know you've been going through a lot lately, but keep an eye on him. I seen [sic] these things spiral" (*Ugly Betty*, "A League of Their Own"). The incident awakens Hilda to the fact that in her own grief, she had lost track of Justin, and the two have a heart-to-heart about their shared loss that restores Justin to his feminine self.

The moment is notable for its affirmation of Justin's femininity, as it prompts the end of a butch masquerade that allowed him to evade his grief—passing as masculine to avoid the emotional travails of mourning the passing of his macho father. But more importantly, the appearance of a butch officer who presents as an actualized gay adult links policing to the anxiety that surrounds the wild queerness of the child, "moving the question of policing out of the streets and into the closet—into the private domestic sphere on which the very identity of the liberal subject depends" (Miller, *The Novel and the Police* ix). The white police officer becomes the agent of normativity, intervening in the Latina household on behalf of the putatively gay child, teaching the mother to intervene on the child's identity crisis.

Ugly Betty's forward-thinking posture with regard to gender and sexuality is often leveraged, for better or for worse, on this appearance and intervention by white characters. There is a pattern in *Ugly Betty* according to which nearly every time Justin faces a dramatic rite of passage, a white male or masculine character enters the scene as an exemplary and mediating figure. Similarly, before turning a new leaf, his father delivers the show's first homophobic outburst—"Give the glitter a rest. C'mon, come out and be a normal kid for an hour"—and it is Betty's hungover boss Daniel who, present at the Suarez household by some narrative contrivance involving drinking and an impromptu visit to Queens for Betty's emotional support, steps in and praises Justin's queerness as a gift: "I don't know, Santos. I mean, if Justin deserts me now, the tree will end up looking like overdressed firewood. I need Justin's eye. He's . . . he's got a gift" (*Ugly Betty*, "Lose the Boss?"). We might conceive of Justin's eye, this gift, as a kind of second sight or *facultad* through which Justin achieves narrative focalization and peers into his own queer future. And, as Anzaldúa's theory posits, it is not a nascent talent but one borne of proximity to the very structures that marginalize the queer other (Anzaldúa 60). Justin's relations with white men, his sometimes involuntary though not necessarily infelicitous stewardship by white sojourners, provide occasion for this vision of an alternative way of being to develop. The dynamic culminates with the episode to which I turn below, when Hilda recruits a man named Marc—Betty's supercilious coworker at *MODE* who is regularly used by the show's writers as a mouthpiece for campy, racist humor—to help mentor Justin out of the closet.

In a mid-season cliffhanger titled "Backseat Betty," Justin gets framed by a small group of popular kids who countermand the homecoming election and, as a means of humiliation, pronounce him homecoming queen in front of his family and a gymnasium full of classmates. Justin obeys advice offered by Marc: "Get ahead of the joke, son. . . . If you show them that you're in on the joke, then they'll think they're not getting to you, and they'll stop making fun of you" (*Ugly Betty*, "Backseat Betty"). With fabulous theatricality, he turns a potentially humiliating homecoming ceremony into an act fit for gay cabaret.

He climbs onto the stage and graciously accepts the flowers and tiara, feigning the utmost delight. In his speech, he takes a few witty jabs at the audience and receives, at first, a smattering of tentative laughs. Then he dedicates the title to his mother, who missed her own homecoming coronation because she was pregnant with Justin at the time. With the audience rapt, cooing and sighing as he tells this story, the jocks who announced his name with mean exuberance now sulk on the sidelines. Justin uses the control he gains over the scene to clear the toxic atmosphere created by the bullies and nimbly reset the tone of the ceremony. Simultaneously, he also enacts a rejoinder to another racial homo-narrative that pathologizes teen mothers as a matter of course, a stigmatizing cultural foundation laid by sociological touchstones like the Moynihan Report. Justin claims his mother as a prefiguration of himself, rather than as the origin point of a story about hardship and self-improvement. The audience gives him a standing ovation as he walks offstage to the center of the gym to hand his mother the tacky bouquet of red carnations and baby's breath and fondly place the tiara on her head as her eyes well up with tears. An aerial shot captures Justin, Hilda, Betty, and Betty's father Ignacio in a family hug at the center of the basketball court, right on top of the "Wildcats" school seal—a Latina invasion of a space represented as a site of white normativity.

This scene seems at first like a major triumph for Justin's character. From a standpoint invested in queer vindication, there is something profoundly satisfying about a smart, femme character not only stamping out a classic maneuver in high school bullying—the freak-baiting popularity contest—but also managing through wit and sincerity to win over a crowd of his peers. Moreover, his campy, mother-possessed deflection of his peers' homophobia is staged as an act reminiscent of a drag queen's style of "reading," and in this way Justin's act is portrayed as a queer femme coming out and coming into his own. There is an almost compulsory understanding, enacted by the characters but also reflected in the show's fandom on blogs and message boards, that to come out as gay, even against his will, is Justin's rite of passage into adolescent maturity. But this liberal expectation of self-actualization is complicated back at home when Justin rejects the family and Marc's buoyant triumphalism. "Honey, you know I love you, right?" says his mother. "No matter who you are. So what those kids are saying about you—." Before she can denotatively utter a shape for Justin's sexuality, Justin retorts, "Mom, it's a joke. I'm just playing along. I'm not gay." Thus Justin rewrites what people around him perceived as a positive, rousing coming-out scene into a performance of pure gay negation, mother honor, and queer deferral. Ostensibly tragic, Justin's departure from the path of well-adjusted, high self-esteem gayness popularly prized by neoliberal culture can appear as a failure, a phase, or a bump in the road.

The scene ends with a tone of disenchantment and pity. After Justin leaves the room, his family's previously ecstatic expressions turn into brows furrowed with dejection. "Then he's not gay," offers Marc to Hilda, championing self-determination over the connotations of gender presentation. The implicit tragedy is that by "playing along," Justin has internalized his classmates' homophobia—that he has not yet parsed the schoolyard epithet from the realizable identity. But can't we take Justin at his word without assuming that he longs for heterosexuality? Does his departure from one narrative necessarily indicate his succumbing to a normative one? Are we unable to read the ways in which his rejection of one "gay" narrative articulates a commitment to *something else* unimaginable to his normative and homonormative guardians? I would like to reframe Justin's negation of gay sexuality as a negation of the social homonormativity Marc represents. Marc is on his own journey—a privileged, upper-middle-class man from Connecticut who aspires to run a fashion empire, idolizes glamorous hyper-competent women, despises average women, and makes constant jokes about Betty's race and weight, and whose romantic life is constantly at odds with his careerism. Although he is cast as Justin's mentor, it is largely Marc's character that experiences reparation through this relationship. His proximity to the Suarez family ironically offers him the necessary ideological distance from his Manhattanized self to reflect on the annoying chauvinism that had been rhetorically instrumental in putting the "Ugly" in *Ugly Betty* for four entire seasons. I would like to forestall the tragedy with which the adults imbue the scene, what I would call a homonormative logic embodied and promulgated by Marc, by reimagining Justin's performance in the gymnasium. In his performance, he makes a claim on his matrilineal extraction. He channels a diva sensibility. He acts in a manner quite savvy to the plasticity of gender, just as he does when he attempts to make himself in his murdered father's image, which is framed as a tragic departure from his "being himself" but is also legible as self-education in gender performativity, an experiment in identity as protracted becoming rather than singular discovery. These strategies of gender-queer resistance present a different Justin from the one a homo-narrative of gay health and actualization asks us to see.

In the sexual/racial tug-of-war taking place among the adults, Justin nonetheless makes agentic moves to guard himself, experimenting in sometimes difficult ways with forms of gender expression that emerge from a Latino sensibility. Instead of bemoaning something like Justin's internalized homophobia—an increasingly empty pop diagnosis—we can instead imagine Justin painstakingly building radical gender and sexual possibility out of a different set of materials: the matrifocal, the brown, and the gender-queer. When Justin says, "I'm not gay, Mom," we don't *have* to hear Justin clinging to the possibility of being straight. As his performance in the gymnasium attests, Justin's identity is simply not hooked on straightness. Justin is engaged in something altogether new for prime time, an important narrative of gender-becoming that challenges not only heteronormativity but the homo-narrative of coming out, too, through performative gender experiments that challenge the racial, economic, and gender regimes of the new gay normal.

AFTERWORD

Intersections and Future Connections

JENNIFER ANN HO

NARRATIVES ARE constructions, fabrications that develop from their authors' imaginations. Race is a construction, a fabrication of society based on the societal will to believe that the human body can be catalogued and differentiated by phenotypic markers (ones that are imperfectly and inconsistently applied). Nations are constructions, fabrications of governments based on the manipulation of geographical territories into distinct regions bounded by imaginary borders that translate into lines on a map. *Narrative, Race, and Ethnicity in the United States* highlights the different constructions of narrative, race, and nation, and the essays that form this collection speak to various narratological elements (Blake Wilder and Deborah Noel's interrogation of narrative worldmaking, Patrick Horn's analysis of paralipsis) applied to U.S. texts (Toni Morrison's *Song of Solomon,* Leslie Marmon Silko's *Ceremony,* Junot Díaz's *The Brief Wondrous Life of Oscar Wao*) with a focus on race and ethnicity (the role of the white narrator of Ann Petry's *Country Place,* the depiction of Latina/os in the television series *Ugly Betty*). While distinctly different in the narratological elements they analyze and the primary and secondary texts they draw from, what all our contributors have in common is the desire to place critical race theory in conversation with narrative theory, to show the primacy of reading race and ethnicity through various narrative constructs.

The constructed, denaturalized nature of these terms—narrative, race, ethnicity, nation—are paramount to our collection because one of our major goals is to demonstrate the ways in which these various fabrications both reflect and shape our sense of reality; thus, it matters who creates these fabrications, who reads and interprets, and the ethical judgments that are made. As James Phelan incisively observes in *Living to Tell about It: A Rhetoric and Ethics of Character Narration*: "literature in general and narrative in particular, through their attention to the concrete particularities of human situations and their capacity to engage our emotions, provide an especially rich arena for the exploration of ethical issues" (21). Narratives, especially fictional narratives, exist because authors (implied and flesh-and-blood) construct these worlds and populate them with characters who are imaginative creations. Characters exist in fictional worlds and may or may not be realistic or representational with respect to actual living people. Race, as has been amply documented by various scholars over the last few decades, is also a construction. Race has no natural essence, cannot be reducible to genetics or DNA, and is, instead, a political category, one created in the modern era to uphold hierarchies in which those of darker phenotypes were deemed to be of lesser value than those of lighter phenotypes, which also generally aligned with specific regions around the globe. Those of European heritage were said to be superior to those of African ancestry, and this belief system created one of the most brutal ideological eras: the spread of the transatlantic slave trade triangulated from Europe to Africa to the Americas and the continued effects of systemic racism in the United States.[1]

Like narratives and race, nation-states are also constructed entities. Benedict Anderson's landmark book *Imagined Communities: Reflections on the Origin and Spread of Nationalism* aptly charts the constructed nature of nations, which he defines as "an imagined political community" (49). For Anderson, nations are cultural and political constructions that are, in large part, maintained through print culture. One could say that the narratives we imagine about nations have a tautological relationship to nationhood: narratives about nations create nationhood, and nationhood propels narratives about nations. Nations are also imagined constructs because they often exceed boundaries, both in literal geographic terms as well as in the larger symbolic realm. The United States, as a concept, exceeds its geopolitical boundaries, particularly when we are reminded of the colonial histories of U.S. territories. Indeed, invocations of Hawaii that occur in various narratives are redolent with the traces of a colonial history in which Hawaii was forcibly annexed as part of the United States, first as a territory and then incorporated as the fiftieth and (currently) last state in the union. Imagining Hawaii as part of the United States is

---

1. For more on the social construction of race and the ideology of racial formation and white supremacy, see Omi and Winant; I. H. López; and Lipsitz.

possible because the larger narratives we have of U.S. manifest destiny (or U.S. imperialism) is that the actual geography of the United States cannot be contained within a single land mass but, instead, traverses oceans and continents, highlighting that the United States is, indeed, a literal construction or amalgamation of various territories acquired (purchased or forcibly taken) over time.

Within this collection, both Joseph Coulombe and Stephen Spencer question the hegemony of the U.S. nation-state in their analyses of American Indian narratives, reminding readers that the notion of a united America is certainly a construction from the perspective of indigenous people. In their respective analyses of Thomas King's *Green Grass, Running Water* and Leslie Marmon Silko's *Ceremony,* Coulombe and Spencer reinforce that these narratives are not simply ethnography; they exist as aesthetic literary productions that they put in dialogue with narrative theory. As Coulombe emphasizes through his reading of the non-mimetic qualities of *Green Grass, Running Water,* "contemporary written Native texts encourage readers to rethink entrenched Euro-American narratives of discovery and exceptionalism and to consider constructive alternatives" (123 in this volume). For Spencer, applying Bakhtin to Silko's novel allows him to see that "the polyvocal nature of *Ceremony* thus undermines Western narrative tropes such as the quest motif and *bildungsroman*" (68 in this volume). Claudia Breger also focuses on polyvocality and dialogism in her analysis of Teju Cole's *Open City,* arguing for the cosmopolitan nonsovereignty of the character-narrator, Julius, who exceeds the boundaries of U.S. racial markers and their concomitant histories, so that the world that Cole creates exists beyond the binary of the black-and-white Atlantic: "As Julius's nonsovereign, polyvocal narrative performance unfolds the novel's open-ended process of affective-cognitive worldmaking, it traces the complexities of dis/connection and non/belonging in the contemporary world, in which the legacies of modern regimes of racialized violence no longer easily translate into collective identities" (176 in this volume). Coulombe, Spencer, and Breger reinforce that narrative theory in conversation with postcolonial and critical race theory yields textual interpretations that question the very categories of race and nation.

Besides being constructions, "narrative," "race," and "nation" also act as representations, especially when they are broken down into their categorical forms and especially when they are connected to one of the other two terms. Narratives about specific nations are seen as representing the values, histories, and experiences of the people in that land. Nations are often described as representing races of people. And narratives about race are understood as representations of racial groups. Where the water gets muddy is when suppositions of correspondences break down, between author and narrative, between race and nation, and among author, narrative, and race.

Blake Wilder and Stephanie Li examine works written by African American flesh-and-blood writers that are narrated by white characters, and in their analyses they demonstrate the ways narratology and critical race theory can most productively be in conversation, especially when there is a disconnect between the expectations of the race of the writer and the race of the narrator. Wilder looks at James Baldwin's short story "Going to Meet the Man" in order to show that "Baldwin depicts Jesse's narrative acts within the story as attempts to force order onto the disruptive social world around him through narrative worldmaking. In doing so, Baldwin draws attention to the blind spots of master narratives and implicitly suggests the collective benefit of moving beyond Jim Crow definitions of white masculinity" (72 in this volume). In Li's analysis of Ann Petry's *County Place,* the disjunction between author and narrator provides the critical place to think through issues of race, since "by emphasizing distinctions between the narrator and the implied author, we may recognize the novel's deft critique of the false entitlements of whiteness" (96 in this volume). Similarly, Christian Schmidt also questions the racial assumptions of author and narrator by considering the distinctly non-mimetic and postblack qualities of Percival Everett's *I Am Not Sidney Poitier.* As Schmidt maintains, "since an implied author by definition is a disembodied narrative entity, the novel's postblack implied authorial agency self-consciously points to the gap between text and world and between raced reality and raced/unraced diegesis, as it highlights the oxymoronic and non-naturalizable nature of postblackness" (83 in this volume). Wilder's, Li's, and Schmidt's contributions illustrate that narrative theory as applied to works written by black writers illuminates the various raced assumptions and worlds created in and through narrative, particularly ones adhering to notions of whiteness.

The concept of whiteness is so pervasive and universally accepted that one comes to expect that only nonwhite characters will be racially marked. As Patrick Horn observes, the strategic paralipsis or "the 'infractionary' or transgressive omission of Linda's racial identity" invites readers to assume whiteness, only to have their assumptions upended when her last name, Nguyen, is revealed (113 in this volume). Horn deftly unpacks assumptions of whiteness linked with assumptions of narratives: that unmarked narrators are presumed to be white and our interpretations of texts are thus influenced by these racial and narratological assumptions. Shaun Morgan provides a similar intervention into whiteness by explicating the two structural levels of focalization in Jhumpa Lahiri's "Sexy," the only story in her Pulitzer Prize–winning short story collection *Interpreter of Maladies* focalized through a white female protagonist. According to Morgan, "by alternating between the position of an externally focalized narrator and an internal character focalizer, Lahiri represents race as an ideological component of character perception" (151 in this volume). Whiteness takes on a universalized and hence naturalized essence in standard approaches to narrative studies as well as narrative theory, yet both Horn's and Morgan's essays unpack the assumptions of whiteness made by readers through narratological tools—their applications of paralipsis and focalization, respectively, reveal the ideological constructions of whiteness as much as (or more) than the Asian as exotic other.

Deborah Noel and Roy Pérez address issues of white ideology through worldmaking as not just a narrative device but as a strategy for survivorship for people of color. Noel looks at the constructions of "possible worlds" in works by Judith Cofer and Junot Díaz and argues that "the bibliophile characters featured in *The Latin Deli* and *Oscar Wao* identify with literary subcultures as a means of resistance against cultural hegemony and tradition. They become immersed in alternative possible worlds, and in the process, they imagine possible selves in order to cope with their existence in hostile text-actual-worlds" (180 in this volume). Pérez focuses on issues of performativity and the body in representations of queer Latina/o childhood in order to demonstrate how narratology can speak to embodied performers and performances: "narrative acts, theorized as performances in their worldmaking capacity, can approximate something other than the familiar, rote, and even deadening affects of racial and sexual normativity" (194 in this volume). For both Noel and Pérez, the possibility of creating other worlds or producing alternative narratives provides the Latina/o characters with a strategy for combatting normalizing narratives and allows readers to experience counter-narratives to prevailing discourses that privilege whiteness as the norm.

If we view narratives as rhetorical acts, then stories are told with a communicative purpose and are defined, according to James Phelan, as "somebody telling somebody else on some occasion and for some purpose(s) that something happened" (*Living to Tell* 18). One communicative purpose that all our contributors have touched on in their respective essays is the significance of race in the construction and reception of narratives. Just as Susan Lanser trenchantly argues for the primacy of gender in narrative constructions in her pioneering essay, "The 'I' of the Beholder: Equivocal Attachments and the Limits of Structuralist Narratology," so too do our contributors reinforce the integral and integrated nature of interpreting race within narrative and narrative within race. Sterling Bland and Catherine Romagnolo each demonstrate the ways in which form is content and content is form through analyzing the distinctiveness of race, generally, and blackness, specifically. As Bland asserts, "In a larger narrative sense, what is important about the novel [*Invisible Man*] is that it is only through the imperfect frame surrounding the narrative—its prologue and ambiguously universalized epilogue—that many of the questions raised by the narrator's recitation of experience can be addressed. The narrative structure itself is the primary lens through which the relationship between race, history, social structure, writing, and speech can be understood" (148 in this volume). Attending to the structure of narrative beginnings, Romagnolo questions the divide between form and content particularly for writers of color like Toni Morrison, proclaiming that "examining form, content, and ideology as mutually constitutive is not merely an option when studying minoritized writers, it is essential—integral to a full understanding of the work their texts perform. As my reading will suggest, narrative elements such as beginnings can signify in vastly different ways for writers of color who have not had the luxury of assuming narrative authority and agency" (45 in this volume). What Bland, Romagnolo, and all the contributors to this collection make abundantly clear is that race matters—it matters as a representation of reality, as a hermeneutics of narrative, and as a sociohistorical element that has aesthetic and narratological significance.

Race matters for ethnic American literature and for narratology, which all the essays in this volume confirm. And more to the point, the fields of narratology and critical race theory are also not so dissimilar. Chris González and Sue Kim astutely illustrate, in their respective opening essays to this collection, the relationship of narrative theory to Latina/o and Asian American literature. González's essay insightfully examines the multifaceted nature of how Latina/o literature is produced, read, and received through an exploration of narrative concepts such as storyworld, ideal readers, and actual readers. According to González:

> While there are many aspects of Latina/o narratives that might greatly expand our understanding of narrative writ large, my aim here is to propose a model for understanding how storyworlds invite readers to take up the task of not just understanding Latina/o narratives but also actually participating in the creation of these richly textured worlds as a hospitable, ideal readership might. My reason for concentrating on the reception end of the narrative and the reconstructed storyworld is that often in Latina/o literary scholarship, the narrative design itself is viewed the way some view the package of something purchased—as a necessary means of conveyance for its contents, but little more than that. (41–42 in this volume)

Attending to similar field-level analyses, Sue Kim's contribution, "What Asian American Studies and Narrative Theory Can Do for Each Other" ably maps out the foundational texts of each field in order to show "not only productive differences but also surprising resonances between early Asian Americanist and narratological texts" (14 in this volume). Comparing Dorrit Cohn's concept of "cognitive privilege" with early Asian American criticism, which has been "centrally concerned with this struggle for 'cognitive privilege'—in particular, *which* minds have been seen to be legible or inscrutable, and how 'minds' (i.e., subjectivity, agency, identity) have been defined" (25 in this volume), Kim makes a persuasive case for understanding "the potential common ground between narratology and Asian American literary studies" (26 in this volume). Seeing points of productive convergence in critical race and narrative theories, González's and Kim's essays validate the emergence of a critical race narratology.

The intersections between narrative and critical race theories, as exemplified in the essays within *Narrative, Race, and Ethnicity in the United States,* are rich, manifold, and mutually illuminating. From macro examinations of the fields of narratology and ethnic American literature to the micro explications of various narratives written by writers of color and narrated by an assortment of racialized narrators, the works in this collection offer a multipronged and prodigious engagement of thinking through constructions of race, ethnicity, and narrative. However, the one thing they do not offer is an exhaustive examination of these topics. Returning to the introduction of this collection, the editors wish to reiterate that "these essays open up some of the many avenues for discussion that exist at this exciting intersection. As such, this volume is intended not as the final word, but as an opening salvo; we hope we have demonstrated not the limitations of the potential threads that can be teased out of the larger fabric, but rather the variety of possibilities that exist" (8 in this volume). So let us turn, now, to further possibilities, future connections if you will, between critical race theory and narratology: What other subjects should be mined in the nascent field of critical race narratology?

Certainly this collection of essays has not exceeded coverage of either narratological concepts or ethnic and racial groups in the United States. We received far more essays examining African American literature than any other category, and we received no essays investigating whiteness in a white-authored text (more on that later). Though there are essays in our collection looking at Asian American novels, the sheer diversity of ethnicities that the term "Asian American" encompasses is dizzying since it covers ethnic-nationalities from China, Japan, Korea, the Philippines, Viet Nam, Cambodia, Thailand, Singapore, Malaysia, Laos, Bhutan, India, Pakistan, Sri Lanka, Mongolia,

Tibet, Taiwan, Syria, Iran, Iraq, and other countries too numerous to catalog. Added to this complexity is deciding which type of Asian American literature one will analyze: Early Asian American literature written before World War II? Contemporary Asian American literature after the term was officially coined during the Third World strikes of the late 1960s? And what about mixed-race Asian American literature—should a work written by someone who is half black and half Japanese count as Asian or African American literature? As neither/both? In what ways would the concept of flesh-and-blood and implied author be useful to teasing out the distinctions for authorship and hence categorization of these kinds of embodied ethnic literatures?[2]

Nor did we receive essays that looked at intersections of race and religion, a definite lacunae since so often religious identities become elided with racial identities, especially when discussing non-Christian religious identities. One need only consider our public discourse in a post-9/11 world to understand how terms such as "Muslim," "Middle-Eastern," and "Arab" have become confused for one another and conflated into a singularly charged and newly racialized term: terrorist. A comparison of Jewish American literary texts and Muslim American literary texts of the late twentieth and early twenty-first century, particularly in terms of the ethical and rhetorical function of the audience in light of global events that have deeply impacted U.S. history, would be a very rich contribution to critical race narratology.

Questions of nationality are another arena that should be pursued more trenchantly in critical race narratology. Though the contributors to this volume who worked on Native American authors gestured toward this concept, understanding the position of indigenous authors as not simply raced but nationalized is crucial. American Indian literature is not so much a racialized or ethnicized literature as it is a national literature, one that reflects the sovereign authority of the different tribal nation-states that indigenous authors represent. Louise Erdrich's novels are labeled Native American, but more specifically and accurately, she is an enrolled member of the Turtle Mountain Band of Chippewa Indians and has publicly identified herself as Ojibwe. Using narratological tools when examining issues of nationality and race, especially as they pertain to indigenous writers, provides a much-needed intervention in understanding American Indian literature not simply

---

2. There are critics of Asian American literature who have taken up this issue of authorship and categorization of Asian American literature. See Song; Sohn; and in a shameless self-promotion plug, my own book *Racial Ambiguity in Asian American Culture*, where I take up this issue in chapter 5: "Transgressive Texts and Ambiguous Authors: Racial Ambiguity in Asian American Literature." I also look at the issue of race and the implied author in my paper "Racial Constructs and Narratological Constructs in David Mitchell's *Cloud Atlas*."

as a subset of ethnicized American literature but as a field that has a set of political issues embedded in its narratives, ones that consolidate nationality for Ojibwe writers like Erdrich, even as they are being appropriated and categorized in other ways.

And while the list of interventions needed in critical race narratology can also not be exhaustively listed in this afterword, one area that needs especial attention is whiteness, especially in all its imaginary and imagined forms. Whiteness, like other types of racial formation, is a construct created by society as a means of hierarchization. Too often we forget to think about whiteness as a racial category, which, as critic Richard Dyer notes, becomes problematic since "as long as race is something only applied to non-white peoples, as long as white people are not racially seen and named, they/we function as a human norm. Other people are raced, we are just people" (10). Invocations of gender, sex, race, and ethnicity are almost invariably linked to those who are qualified as some type of "other" through their difference from the human norm that Dyer discusses: the non-male, the nonwhite, the non-hetero, the non-American. Thus, a collection of essays focusing on race and ethnicity in American narratives would be certainly remiss without mentioning, even if briefly in an afterword, the way that whiteness operates, narratologically. If we ignore whiteness and the ways in which whiteness operates as a trope, theme, character element, and plot device, we perpetuate the notion that race is something that only nonwhite people have and that racism is only a problem for the nonwhite. As Peggy McIntosh writes in her groundbreaking essay, "White Privilege: Unpacking the Invisible Knapsack": "I did not see myself as a racist because I was taught to recognize racism only in individual acts of meanness by members of my group, never in invisible systems conferring unsought racial dominance on my group from birth" (113). More scholarship examining whiteness that interrogates the norms of whiteness as universal in discussions of narratives, particularly those written by white authors, is a necessity for critical race narratology. We need to unpack the assumptions we are making as critics so that we do not unthinkingly privilege white-authored texts over others or make pronouncements about narrative functions without recognizing the impact of race and the privilege and power that has cohered to which texts are even published or made available to audiences, especially when considering U.S. literature and the history of the United States with respect to how people have become racialized over the last three centuries.

Race is as constructed a category as fictional characters: both are, at the end of the day, creations rather than natural essences. Nations, too, are but imagined constructions built from the collective will to believe in the geopolitical power of nation-states. Scholarship that interrogates the construction of all three of these terms can only strengthen the fields of ethnic American literature and narrative theory, creating insightful research and productive connections across both fields. There is much that critical race theory and narratology can do together, and we hope that *Narrative, Race, and Ethnicity in the United States* is but one example of the generative and fruitful scholarship that results from these discourses in dialogue with one another.

WORKS CITED

Abbott, H. Porter. "Story, Plot, and Narration." *The Cambridge Companion to Narrative*. Ed. David Herman. Cambridge: Cambridge UP, 2007. 39–51.

Acosta, Oscar "Zeta." *The Autobiography of a Brown Buffalo*. 1972. New York: Vintage Books, 1989.

———. *The Revolt of the Cockroach People*. 1973. New York: Vintage, 1989.

Adell, Sandra. *Double Consciousness/Double Bind: Theoretical Issues in Twentieth-Century Black Literature*. Urbana: U of Illinois P, 1994.

Adelson, Leslie. *The Turkish Turn in German Literature: Toward a New Critical Grammar of Migration*. New York: Palgrave, 2005.

Ahmed, Sara. *The Cultural Politics of Emotions*. Edinburgh: Edinburgh UP, 2004.

———. "Happy Objects." *The Affect Theory Reader*. Ed. Melissa Gregg and Gregory J. Seigworth. Durham: Duke UP, 2010. 30–51.

Akins, Adrienne. "'Next Time, Just Remember the Story': Unlearning Empire in Silko's *Ceremony*." *Studies in American Indian Literatures* 24.1 (2012): 1–14.

Alarcón, Norma, et al. "Introduction: Between Woman and Nation." *Between Woman and Nation: Nationalisms, Transnational Feminisms, and the State*. Ed. Caren Kaplan, Norma Alarcón, and Minoo Moallem. Durham: Duke UP, 1999.

Alber, Jan, and Monika Fludernik. Introduction. *Postclassical Narratology: Approaches and Analyses*. Ed. Jan Alber and Monika Fludernik. Columbus: The Ohio State UP, 2010. 1–31.

———, eds. *Postclassical Narratology: Approaches and Analyses*. Columbus: The Ohio State UP, 2010.

Alber, Jan, et al. Introduction. *A Poetics of Unnatural Narrative*. Ed. Jan Alber et al. Columbus: The Ohio State UP, 2013. 1–15.

Alberski, Wokciech. "Selected Functions of Narrative Structures in the Process of Social and Cultural Communication." *Styles of Communication* 4.1 (2012): 7–24.

Alcoff, Linda Martin. "The Problem of Speaking for Others." *Who Can Speak? Authority and Critical Identity*. Ed. Judith Roof and Robyn Wiegman. Urbana: U of Illinois P, 1995. 97–119.

Aldama, Arturo J. "Tayo's Journey Home: Crossblood Agency, Resistance, and Transformation in *Ceremony* by Leslie Marmon Silko." *Cross-Addressing: Resistance Literature and Cultural Borders*. Ed. John C. Hawley. New York: SUNY Press, 1996. 157–80.

Aldama, Frederick Luis, ed. *Analyzing World Fiction: New Horizons in Narrative Theory*. Austin: U of Texas P, 2011.

———. "Ethnicity." *Teaching Narrative Theory*. Ed. David Herman et al. New York: The Modern Language Association of America, 2010. 252–65.

———. "How to Use This Book." *Analyzing World Fiction: New Horizons in Narrative Theory*. Ed. Frederick Luis Aldama. Austin: U of Texas P, 2011. vii–xiii.

———. *Multicultural Comics: From Zap to Blue Beetle*. Austin: U of Texas P, 2010.

———. *Postethnic Narrative Criticism: Magicorealism in Oscar "Zeta" Acosta, Ana Castillo, Julie Dash, Hanif Kureshi, and Salman Rushdie*. Austin: U of Texas P, 2003.

———. *A User's Guide to Postcolonial and Latino Borderlands Fiction*. Austin: U of Texas P, 2009.

———. *Your Brain on Latino Comics*. Austin: U of Texas P, 2009.

Aldama, Frederick Luis, and Patrick Colm Hogan. *Conversations on Cognitive Cultural Studies: Literature, Language, and Aesthetics*. Columbus: Ohio State UP, 2014.

Ali, Suki. *Mixed-Race, Post-Race: Gender, New Ethnicities, and Cultural Practices*. New York: Berg, 2003.

Allen, Dennis. "Why Things Don't Add up in 'The Sum of Us': Sexuality and Genre Crossing in the Romantic Comedy." *Narrative* 7.1 (1999): 71–88.

Allen, Paula Gunn. *The Sacred Hoop: Recovering the Feminine in American Indian Traditions*. Boston: Beacon Press, 1986.

Anderson, Benedict. *Imagined Communities: Reflections on the Origins and Spread of Nationalism*. London: Verso, 1983.

Anzaldúa, Gloria. *Borderlands/La Frontera: The New Mestiza*. San Francisco: Aunt Lute Press, 1999.

Appiah, Kwame Anthony. *Cosmopolitanism: Ethics in a World of Strangers*. New York: Norton, 2006.

Aristotle. *Poetics*. Trans. Malcolm Heath. New York: Penguin Books, 1996.

Asian Women's Coalition, ed. *Asian Women*. Berkeley: U of California P, 1971.

Awkward, Michael. "A Black Man's Place(s) in Black Feminist Criticism." *Who Can Speak? Authority and Critical Identity*. Ed. Judith Roof and Robyn Wiegman. Urbana: U of Illinois P, 1995. 70–91.

Baker, Lisa. "Storytelling and Democracy (in the Radical Sense): A Conversation with John Edgar Wideman." *African American Review* 34.2 (2000): 263–72.

Bakhtin, M. M. *The Dialogic Imagination: Four Essays*. Trans. Caryl Emerson and Michael Holquist. Austin: U of Texas P, 1981.

Bal, Mieke. *Narratology: An Introduction to the Theory of Narrative*. 2nd ed. Toronto: U of Toronto P, 1997.

Baldwin, James. *Collected Essays*. New York: Library of America, 1998.

———. *Going to Meet the Man*. New York: Dial Press, 1965.

Barthold, Bonnie. *Black Time: Fiction of Africa, the Caribbean and the United States*. New Haven: Yale UP, 1981.

Bauerkemper, Joseph. "Narrating Nationhood: Indian Time and Ideologies of Progress." *Studies in American Indian Literatures* 19.4 (2007): 27–53.

Bell, Bernard W. "Ann Petry's Demythologizing of American Culture and Afro-American Character." *Conjuring: Black Women, Fiction, and Literary Tradition.* Ed. Marjorie Pryse and Hortense J. Spillers. Bloomington: Indiana UP, 1985. 105–15.

Bell, Derrick. "*Brown v. Board of Education* and the Interest Convergence Dilemma." *Critical Race Theory: The Key Writings That Formed the Movement.* Ed. Kimberlé Crenshaw et al. New York: New Press, 1996. 20–29.

Bernard, Emily. "'Raceless' Writing and Difference: Ann Petry's *Country Place* and the African-American Literary Canon." *Studies in American Fiction* 33.1 (2005): 87–117.

Best, Stephen, and Sharon Marcus. "Surface Reading: An Introduction." *Representations* 108.1 (2009): 1–16.

Bonilla-Silva, Eduardo. *Racism without Racists: Color-Blind Racism and the Persistence of Racial Inequality in the United States.* Lanham: Rowman & Littlefield, 2003.

Booth, Wayne. *The Company We Keep: An Ethics of Fiction.* Oakland: U of California P, 1989.

———. *The Rhetoric of Fiction.* 2nd ed. Chicago: U of Chicago P, 1983.

Bow, Leslie. *Asian Americans and Racial Anomaly in the Segregated South.* New York: New York UP, 2010.

Bracher, Mark. *Literature and Social Justice: Protest Novels, Cognitive Politics, and Schema Criticism.* Austin: U of Texas P, 2013.

Breger, Claudia. *An Aesthetics of Narrative Performance: Transnational Theater, Literature and Film in Contemporary Germany.* Columbus: The Ohio State UP, 2012.

———. "Configuring Affect: Complex Worldmaking in Fatih Akın's *Auf der anderen Seite* (*The Edge of Heaven*)." *Cinema Journal* 54.1 (2014): 65–87.

Bruce-Novoa, Juan. *Chicano Poetry: A Response to Chaos.* Austin: U of Texas P, 1982.

Bruhm, Steven, and Natasha Hurley, eds. *Curiouser: On the Queerness of Children.* Minneapolis: Minnesota UP, 2004.

Butler, Judith. *Excitable Speech: A Politics of the Performative.* New York: Routledge, 1997.

———. *Gender Trouble: Feminism and the Subversion of Identity.* New York: Routledge, 1990.

Callahan, John F. *In the African-American Grain: The Pursuit of Voice in Twentieth-Century Black Fiction.* Urbana: U of Illinois P, 1998.

Campbell, Joseph. *The Hero with a Thousand Faces.* Novato: New World Library, 2008.

Campbell, Josie P. "To Sing the Song, to Tell the Tale: A Study of Toni Morrison and Simone Schwarz-Bart." *Comparative Literature Studies* 3 (1985): 394–412.

Carbado, Devon W. "Colorblind Intersectionality." *Signs* 38.4 (2013): 811–45.

Carpio, Glenda R., et al. "What Was African American Literature?" *PMLA* 128.2 (2013): 386–409.

Carr Lee, Catherine. "The South in Toni Morrison's *Song of Solomon: Initiation, Healing, and Home.*" *Studies in the Literary Imagination* 31.2 (1998): 109–23.

Carrasquillo, Marci L. "Oscar 'Zeta' Acosta's American Odyssey." *MELUS* 35.1 (2010): 77–97.

Carvajal, Doreen. "Of Hispanic Literature and Not So Equal Opportunities." *New York Times* 4 May 1996.

Chanady, Amaryll. "Cultural Memory and the New World Imaginary." *Colonizer and Colonized.* Ed. Theo D'Haen and Patrick Krus. Amsterdam: Rodopi, 2000. 183–92.

Charles, John C. *Abandoning the Black Hero: Sympathy and Privacy in the Postwar African American White-Life Novel.* New Brunswick, NJ: Rutgers UP, 2013.

Chatman, Seymour. *Story and Discourse: Narrative Structure in Fiction and Film*. Ithaca: Cornell UP, 1978.

Chavkin, Allan, ed. *Leslie Marmon Silko's* Ceremony: *A Casebook*. Oxford: Oxford UP, 2002.

Cheah, Pheng. "Cosmopolitanism." *Theory, Culture & Society* 23.2–3 (2006): 486–96.

Cheng, Anne Anlin. "Ellison and the Politics of Melancholia." *The Cambridge Companion to Ralph Ellison*. Cambridge: Cambridge UP, 2005. 121–36.

Chesnutt, Charles W. *Conjure Tales and Stories of the Color Line*. Penguin Classics. New York: Penguin, 2000.

———. *The Wife of His Youth, and Other Stories of the Color Line*. Ridgewood, NJ: Gregg Press, 1967.

Cheung, King-Kok. "*Aiiieeeee!* and Asian American Literature: Forty Years Later." Annual Convention of the Modern Language Association, Chicago. 10 Jan. 2014. Roundtable discussion.

Cheyfitz, Eric. "The (Post)Colonial Predicament of Native American Studies." *interventions* 4.3 (2002): 405–27.

Chin, Frank, et al., eds. *Aiiieeeee!: An Anthology of Asian-American Writers*. Washington, DC: Howard UP, 1974.

Chow, Rey. *Entanglements, or Transmedial Thinking about Capture*. Durham: Duke UP, 2012.

Clayton, Jay. *The Pleasures of Babel: Contemporary American Literature and Theory*. New York: Oxford UP, 1993.

Cofer, Judith. *The Latin Deli*. New York: W. W. Norton & Co., 1993.

Cohn, Dorrit. *Transparent Minds: Narrative Modes for Presenting Consciousness in Fiction*. Princeton: Princeton UP, 1978.

Cole, Teju. *Open City*. New York: Random House, 2012.

Conrad, Joseph. *Heart of Darkness*. New York: Penguin Group, 2012.

Cook-Lynn, Elizabeth. "Who Gets to Tell Stories?" *Wicazo Sa Review* 9.1 (1993): 60–64.

Cuddy-Keane, Melba. "Virginia Woolf and Beginning's Ragged Edge." *Narrative Beginnings: Theories and Practices*. Ed. Brian Richardson. Lincoln: U of Nebraska P, 2008. 96–112.

Culler, Jonathan. "Omniscience." *Narrative* 12.1 (2004): 22–34.

———. "Story and Discourse in the Analysis of Narrative." *The Pursuit of Signs: Semiotics, Literature, Deconstruction*. Ithaca: Cornell UP, 1981. 169–87.

Cvetkovich, Ann. "Public Feelings." *After Sex: On Writing since Queer Theory*. Ed. Janet Halley and Andrew Parker. Durham: Duke UP, 2011. 169–79.

de Saussure, Ferdinand. *Course in General Linguistics*. New York: HardPress Publishing, 2013.

Delany, Samuel, and Joseph Beam. "Samuel R. Delany: The Possibility of Possibilities." *Conversations with Samuel R. Delany*. Ed. Carl Freedman. Jackson: U of Mississippi P, 2009.

Delgado, Richard. *Critical Race Theory: An Introduction*. New York: New York UP, 2001.

———. "Storytelling for Oppositionists and Others: A Plea for Narrative." *Michigan Law Review* 87.8 (1989): 2411–41.

Demirtürk, E. Lâle. "Rescripted Performances of Blackness as 'Parodies of Whiteness': Discursive Frames of Recognition in Percival Everett's *I Am Not Sidney Poitier*." *The Contemporary African American Novel: Multiple Cities, Multiple Subjectivities, and Discursive Practices of Whiteness in Everyday Urban Encounters*. Madison, NJ: Fairleigh Dickinson UP, 2012. 85–109.

Díaz, Junot. *The Brief Wondrous Life of Oscar Wao*. New York: Penguin, 2007.

Donahue, James J. "Focalization, Ethics, and Cosmopolitanism in James Welch's *Fools Crow*." *JNT: Journal of Narrative Theory* 44.1 (2014): 54–80.

Dubek, Laura. "White Family Values in Ann Petry's *Country Place*." *MELUS* 29.2 (2004): 55–76.

Du Bois, W. E. B. *The Souls of Black Folk*. New York: Modern Library, 2003.

Duggan, Lisa. *Twilight of Equality?: Neoliberalism, Cultural Politics, and the Attack on Democracy*. Boston: Beacon, 2003.

Dunbar, Paul Laurence. *Lyrics of Lowly Life*. Upper Saddle River, NJ: Gregg Press, 1968.

Dyer, Richard. "The Matter of Whiteness." *White Privilege: Essential Readings on the Other Side of Racism*. Ed. Paula S. Rothenberg. New York: Worth Publisher, 2005. 9–14.

Edelman, Lee. *No Future: Queer Theory and the Death Drive*. Durham: Duke UP, 2004.

Ellison, Ralph. "Change the Joke and Slip the Yoke." *The Collected Essays of Ralph Ellison*. Ed. John F. Callahan. New York: The Modern Library, 1995. 100–112.

——. "Harlem Is Nowhere." *The Collected Essays of Ralph Ellison*. Ed. John F. Callahan. New York: The Modern Library, 1995. 320–27.

——. "Introduction to Shadow and Act." *The Collected Essays of Ralph Ellison*. Ed. John F. Callahan. New York: The Modern Library, 1995. 49–60.

——. *Invisible Man*. Random House: New York, 1995.

——. "On Initiation Rites and Power." *The Collected Essays of Ralph Ellison*. Ed. John F. Callahan. New York: The Modern Library, 1995. 520–41.

——. "Twentieth-Century Fiction and the Black Mask of Humanity." *The Collected Essays of Ralph Ellison*. Ed. John F. Callahan. New York: The Modern Library, 1995. 81–99.

——. "The World and the Jug." *The Collected Essays of Ralph Ellison*. Ed. John F. Callahan. New York: The Modern Library, 1995. 155–88.

Erdrich, Louise. *Tracks*. New York: HarperCollins, 1988.

Everett, Percival. *Erasure*. London: Faber and Faber, 2004.

——. *I Am Not Sidney Poitier*. Saint Paul: Gray Wolf Press, 2009.

Falk, Richard. "Reflections on Teju Cole's *Open City*." *Global Justice in the 21st Century*. 21 Feb. 2013. Web. <https://richardfalk.wordpress.com/2013/02/21/reflections-on-teju-coles-open-city/>.

Fanon, Frantz. *Black Skins, White Masks*. Trans. Charles Lam Markmann. New York: Grove, 1967.

Farrell, Susan. "'Who'd He Leave Behind?': Gender and History in Toni Morrison's *Song of Solomon*." *Having Our Way: Women Rewriting Tradition in Twentieth-Century America*. Ed. Harriet Pollack. Lewisburg: Bucknell UP, 1995. 131–50.

Fludernik, Monika. "Identity/Alterity." *The Cambridge Companion to Narrative*. Ed. David Herman. Cambridge: Cambridge UP, 2007. 260–73.

Foden, Giles. "*Open City* by Teju Cole—Review." *The Guardian* 17 Aug. 2011.

Foley, Barbara. *Wrestling with the Left: The Making of Ralph Ellison's* Invisible Man. Durham: Duke UP, 2010.

Gates, Henry Louis Jr. *The Signifying Monkey: A Theory of African American Literary Criticism*. New York: Oxford UP, 1989.

Gee, Emma, ed. *Counterpoint: Perspectives on Asian America*. Los Angeles: Asian American Studies Center, UCLA, 1976.

Genette, Gérard. *Narrative Discourse: An Essay in Method.* Trans. Jane E. Lewin. Ithaca: Cornell UP, 1980.

———. *Narrative Discourse Revisited.* Trans. Jane E. Lewin. Ithaca: Cornell UP, 1988.

———. "Order, Duration, Frequency." *Narrative/Theory.* New York: Longman Publishers, 1996. 132–39.

———. *Paratexts: Thresholds of Interpretation.* New York: Cambridge UP, 1997.

Gerber, David. "Haley's *Roots* and Our Own: An Inquiry into the Nature of a Popular Phenomenon." *Journal of Ethnic Studies* 5.3 (1977): 87–111.

Gilroy, Paul. *Against Race: Imagining Political Culture beyond the Color Line.* Cambridge: Harvard UP, 2000.

———. *Postcolonial Melancholia.* New York: Columbia UP, 2005.

Glancy, Diane. *Pushing the Bear.* New York: Harcourt Brace and Company, 1996.

Gohrisch, Jana. "Cultural Exchange and the Representation of History in Postcolonial Literature." *European Journal of English Studies* 10.3 (2006): 231–47.

Golden, Thelma. Introduction. *Freestyle.* Studio Museum in Harlem. Thelma Golden et al. New York: Studio Museum in Harlem, 2001. 14–15.

Goodman, Nelson. *Ways of Worldmaking.* Indianapolis: Hackett, 1978.

Grewal, Inderpal, and Caren Kaplan, eds. *Scattered Hegemonies: Postmodernity and Transnational Feminist Practices.* Minneapolis: U of Minnesota P, 1999.

Hale, Grace Elizabeth. *Making Whiteness: The Culture of Segregation in the South, 1890–1940.* New York: Pantheon Books, 1998.

Hanhardt, Cristina B. *Safe Space: Gay Neighborhood History and the Politics of Violence.* Durham: Duke UP, 2014.

Hanlon, Christopher. "Eloquence and *Invisible Man.*" *College Literature* 32.4 (2005): 74–98.

Hanna, Monica. "'Reassembling the Fragments': Battling Historiographies, Caribbean Discourse, and Nerd Genres in Junot Díaz's *The Brief Wondrous Life of Oscar Wao.*" *Callaloo* 33.2 (2010): 498–520.

Harding, Sandra. "Subjectivity, Experience, and Knowledge: An Epistemology from/for Rainbow Coalition Politics." *Who Can Speak? Authority and Critical Identity.* Ed. Judith Roof and Robyn Wiegman. Urbana: U of Illinois P, 1995. 120–36.

Harris, Keith M. "In the Life on the Down Low: Where's a Black Gay Man to Go?" *Beyond Masculinity: Essays by Queer Men on Gender and Politics.* 17 July 2008. Web. 27 February 2017. <http://www.beyondmasculinity.com/articles/harris.php>

Harris, Leslie A. "Myth as Structure in Toni Morrison's Song of Solomon." *MELUS* 3 (1980): 69–76.

Heinze, Ruediger. "Violations of Mimetic Epistemology in First-Person Narrative Fiction." *Narrative* 16.3 (2008): 279–97.

Herman, David. *Basic Elements of Narrative.* West Sussex: Wiley-Blackwell, 2009.

———. *The Cambridge Companion to Narrative.* Cambridge: Cambridge UP, 2007.

———. *Narratologies: New Perspectives on Narrative Analysis.* Columbus: The Ohio State UP, 1999.

———. *Story Logic: Problems and Possibilities of Narrative.* Lincoln: U of Nebraska P, 2002.

———. *Storytelling and the Sciences of Mind.* Cambridge: MIT Press, 2013.

Herman, David, James Phelan, Peter J. Rabinowitz, Brian Richardson, and Robyn Warhol. *Narrative Theory: Core Concepts and Critical Debates*. Columbus: The Ohio State UP, 2012.

———. *Teaching Narrative Theory*. New York: The Modern Language Association of America, 2010.

Hirsch, Bernard A. "'The Telling Which Continues': Oral Tradition and the Written Word in Leslie Marmon Silko's *Storyteller*." *"Yellow Woman": Leslie Marmon Silko*. Ed. Melody Graulich. New Brunswick, NJ: Rutgers UP, 1993. 151–84.

Ho, Jennifer Ann. *Consumption and Identity in Asian American Coming-of-Age Novels*. New York: Routledge, 2005.

———. *Racial Ambiguity in Asian American Culture*. New Brunswick, NJ: Rutgers UP, 2015.

———. "Racial Constructs and Narratological Constructs in David Mitchell's *Cloud Atlas*." International Society for the Study of Narrative: International Conference on Narrative, University of Amsterdam, Amsterdam, Netherlands, 17 June 2016. Panel.

Hogan, Patrick Colm. *Affective Narratology*. Lincoln: U of Nebraska P, 2011.

———. *Narrative Discourse: Authors and Narrators in Literature, Film, and Art*. Columbus: The Ohio State UP, 2013.

———. *Understanding Nationalism: On Narrative, Cognitive Science, and Identity*. Columbus, Ohio State UP, 2009.

Holladay, Hilary. "Narrative Space in Ann Petry's *Country Place*." *Xavier Review* 16.1 (1996): 21–35.

Holquist, Michael, ed. *The Dialogic Imagination: Four Essays by M. M. Bakhtin*. Austin: U of Texas P, 1981.

Homer, Sean. *Jacques Lacan*. London: Routledge, 2005.

Howe, LeAnne. "Blind Bread and the Business of Theory Making, by Embarrassed Grief." *Reasoning Together: The Native Critics Collective*. Ed. Craig S. Womack et al. Norman: U of Oklahoma P, 2008. 325–52.

Hutchinson, John. "Cultural Nationalism and Moral Regeneration." *Nationalism*. Ed. John Hutchinson and Anthony B. Smith. New York: Oxford UP, 1994. 122–31.

Iser, Wolfgang. *The Implied Reader: Patterns of Communication in Prose Fiction from Bunyan to Beckett*. Baltimore: Johns Hopkins UP, 1974.

It Gets Better Project. "It Gets Better: Dan and Terry." *YouTube*. 21 Sept. 2010. Web. <http://www.itgetsbetter.org/#7lcVyvg2Qlo>.

———. "What Is the It Gets Better Project?" n.d. Web. 26 April 2015. <http://www.itgetsbetter.org/pages/about-it-gets-better-project>.

Iwasaki, Bruce. "Introduction: Literature." *Counterpoint: Perspectives on Asian America*. Ed. Emma Gee. Los Angeles: Asian American Studies Center, UCLA, 1976. 452–63.

Jablon, Madelyn. *Black Metafiction: Self-Consciousness in African American Literature*. Iowa City: U of Iowa P, 1997.

Jackson, Elizabeth. "Transcending the Politics of 'Where You're From': Postcolonial Nationality and Cosmopolitanism in Jhumpa Lahiri's *Interpreter of Maladies*." *ARIEL: A Review of International English Literature* 43.1 (2012): 109–26.

Jauss, Hans Robert. *Aesthetic Experience and Literary Hermeneutics*. 1977. Trans. Michael Shaw. Minneapolis: U of Minnesota P, 1982.

———. *Toward an Aesthetic of Reception*. 1977. Trans. Timothy Bahti. Minneapolis: U of Minnesota P, 1982.

Jennings, La Vinia Delois. *Toni Morrison and the Idea of Africa*. Cambridge: Cambridge UP, 2008.

Johnson, James Weldon. *The Autobiography of an Ex-Colored Man*. New York: Vintage Books, 1989.

Joyce, Joyce A. *Warriors, Conjurers and Priests: Defining African-centered Literary Criticism*. Chicago: Third World Press, 1994.

Justice, Daniel Heath. "'Go Away, Water!' Kingship Criticism and the Decolonization Imperative." *Reasoning Together: The Native Critics Collective*. Ed. Craig S. Womack et al. Norman: U of Oklahoma P, 2008. 147–68.

Kacandes, Irene. *Talk Fiction: Literature and the Talk Explosion*. Lincoln: U of Nebraska P, 2001.

Kakutani, Michiko. "Roaming the Streets, Taking Surreal Turns." *The New York Times* 18 May 2011.

Kaplan, Amy. *The Anarchy of American Empire in the Making of U. S. Culture*. Cambridge: Harvard UP, 2005.

———. "Left Alone with America." *Cultures of United States Imperialism*. Ed. Amy Kaplan and Donald Pease. Durham: Duke UP, 1993. 3–21.

Kaufman, Geoff F., and Lisa K. Libby. "Changing Beliefs and Behavior through Experience-Taking." *Journal of Personality and Social Psychology* 103.1 (2012): 1–19.

Keen, Suzanne. *Empathy and the Novel*. Oxford: Oxford UP, 2007.

Kim, Elaine. *Asian American Literature: An Introduction to the Writings and Their Social Context*. Philadelphia: Temple UP, 1982.

Kim, Sue J. "Introduction: Decolonizing Narrative Theory." *Journal of Narrative Theory* 42.3 (2012): 233–47.

King, Thomas. *Green Grass, Running Water*. New York: Bantam Books, 1993.

———. *The Truth about Stories: A Native Narrative*. Minneapolis: U of Minnesota P, 2005.

Koshy, Susan. "Minority Cosmopolitanism." *PMLA* 126.3 (2011): 592–609.

Krupat, Arnold. "The Dialogic of Silko's *Storyteller*." *Narrative Chance: Postmodern Discourse on Native American Indian Literatures*. Albuquerque: U of New Mexico P, 1989. 58–68.

———. "Postcolonialism, Ideology, and Native American Literature." *Postcolonial Theory and the United States: Race, Ethnicity, and Literature*. Ed. Amritjit Singh and Peter Schmidt. Jackson: U of Mississippi P, 2000. 73–94.

Lacan, Jacques. *Écrits: A Selection*. Trans. Alan Sheridan. New York: Norton, 1977.

Lahiri, Jhumpa. "Sexy." *Interpreter of Maladies*. Boston: Houghton Mifflin, 1999. 83–110.

Lanser, Susan. *Fictions of Authority: Women Writers and Narrative Voice*. Ithaca: Cornell UP, 1992.

———. "The 'I' of the Beholder: Equivocal Attachments and the Limits of Structuralist Narratology." *A Companion to Narrative Theory*. Ed. James Phelan and Peter J. Rabinowitz. Malden, MA: Blackwell, 2005. 206–19.

———. "(Im)plying the Author." *Narrative* 9 (2001): 153–60.

———. *The Narrative Act: Point of View in Prose Fiction*. Princeton: Princeton UP, 1981.

———. "Queering Narratology." *Ambiguous Discourse: Feminist Narratology and British Women Writers*. Chapel Hill: U of North Carolina P, 1996. 250–61.

———. "Sexing the Narrative: Propriety, Desire, and the Engendering of Narratology." *Narrative* 3.1 (1995): 85–94.

———. "Susan S. Lanser." *Narrative Theories and Poetics: 5 Questions.* Ed. Peer F. Bundgård et al. Copenhagen: Automatic Press, 2012. 95–101.

———. "Toward a Feminist Narratology." *Essentials of the Theory of Fiction.* Ed. Michael J. Hoffman and Patrick D. Murphy. Durham: Duke UP, 1996. 453–72.

Lee, Christopher. *The Semblance of Identity: Aesthetic Mediation in Asian American Literature.* Stanford: Stanford UP, 2012.

Lee, Kun Jong. "Ellison's *Invisible Man*: Emersonianism Revised." *PMLA* 107.2 (1992): 331–44.

Lewek, Thomas. "City of the Body." *The Critical Flame.* 5 March 2012. Web. <http://criticalflame.org/city-of-the-body/>

Lewis, David. "Scorekeeping in a Language Game." *Journal of Philosophical Logic* 8.1 (1979): 339–59.

Li, Stephanie. *Signifying without Specifying: Racial Discourse in the Age of Obama.* New Brunswick: Rutgers UP, 2012.

Ling, Amy. Rev. of *Asian American Literature: An Introduction to the Writings and Their Social Context,* by Elaine Kim. *MELUS* 10.3 (1983): 89–92.

Lingan, John. Rev. of *I Am Not Sidney Poitier,* by Percival Everett. *The Quarterly Conversation.* 7 Dec. 2009. Web. 30 Oct. 2012.

Lipsitz, George. *The Possessive Investment in Whiteness: How White People Profit from Identity Politics.* Philadelphia: Temple UP, 1998.

Littlejohn, David. *Black on White: A Critical Survey of Writing by American Negroes.* New York: Grossman Publishers, 1966.

López, Ian Haney. *White By Law, 10th Anniversary Edition: The Legal Construction of Race.* New York: NYU Press, 2006.

Lowe, Lisa. *Immigrant Acts.* Durham: Duke UP, 1996.

Manning, Brandon. "'I Felt Like I Was Part of the Troop': Satire, Feminist Narratology, and Community." Ed. Derek Maus and James J. Donahue. *Post-Soul Satire: Black Identity After Civil Rights.* Jackson: UP of Mississippi, 2014. 125–36.

Markus, Hazel Rose, and Paula M. L. Moya. *Doing Race: 21 Essays for the 21st Century.* New York: W. W. Norton & Co., 2010.

Martín-Rodríguez, Manuel M. *Life in Search of Readers: Reading (in) Chicano/a Literature.* Albuquerque: U of New Mexico P, 2003.

Martínez, M. Angeles. "Storyworld Possible Selves and the Phenomenon of Narrative Immersion: Testing a New Theoretical Construct" *Narrative* 22.1 (2014): 110–31.

Mason, Theodore O., Jr. "The Novelist as Conservator: Stories and Comprehension in Toni Morrison's *Song of Solomon*." *Contemporary Literature* 29.4 (1998): 564–81.

Massaro, Toni M. "Empathy, Legal Storytelling, and the Rule of Law: New Words, Old Wounds?" *Michigan Law Review* 87.8 (1989): 2099–127.

Matz, Jesse. "'No Future' vs. 'It Gets Better': Queer Prospects for Narrative Temporality." *Narrative Theory Unbound: Queer and Feminist Interventions.* Ed. Robyn Warhol and Susan S. Lanser. Columbus: Ohio State UP, 2015. 227–50.

Maus, Derek C., and James J. Donahue, eds. *Post-Soul Satire: Black Identity after Civil Rights.* Jackson: UP of Mississippi, 2014.

McGurl, Mark. *The Program Era: Postwar Fiction and the Rise of Creative Writing.* Cambridge: Harvard UP, 2009.

McIntosh, Peggy. "White Privilege: Unpacking the Invisible Knapsack." *White Privilege: Essential Readings on the Other Side of Racism.* Ed. Paula S. Rothenberg. New York: Worth Publisher, 2005. 109–13.

Mercer, Kobena. "Diaspora Aesthetics and Visual Culture." *Black Cultural Traffic: Crossroads in Global Performance and Popular Culture.* Ed. Harry J. Elam Jr. and Kennell Jackson. Ann Arbor: U of Michigan P, 2005. 141–61.

Messud, Claire. "The Secret Sharer." *New York Review of Books* 14 July 2011.

Miller, D. A. *The Novel and the Police.* Berkeley: U of California P, 1988.

Miller, J. Hillis. *Reading Narrative.* Norman: U of Oklahoma P, 1998.

Millican, Arthenia Bates. "Fire as the Symbol of a Leadening Existence in 'Going to Meet the Man.'" *James Baldwin: A Critical Evaluation.* Ed. Therman O'Daniel. Washington DC: Howard UP, 1977. 170–80.

Mills, Elizabeth Shown, and Gary B. Mills. "*Roots* and the New 'Faction': A Legitimate Tool for Clio?" *The Virginia Magazine of History and Biography* 89.1 (1981): 4–12.

Miron, Louis, and Jonathan Inda. "Race as a Kind of Speech Act." *Cultural Studies* 5 (2000): 85–107.

Morrison, Toni. "The Language Must Not Sweat: A Conversation with Toni Morrison." Thomas LeClair. *New Republic* 184 (1981): 25–29.

———. *Playing in the Dark: Whiteness and the Literary Imagination.* New York: Vintage Books, 1992.

———. *Song of Solomon.* New York: Penguin Books, 1987.

———. "Unspeakable Things Unspoken: The Afro-American Presence in American Literature." The Tanner Lectures on Human Values, University of Michigan. 7 Oct. 1988.

Muñoz, José. *Cruising Utopia: The Then and There of Queer Futurity.* New York: New York UP, 2009.

———. *Disidentifications: Queers of Color and the Performance of Politics.* Minneapolis: U of Minnesota P, 1999.

Nelles, William. "Historical and Implied Authors and Readers." *Comparative Literature* 45 (1993): 22–46.

———. "A Hypothetical Implied Author." *Style* 45.1 (2011): 109–18.

Nericcio, William Anthony. Afterword. "How This Book Reads You: Looking beyond *Analyzing World Fiction: New Horizons in Narrative Theory.*" *Analyzing World Fiction New Horizons in Narrative Theory.* Ed. Frederick Luis Aldama. Austin: U of Texas P, 2011. 269–76.

Nielsen, Henrik Skov. "Naturalizing and Unnaturalizing Reading Strategies: Focalization Revisited." *A Poetics of Unnatural Narrative.* Ed. Jan Alber et al. Columbus: The Ohio State UP, 2013. 67–93.

Nuttall, A. D. *Openings: Narrative Beginnings from the Epic to the Novel.* Oxford: Clarendon Press, 1992.

Nyong'o, Tavia. "School Daze." *Bully Bloggers.* 30 Sept. 2010. Web. 27 April 2013. <http://bullybloggers.wordpress.com/2010/09/30/school-daze/>.

Ochs, Elinor, and Lisa Capps. "Narrating the Self." *Annual Review of Anthropology* 25 (1996): 19–43.

Omi, Michael, and Howard Winant. *Racial Formation in the United States: From the 1960s to the 1990s.* New York: Routledge, 1994.

Ong, Aihwa. *Flexible Citizenship: The Cultural Logics of Transnationality.* Durham: Duke UP, 1999.

———. *Neoliberalism as Exception: Mutations in Citizenship and Sovereignty.* Durham: Duke UP, 2006.

Owens, Louis. "As If an Indian Were Really an Indian: Native American Voices and Postcolonial Theory." *Native American Representations: First Encounters, Distorted Images, and Literary Appropriations.* Ed. Gretchen M. Bataille. Lincoln: U of Nebraska P, 2001. 11–24.

———. "'The Very Essence of Our Lives': Leslie Silko's Webs of Identity." *Leslie Marmon Silko's Ceremony: A Casebook.* Ed. Allan Chavkin. Oxford: Oxford UP, 2002. 91–116.

Palmer, Alan. *Fictional Minds.* Lincoln: U of Nebraska P, 2004.

Paredes, Américo. *With His Pistol in His Hand: A Border Ballad and Its Hero.* 1958. Austin: U of Texas P, 2004.

Pavel, Thomas G. *Fictional Worlds.* Cambridge: Harvard UP, 1986.

———. "Narrative Domains." *Poetics Today* 1.4 (1980): 105–114.

Petry, Ann. *Country Place.* Cambridge: The Riverside Press, 1947.

Phelan, James. *Experiencing Fiction: Judgments, Progressions and the Rhetorical Theory of Narrative.* Columbus: The Ohio State UP, 2007.

———. *Living to Tell about It: A Rhetoric and Ethics of Character Narration.* Ithaca: Cornell UP, 2005.

———. "Narrative Judgments and the Rhetorical Theory of Narrative." *A Companion to Narrative Theory.* Ed. James Phelan and Peter J. Rabinowitz. Oxford: Blackwell Publishing, 2005. 322–36.

———. *Reading the American Novel 1920–2010.* Chichester: Wiley-Blackwell, 2013.

———. "Rhetoric/ethics." *The Cambridge Companion to Narrative.* Ed. David Herman. Cambridge: Cambridge UP, 2007. 203–16.

———. "Voice, Politics, and Judgments in *Their Eyes Were Watching God*: The Initiation, the Launch, and the Debate about the Narration." *Analyzing World Fiction: New Horizons in Narrative Theory.* Ed. Frederick Luis Aldama. Austin: U of Texas P, 2011. 57–73.

Phelan, James, and Peter J. Rabinowitz, eds. *A Companion to Narrative Theory.* Oxford: Blackwell Publishing, 2005.

Pratt, Louis H. *James Baldwin.* Boston: Twayne Publishers, 1978.

Prince, Gerald. *A Grammar of Stories: An Introduction.* The Hague: Mouton, 1973.

Prince, Valerie Sweeney. "Keep on Moving Don't Stop: *Invisible Man*." *Ralph Ellison: New Edition.* Ed. Harold Bloom. New York: Bloom's Literary Criticism, 2010. 155–72.

Propp, Vladimir. *Morphology of the Folktale.* Austin: U of Texas P, 1968.

Puar, Jasbir. "In the Wake of It Gets Better." *The Guardian.* 16 Nov. 2010. Web. 13 June 2013. <http://www.guardian.co.uk/commentisfree/cifamerica/2010/nov/16/wake-it-gets-better -campaign>.

———. *Terrorist Assemblages: Homonationalism in Queer Times.* Durham: Duke UP, 2007.

Purdy, John. "The Transformation: Tayo's Genealogy in *Ceremony*." *Leslie Marmon Silko's Ceremony: A Casebook.* Ed. Allan Chavkin. Oxford: Oxford UP, 2002. 63–70.

Rabinowitz, Peter J. "'The Absence of Her Voice from That Concord': The Value of the Implied Author." *Style* 45.1 (2011): 99–108.

———. "'Betraying the Sender': The Rhetoric and Ethics of Fragile Texts." *Narrative* 2.3 (1994): 201–13.

Rader, Dean. Prologue. *Engaged Resistance: American Indian Art, Literature, and Film from Alcatraz to the National Museum of the American Indian.* Austin: U of Texas P, 2011. 1–6.

Rice, H. William. *Ralph Ellison and the Politics of the Novel.* Lanham, MD: Lexington Books, 2003.

Richardson, Brian. Introduction. *Narrative Beginnings: Theories and Practices.* Ed. Brian Richardson. Lincoln: U of Nebraska P, 2009. 1–10.

———. "Singular Text, Multiple Implied Readers." *Style* 41.3 (2007): 259–74.

———. "Unnatural Stories and Sequences." *A Poetics of Unnatural Narrative.* Ed. Jan Alber et al. Columbus: The Ohio State UP, 2013. 16–30.

———. "U. S. Ethnic and Postcolonial Fiction: Toward a Poetics of Collective Narratives." Ed. Frederick Luis Aldama. *Analyzing World Fiction: New Horizons in Narrative Theory.* Austin: U of Texas P, 2011. 3–16.

Rimstead, Roxanne. "Cultural Memory and Social Identity." *Essays on Canadian Writing* 80 (2003): 1–14.

Ritivoi, Andreea Deciu. "Explaining People: Narrative and the Study of Identity." *StoryWorlds: A Journal of Narrative Studies* 1.1 (2009): 25–41.

Rivera-Servera, Ramón H. *Performing Latinidad: Dance, Sexuality, Politics.* Ann Arbor: U of Michigan P, 2012.

Robinson, Sally. *Engendering the Subject.* New York: SUNY Press, 1991.

Robles, Mario Ortiz. *The Novel as Event.* Ann Arbor: U of Michigan P, 2010.

Rockwell, Daisy. "*Open City* by Teju Cole." *Bookslut.* February 2011. Web. <http://www.bookslut.com/fiction/2011_02_017145.php>.

Rodríguez, Juana María. *Queer Latinidad: Identity Practices, Discursive Spaces.* New York: New York UP, 2003.

———. *Sexual Futures, Queer Gestures, and Other Latina Longings.* New York: New York UP, 2014.

Roediger, David. *Working toward Whiteness: How America's Immigrants Became White: The Strange Journey from Ellis Island to the Suburbs.* Cambridge, MA: Basic Books, 2005.

Romagnolo, Catherine. "Initiating Dialogue: Narrative Beginnings in Multicultural Narratives." *Analyzing World Fiction: New Horizons in Narrative Theory.* Ed. Frederick Luis Aldama. Austin: U of Texas P, 2011. 183–98.

———. *Opening Acts: Narrative Beginnings in Twentieth-Century Feminist Fiction.* Lincoln: U of Nebraska P, 2015.

———. "Recessive Origins in Julia Alvarez's *Garcia Girls*: A Feminist Exploration of Narrative Beginnings." *Narrative Beginnings: Theories and Practices.* Ed. Brian Richardson. Lincoln: U of Nebraska P, 2008. 149–65.

Roof, Judith. *Come as You Are: Sexuality and Narrative.* New York: Columbia UP, 1996.

Roof, Judith, and Robyn Wiegman, eds. *Who Can Speak? Authority and Critical Identity.* Urbana: U of Illinois P, 1995.

Roppolo, Kimberly. "Samson Occom as Writing Instructor: The Search for an Intertribal Rhetoric." *Reasoning Together: The Native Critics Collective.* Ed. Craig S. Womack, Daniel Heath Justice, and Christopher B. Teuton. Norman: U of Oklahoma P, 2008. 303–24.

Rose, Margaret A. *Parody//Meta-Fiction: An Analysis of Parody as a Critical Mirror to the Writing and Reception of Fiction.* London: Croom Helm, 1979.

Rothenberg, Paula S., ed. *White Privilege: Essential Readings on the Other Side of Racism*. New York: Worth Publisher, 2005.

Royster, Philip M. "Milkman's Flying: The Scapegoat Transcended in Toni Morrison's *Song of Solomon*." *College Language Association Journal* 24.4 (1981): 419–40.

Ryan, Marie-Laure. *Possible Worlds, Artificial Intelligence and Narrative Theory*. Bloomington: Indiana UP. 1991.

———. "Possible Worlds." *the living handbook of narratology*. Ed. Peter Huhn et al. Hamburg: Hamburg University. 27 Sept. 2013. Web. 12 Dec. 2013.

Said, Edward W. *Beginnings*. New York: Basic Books, 1975.

———. *Culture and Imperialism*. New York: Knopf, 1993.

Saldívar, Ramón. "Historical Fantasy, Speculative Realism, and Postrace Aesthetics in Contemporary American Fiction." *American Literary History* 23.33 (2011): 574–99.

———. "The Second Elevation of the Novel: Race, Form, and the Postrace Aesthetic in Contemporary Narrative." *Narrative* 21.1 (2013): 1–18.

San Juan, E., Jr. "From Carlos Bulosan and the Imagination of the Class Struggle." *Counterpoints: Perspectives on Asian America*. Ed. Emma Gee. Los Angeles: Asian American Studies Center, UCLA, 1976. 190–94.

Sandoval Sanchez, Alberto. "*West Side Story*: A Puerto Rican Reading of 'America.'" *Jump Cut: A Review of Contemporary Media* 39 (1994): 59–66.

Savage, Dan, and Terry Miller, eds. *It Gets Better: Coming Out, Overcoming Bullying, and Creating a Life Worth Living*. New York: Penguin, 2011.

Schaub, Thomas. "Ellison's Masks and the Novel of Reality." *New Essays on Invisible Man*. Ed. Robert O'Meally. New York: Cambridge UP, 1988. 123–56.

Schmidt, Christian. "Dissimulating Blackness: The Degenerative Satires of Paul Beatty and Percival Everett." *Post-Soul Satire: Black Identity after Civil Rights*. Ed. Derek C. Maus and James J. Donahue. Jackson: UP of Mississippi, 2014. 150–61.

———. "The Parody of Postblackness in Percival Everett's *I Am Not Sidney Poitier* and the End(s) of African American Literature." *Black Studies Papers* 2.1 (2016): 113–32. Web. 2 June 2016. <http://elib.suub.uni-bremen.de/edocs/00105252-1.pdf>.

———. *Postblack Aesthetics: The Freedom to Be Black in Contemporary African American Fiction*. Heidelberg: Universitätsverlag Winter, 2017.

Sebald, W. G. *Austerlitz*. Frankfurt/M: Fischer, 2003.

———. *Die Ausgewanderten*. Frankfurt/M: Eichbom, 1993.

Sedgwick, Eve Kosofsky. "How to Bring Your Kids Up Gay." *Tendencies*. Durham: Duke UP, 1993. 154–64.

———. *Touching Feeling: Affective, Pedagogy, Performativity*. Durham: Duke UP, 2003.

Shen, Dan. "Why Contextualist and Formal Narratologies Need Each Other." *JNT: Journal of Narrative Theory* 35.2 (2005): 141–71.

Shklovsky, Viktor. *Theory of Prose*. Trans. Benjamin Sher. Intro. Gerald L. Bruns. Elmwood Park: Dalkey Archive, 1991.

Silko, Leslie Marmon. *Ceremony*. New York: Penguin, 1977.

Smith, Adam. *The Theory of Moral Sentiments*. New York: Penguin, 2009.

Smith, Valerie. "The Quest for and Discovery of Identity in Toni Morrison's *Song of Solomon*." *The Southern Review* 21.3 (1985): 721–32.

Sohn, Stephen. *Racial Asymmetries: Asian American Fictional Worlds*. New York: New York UP, 2014.

Song, Min. *The Children of 1965: On Writing, and Not Writing, as an Asian American*. Durham: Duke UP, 2013.

Spallino, Chiara. "*Song of Solomon*: An Adventure in Structure." *Callaloo* 8.3 (1985): 510–24.

Stavans, Ilan. *Bandido: Oscar "Zeta" Acosta and the Chicano Experience*. New York: HarperCollins, 1995.

———, ed. *The Norton Anthology of Latino Literature*. New York: Norton, 2011.

Steele, Meili. "Metatheory and the Subject of Democracy in the Work of Ralph Ellison." *New Literary History* 27.3, Literary Subjects (1996): 473–502.

Stein, Gertrude. *Tender Buttons: Objects—Food—Rooms*. Champaign, IL: Standard P, 2008.

Stockton, Kathryn Bond. *The Queer Child, or Growing Sideways in the Twentieth Century*. Durham: Duke UP, 2009.

Sullivan, Richard. "Injustice, Out of Focus." *New York Times Book Review* 28 Sept. 1947: 12.

Sylvander, Carolyn Wedin. 1980. "Charting Racism in America 1945–1965: Going to Meet the Man." *James Baldwin*. New York: Ungar. 109–24.

Teorey, Matthew. "Spinning a Bigendered Identity in Silko's *Ceremony* and Puig's *Kiss of the Spider Woman*." *Comparative Literature Studies*. 47.1 (2010): 1–20.

Touré. *Who's Afraid of Post-Blackness?: What It Means to Be Black Now*. New York: Free Press, 2011.

Tripathy, Jyotirmaya. "Postcolonialism and the Native American Experience: A Theoretical Perspective." *Asiatic* 3.1 (2009): 40–53.

Truong, Monique. "American Like Me." *Gourmet: The Magazine of Good Living*. Reading supplement, Aug. 2006. Web. 14 Jan. 2014 <http://monique-truong.com/cms/wp-content/uploads/2017/03/American-Like-Me.pdf>.

———. *Bitter in the Mouth*. New York: Random House, 2011.

Turner, Edwin. "Teju Cole's *Open City* Is a Strange, Marvelous Novel That Captures the Post-9/11 Zeitgeist." *Biblioklept*, 21 Feb. 2012.

Turner, Jack. "Awakening to Race: Ralph Ellison and Democratic Individuality." *Political Theory* 35.5 (2008): 655–82.

Ugly Betty. "Backseat Betty." ABC Network. 13 Nov. 2009. Television.

———. "A League of Their Own." ABC Network. 25 Oct. 2007. Television.

———. "Lose the Boss?" ABC Network. 23 Nov. 2006. Television.

———. "Pilot." ABC Network. 28 Sept. 2006. Television.

Villarejo, Amy. *Ethereal Queer: Television, Historicity, Desire*. Durham: Duke UP, 2014.

Vincent, Keith. "Hamaosociality: Narrative and Fascism in Hamao Shiro's *The Devil's Disciple*." *The Culture of Japanese Fascism*. Ed. Alan Tansman. Durham: Duke UP, 2009. 381–408.

Wald, Priscilla. *Constituting Americans: Cultural Anxiety and Narrative Form*. Durham: Duke UP, 1995.

Walton, Kendall. "How Remote Are Fictional Worlds from the Real World?" *The Journal of Aesthetics and Art Criticism* 37.1 (1978): 11–23.

Wand, David Hsin-Fu, ed. *Asian-American Heritage: An Anthology of Prose and Poetry.* New York: Washington Square, 1974.

Warhol, Robyn R. *Gendered Interventions: Narrative Discourse in the Victorian Novel.* New Brunswick: Rutgers UP, 1989.

———. "Neonarrative; or, How to Render the Unnarratable in Realist Fiction and Contemporary Film." *A Companion to Narrative Theory.* Ed. James Phelan and Peter J. Rabinowitz. Oxford: Blackwell Publishing, 2005. 220–31.

Warhol, Robyn, et al. *Narrative Theory: Core Concepts and Critical Debates. See* Herman, David, et al. 2012.

Warren, Kenneth W. *What Was African American Literature?* Cambridge: Harvard UP, 2011.

Watkins, S. Craig. *Representing: Hip Hop Culture and the Production of Black Cinema.* Chicago: U of Chicago P, 1999.

Willis, Suzanne. *Specifying: Black Women Writing the American Experience.* Madison: U of Wisconsin P, 1989.

Womack, Craig. "A Single Decade: Book-Length Native Literary Criticism between 1986 and 1997." *Reasoning Together: The Native Critics Collective.* Ed. Craig S. Womack et al. Norman: U of Oklahoma P, 2008. 3–104.

———. "Theorizing American Indian Experience." *Reasoning Together: The Native Critics Collective.* Ed. Craig S. Womack et al. Norman: U of Oklahoma P, 2008. 353–410.

Womack, Craig S., et al., eds. *Reasoning Together: The Native Critics Collective.* Norman: U of Oklahoma P, 2008.

Wood, James. "The Arrival of Enigmas." *New Yorker* 28 Feb. 2011.

Wright, John S. "The Conscious Hero and the Rites of Man: Ellison's War." *New Essays on Invisible Man.* Ed. Robert O'Meally. New York: Cambridge UP, 1988. 157–86.

Wright, Richard. *Eight Men.* New York: Harper Perennial, 1996.

———. *Native Son, And, How "Bigger" Was Born.* Cutchogue, NY: Buccaneer Books, 1993.

Yancy, George. "Introduction: Fragments of a Social Ontology of Whiteness." *What White Looks Like: African-American Philosophers on the Whiteness Question.* Ed. George Yancy. New York: Routledge, 2004. 1–24.

Yglesias, José. "Classy-Type People." *New Masses* (9 Dec. 1947): 18.

Zunshine, Lisa. *Why We Read Fiction: Theory of Mind and the Novel.* Columbus: The Ohio State UP, 2006.

CONTRIBUTORS

EDITORS

JAMES J. DONAHUE is associate professor of English at the State University of New York, Potsdam, where he directs the graduate program in English & Communication. He is the author of *Failed Frontiersmen: White Men and Myth in the Post-Sixties American Historical Romance* (University of Virginia Press, 2015) and editor (with Derek C. Maus) of *Post-Soul Satire: Black Identity after Civil Rights* (University Press of Mississippi, 2014). He is also the author of numerous book chapters and articles on twentieth-century American literatures.

JENNIFER ANN HO is professor of English and comparative literature at the University of North Carolina, Chapel Hill. She is the author of *Consumption and Identity in Asian American Coming-of-Age Novels* (Routledge, 2005), *Racial Ambiguity in Asian American Culture* (Rutgers University Press, 2015), and *Understanding Gish Jen* (University of South Carolina Press, 2015).

SHAUN MORGAN is associate professor of English at Tennessee Wesleyan University.

CONTRIBUTORS

STERLING LECATER BLAND JR. is associate professor of English and American literature at Rutgers University–Newark. He is the author of *Understanding Slave Narratives* (Greenwood, 2016), *Voices of the Fugitives: Runaway Slave Stories and Their*

Fictions of Self-Creation (Praeger, 2001 Contributions in Afro-American and African Studies series), and a three-volume annotated anthology of African American slave narrative writing (Greenwood, 2000).

CLAUDIA BREGER is professor of Germanic languages at Columbia University. She is the author of several books, including *An Aesthetics of Narrative Performance: Transnational Theater, Literature and Film in Contemporary Germany* (Ohio State University Press, 2012; Theory and Interpretation of Narrative series).

JOSEPH COULOMBE is professor of English at Rowan University. He is the author of two books, *Reading Native American Literature* (Routledge, 2011) and *Mark Twain and the American West* (University of Missouri Press, 2003).

CHRISTOPHER GONZÁLEZ is assistant professor of English at Texas A&M University–Commerce. He is coauthor of *Latinos in the End Zone: Conversations on the Brown Color Line in the NFL* (Palgrave, 2013), author of *Reading Junot Díaz* (University of Pittsburgh Press, 2015), and coeditor of *Graphic Borders: Latino Comics Past, Present, and Future* (University of Texas, 2016).

PATRICK E. HORN currently serves as associate director of the Center for the Study of the American South at the University of North Carolina, Chapel Hill. He has published articles and essays in *a/b: Auto/Biography Studies*; *Fifty Years after Faulkner*; the *Encyclopedia of Muslim-American History*; and UNC Libraries' digital archive *Documenting the American South*.

SUE J. KIM is professor of English and codirector of the Center for Asian American Studies at the University of Massachusetts, Lowell. She is the author of *On Anger: Race, Cognition, Narrative* (University of Texas Press, 2013) and *Critiquing Postmodernism in Contemporary Discourses of Race* (Palgrave, 2009), and coeditor of *Rethinking Empathy through Literature* (Routledge, 2014).

STEPHANIE LI is the Susan D. Gubar chair in literature at Indiana University. She is the author of four books, including *Playing in the White: Black Writers, White Subjects* (Oxford University Press, 2015) and *Signifying without Specifying: Racial Discourse in the Age of Obama* (Rutgers University Press, 2011).

DEBORAH NOEL is a senior lecturer in English at the University of Vermont. Her research interests include American historical romance; narrative theory; and race, ethnicity, and gender studies.

ROY PÉREZ is associate professor of English at Willamette University. His book in progress, *Proximities: Queer Configurations of Race and Sex,* forwards a relational account of *latinidad* by examining sexuality and cross-racial representation in U.S. Latina/o narrative, visual art, and performance.

CATHERINE ROMAGNOLO is associate professor of English at Lebanon Valley College. She is the author of *Opening Acts: Feminist Beginnings in Twentieth-Century US Women's Fiction* (University of Nebraska Press, 2015).

CHRISTIAN SCHMIDT is assistant professor in American studies and intercultural Anglophone studies at the University of Bayreuth (Germany). He is the author of *Postblack Aesthetics: The Freedom to Be Black in Contemporary African American Fiction* (forthcoming from Universitätsverlag Winter, 2017).

STEPHEN SPENCER is professor of English and chair of the English Department at the University of Southern Indiana.

BLAKE WILDER is a doctoral candidate at The Ohio State University. His work addresses the intersection of race, masculinity, and violence in American and African American literature.

INDEX

Acosta, Oscar "Zeta": legacy of, 32–34; reception of, 40–41

affect studies, 163

African American literature, 70, 71, 214; and authorial intent, 85; and blackness, 82, 86; implied authors in, 84, 86; as mimetic, 83, 84, 85–86; and narrative theory, 211; postblack, 82–83, 82n2, 85, 88, 93; race in, 84n4; racism in, 84n4; as sociological, 83

African Americans, 1. *See also* blackness

African American studies: and narratology, 89n7

African diaspora aesthetics, 11, 162, 165; and Appiah, 171; and rhetorical narratology, 162, 170

Ahmed, Sara, 172

Aiiieeeee! An Anthology of Asian-American Writers (Chin, et al.), 14–15, 25; historical grounding of, 16–17

Alarcón, Norma, 47

Alber, Jan, 5, 6, 85

Aldama, Frederick Luis, 3n4, 4, 4n6, 12, 43; on Acosta, 32, 36, 38; on recognition, 35; and "world literatures," 6–7

Allen, Paula Gunn, 57–58, 60, 67; on tribal stories, 68; on Western discourse, 57, 59

America Is in the Heart (Bulosan), 20–21

Anaya, Rudolfo, 40–41

Anderson, Benedict, 209

Anzaldúa, Gloria, 38–39, 204

Appiah, Kwame Anthony: and African diaspora aesthetics, 171; cosmopolitanism of, 172; and cultural difference, 168, 172; on universalism, 169

Aristotle, 110

Asian-American Heritage (Wand), 15, 17

Asian American literary studies, 12; and Asian American history, 16; as contextualist, 15, 58, 112; depiction of minds in, 16, 24; discourse of, 16; formalism in, 20–21; and gender, 21; and history, 14, 21; interdisciplinarity in, 15; and narrative theory, 9, 16, 213–14; and narratology, 13–16, 21, 26, 214; and politics, 21; and racism, 21

Asian American literature, 214–15; context and causality in, 19–20; and ethics, 129; and racism, 122; and subjectivity, 122

Asian American Literature (E. Kim), 15, 17

Asian Americans, 1; in the South, 111–12

Asian American studies: and cognitive privilege, 25; and narrative theory, 14; and poststructuralism, 14

Asian Women (Asian Women's Coalition), 14–15, 25; Asian American history in, 16

assimilation: in *Ceremony*, 61, 63; and gay pride, 198; and homo-narratives, 198; in *Ugly Betty*, 194

Austen, Jane, 22; and patriarchy, 22n8

authenticity: and black identity, 46–47, 48, 51; and Native American identity, 128

autobiography: ethnic, 35

Autobiography of a Brown Buffalo (Acosta), 9; audiences of, 36–38; authorial counterself of, 28, 28n3; the body in, 35–36;

Song of Solomon (Morrison), 9, 208; and
    authenticity, 48, 53; beginnings in, 48–51,
    52, 53–55; black identity in, 55; and dis-
    identification, 9, 47, 55–56; flashbacks
    in, 52–53; flight in, 49, 50–51, 53, 54–55;
    gender in, 51, 55–56; myth in, 49–50, 53;
    as quest narrative, 47–48, 49, 52, 53–55;
    subjectivity in, 46–47, 55
Souls of Black Folks, The (Du Bois), 70, 72, 81
sovereignty: and colonialism, 129, 132; in
    Green Grass, Running Water, 131–32; and
    storytelling, 129
Spallino, Chiara, 50
speculative fiction, 179–80; and susceptibil-
    ity, 179
speculative realism, 8
Spencer, Stephen, 9, 126, 210
Stanzel, Franz, 14
Stavans, Ilan, 32; on Acosta, 33–34, 40
Stein, Gertrude, 115–16
stereotypes, 11, 146, 153, 160, 181; of ethnic
    literature, 30, 84, 84n3, 91, 125; and nar-
    rative, 114, 117, 178
storytelling, 72–73, 79; in *Ceremony,* 64–65,
    68; counter-storytelling, 71; in "Going
    to Meet the Man," 72, 79–80; in *Latin
    Deli,* 182; in *Open City,* 175; and rhetoric,
    138n1; and sovereignty, 129; and world-
    making, 77
storyworlds, 9, 31–32, 75; of "Going to Meet
    the Man," 74, 78, 79; of Latina/o litera-
    ture, 28–29, 31, 32, 36, 41–42; principle of
    minimal departure, 75
Street, The (Petry), 95
structuralism, 13–14, 14n2; limits of, 6
structuralist narratology, 17; as ahistorical, 18;
    and context, 17–18; and formalism, 16; as
    objective, 18. *See also* narrative theory;
    narratology
Suarez, Justin, 194, 201
subjectivity: in Asian American literature,
    122; and cosmopolitanism, 152n2; and
    narrative, 58; in *Song of Solomon,* 46–47,
    55
Sullivan, Richard, 100n9

technicity, 8
Tender Buttons (Stein), 115–16
Teorey, Matthew, 64

Tracks (Erdrich), 134–35
trauma theory, 171
Truong, Monique, 10, 109; on Asian Ameri-
    cans in the South, 111; racial identity
    of, 111n3. *See also Bitter in the Mouth*
    (Truong)

Ugly Betty, 194, 201–7, 208; assimilation in,
    194; class in, 201, 202; coming-out in,
    202, 205–7; femininity in, 203; focaliza-
    tion in, 204; gender in, 202; homopho-
    bia in, 203, 204–7; masculinity in, 203,
    204; prolepsis in, 202; sexuality in, 202–
    3; white intervention in, 203–4
universalism, 168; and cosmopolitanism, 172;
    in *Invisible Man,* 147, 148; and narratol-
    ogy, 14
unnatural narrative poetics, 10

Walton, Kendall, 177
Wand, David Hsin-Fu, 15, 17
Warhol, Robyn, 3, 4; on gender, 17n5; on nar-
    ratology as gender-blind, 5; on neo-nar-
    ratives, 135; on susceptible readers, 179
Warren, Kenneth W., 1n1, 15, 71
Washington, Booker T., 143
Wayne, John, 129–30, 131
West Side Story, 200–201
Whitehead, Colson, 7
whiteness, 214; in *Country Place,* 96, 99–100,
    102, 103; entitlements of, 10, 211; feigned
    omniscience of, 103; and femininity, 20;
    and language, 97; and narrators, 122,
    149, 163, 211; presumed authority of, 96;
    presumption of, 98–99, 99n4, 112, 122,
    124, 149, 163, 211; as racial category, 216;
    and silence, 99, 99n5; and universality,
    211; as unmarked, 113, 122
white supremacy, 74, 209; and silencing,
    80–81
Wife of His Youth, The (Chesnutt), 72
Wilder, Blake, 9–10, 32, 43–44, 61, 127, 138,
    211; on identity formation, 191; on narra-
    tive worldmaking, 208
Willis, Susan, 48
Winant, Howard, 19, 46
Womack, Craig, 128
Wong, Shawn, 15

THEORY AND INTERPRETATION OF NARRATIVE

JAMES PHELAN, PETER J. RABINOWITZ, AND ROBYN WARHOL, SERIES EDITORS

Because the series editors believe that the most significant work in narrative studies today contributes both to our knowledge of specific narratives and to our understanding of narrative in general, studies in the series typically offer interpretations of individual narratives and address significant theoretical issues underlying those interpretations. The series does not privilege one critical perspective but is open to work from any strong theoretical position.